NEW YORK CITY ★

Upper West Side & Central Park
Home to the premier performing arts center and the park that helps define the city.
(Map p250)

Midtown
Times Square, Broadway theaters, canyons of skyscrapers, and bustling crowds that rarely thin.
(Map p252)

Grenwich Village, Chelsea & Meatpacking District
Quaint, intimate streets plus trendy nightlife, shopping and art galleries galore. *(Map p246)*

oHo & Chinatown
up dumpling par
rs and hawkers sell-
g bric-a-brac next
oor to cobblestone
reets and stores
ith the biggest name
rands in the world.
Map p246)

Lincoln Center ◉

Broadway ◉

Times Square ◉

Pennsylvania (Penn) Station ◉

High Line ◉

Hudson River

Low
⚏ Ten

◉ Chinatow

One World Trade Center ◉

National September 11 Memorial & Museum ◉

◉ Brooklyn B

◉ Brooklyn

Liberty State Park

◉ Ellis Island

Upper New York Bay

Governors Island

Statue of Liberty ◉

lonely planet

NEW YORK CITY

TOP SIGHTS, AUTHENTIC EXPERIENCES

THIS EDITION WRITTEN AND RESEARCHED BY

Regis St Louis,
Cristian Bonetto, Zora O'Neill

W9-AMR-001

Welcome to New York City

New York City is the great met[...]
large. It's a place of electrifying[...]
where art-deco skyscrapers tow[...]
sidewalks packed with people fr[...]
corner of the globe, and there ar[...]
different stories (8.4 million act[...]
happening all around you.

In the realms of art, fashion, music, film[...]
and dance, New York remains one of th[...]
giants. And its dining scene – more tha[...]
restaurants! – staggers the imagination[...]
spent exploring venerable art collection[...]
the MoMA, the Guggenheim), taking in i[...]
(the Statue of Liberty, the Brooklyn Brid[...]
Park), and delving into fascinatingly dive[...]
borhoods, from Chinatown to Harlem, ea[...]
world of its own.

Nighttime brings limitless possibilities:[...]
tering lights of Broadway, world-renowne[...]
halls uptown or intimate jazz clubs downt[...]
Add in vintage-filled cocktail bars in Brook[...]
glittering rooftop lounges, where all the cit[...]
out before you, for a memorable cap to the[...]

The New York experience is about so ma[...]
things: window-shopping along glamorous[...]
Ave, catching an indie film at an art-house[...]
gallery-hopping in Chelsea, and hearing the[...]
of the crowd at a game in Madison Square G[...]
This is just the beginning...and in NYC, there[...]
is no end.

> *there are a million*
> *different stories happening*
> *all around you*

Fall foliage in Central Park (p36)
GAVIN HELLIER /GETTY IMAGES ©

Plan Your Trip
This Year in New York City

GRANGER WOOTZ / GETTY IMAGES ©

New York City

No matter when you visit, there's always something happening in New York City, with music festivals, holiday markets and costume parades packing the year's calendar. Be sure to plan ahead for the bigger events. Above: Village Halloween Parade (p15); Top Right: Cherry Blossom Festival, Brooklyn Botanic Garden (p9); Bottom Right: Fireworks for Independence Day (p12).

2017

DAVID SACKS / GETTY IMAGES ©

Top Festivals & Events

Tribeca Film Festival – mid- to late April (p9)

Cherry Blossom Festival – April 29-30 (p9)

SummerStage – June–August (p11)

Independence Day – July 4 (p12)

Village Halloween Parade – October 31 (p15)

STEVE KELLEY / GETTY IMAGES ©

Plan Your Trip
This Year in New York City

January

After Christmas and New Year's, the winter doldrums arrive. Despite the long nights, New Yorkers take advantage of the frosty weather, with ice-skating and ski trips to the Catskills.

January 1
🏃 New Year's Day Swim
What better way to greet the new year than with an icy dip in the Atlantic? Join the Coney Island Polar Bear Club (www.polarbearclub. org) for this annual brrrr fest.

January 5–8
☆ Winter Jazzfest
In mid-January, this four-day music fest (www.winterjazzfest.com) brings over 100 acts playing at nearly a dozen venues around the city. Most of the action happens around the West Village.

Mid-January
🏃 No Pants Subway Ride
In January (often on the second Sunday), some 4000 New Yorkers spice things up with a bit of leg nudity on public transit. Anyone can join in, and there's usually an after-party for the cheeky participants. Check the website (www.improveverywhere.com) for meeting times and details. Dates are usually announced in December.

January 28
🎆 Lunar (Chinese) New Year Festival
One of the biggest Chinese New Year celebrations in the country, this display of fireworks and dancing dragons draws mobs of thrillseekers into the streets of Chinatown.

From left: New Year's Day Swim; Lunar (Chinese) New Year parade

February

The odd blizzard and below-freezing tempera-
tures make February a good time to stay indoors
nursing a drink or enjoying a warm meal at a
cozy bar or bistro.

February 9–17
🚪 New York Fashion Week
The infarnous Bryant Park fashion shows
(www.fashionweekonline.com) are sadly
not open to the public. But whether you're
invited or not, being in the city this week
– when the couture world descends upon
Manhattan to swoon over new looks –
could provide a vicarious thrill, especially
if you can find the after-parties.

February 13–14
👁 Westminster Kennel Club Dog Show
Canine lovers from the four corners of
the earth descend on Manhattan during
this showcase of beautiful breeds (www.
wootminsterkennelclub.org). Some 3200
dogs compete for top honors. The best
in show judging takes place in Madison
Square Garden.

February 14
🎊 Valentine's Day
If you're traveling with a special someone,
you'll want to reserve well ahead for a
Valentine's Day dinner. Many restaurants
offer special prix-fixe menus, and it's quite
the popular night for going out.

Late January– Early February
🍴 Winter Restaurant Week
From late January to early February,
celebrate the dreary weather with
slash-cut meal deals at some of the
city's finest eating establishments
during New York's Winter Restaurant
Week (www.nycgo.com/restaurant-
week), which actually runs for about
three weeks. A three-course lunch
costs around $25 ($40 for dinner).

Plan Your Trip
This Year in New York City

March

After months of freezing temperatures and winter coats, the odd warm spring day appears and everyone rejoices – though it's usually followed by a week of sub-zero drear as winter lingers on.

March 2–5
⊙ The Armory Show
New York's biggest art show (www.thearmoryshow.com) brings together some of the world's top galleries, with art collectors and curators in a dazzling showcase of what's new on the art scene. It happens on Piers 92 and 94, off Twelfth Ave (near 53rd St).

Mid- to Late March
☆ New Directors/New Films
Hosted by the Film Society of Lincoln Center, this 12-day film fest (www.newdirectors.org) is a great place to discover emerging directors from around the globe. It's now in its 46th year, so you can count on an impressive lineup.

STUART MONK / SHUTTERSTOCK ©

March 17
✺ St Patrick's Day Parade
A massive audience, rowdy and wobbly from cups of green beer, lines Fifth Ave for this popular parade (www.nycstpatricksparade.org) of bagpipe blowers, sparkly floats and clusters of Irish-lovin' politicians. The parade, which was first held here in 1762, is the city's oldest and largest.

04

April

Spring finally appears: optimistic alfresco joints have a sprinkling of street-side chairs as the city squares overflow with bright tulips and blossom-covered trees.

April 1

🎋 Pillow Fight Day

For a bit of old-fashioned fun, grab a pillow (of the non-feather variety), take off your glasses and join the fray. Hundreds participate in this soft, cushiony battle (www.pillowfightday.com), typically held in Washington Square Park or Union Square.

Mid- to Late April

☆ Tribeca Film Festival

Created in response to the tragic events of September 11, Robert De Niro's downtown film festival (www.tribecafilm.com) has quickly become a star in the indie-movie circuit. You'll have to make some tough choices: over 150 films are screened during the 10-day fest.

April 16

🎋 Easter Parade

Dating back to the 1870s, this parade features a line up of well-dressed, bonnet-wearing participants who show off their finery along Fifth Ave (from 49th to 57th Sts). Bring your wildest hat, and join in the action. It typically kicks off at 10am.

April 22

🎋 Earth Day

New York hosts a packed day of events at Union Square, with live music, presentations on sustainability and hands on activities for kids (www.earthdayinitiative.org). Grand Central Terminal also has displays on green initiatives.

April 29–30

🎋 Cherry Blossom Festival

Known in Japanese as Sakura Matsuri, this annual tradition celebrates the magnificent flowering of cherry trees in the Brooklyn Botanic Garden, complete with entertainment and activities (*taiko* drumming, origami workshops, ikebana flower displays, samurai sword showmanship), plus refreshments and awe-inspiring beauty.

Cherry Blossom Festival

ANDREA CAROLINA SANCHEZ GONZALEZ / GETTY IMAGES ©

Plan Your Trip
This Year in New York City

May

April showers bring May flowers in the form of blossoms adorning the trees all around the city. The weather is warm and mild without the unpleasant humidity of summer.

May 7
🚴 TD Bank Five Boro Bike Tour
May is Bike Month, featuring two-wheelin' tours, parties and other events for pedal-pushing New Yorkers. TD Bank Five Boro Bike Tour (www.bike.nyc), the main event, sees thousands of cyclists hit the pavement for a 42-mile ride through each of the city's five boroughs.

May 29
🎖 Memorial Day
Held on the last Monday of May, this holiday commemorates Americans who've died in combat. The boroughs host parades featuring marching bands, vintage cars and flag-waving seniors, the biggest of which is Queens' Little Neck-Douglaston Memorial Day Parade (www.lndmemorialday.org).

Late May–August
☆ Shakespeare in the Park
The much-loved Shakespeare in the Park (www.publictheater.org) pays tribute to the Bard, with free performances in Central Park. The catch? You'll have to wait hours in line to score tickets, or win them in the online lottery. Tickets are given out at noon on show days; arrive no later than 10am for a seat.

GARY718 / SHUTTERSTOCK ©

Late May
⊙ Fleet Week
For one week at the end of May, Manhattan resembles a 1940s movie set as clusters of fresh-faced, uniformed sailors go 'on the town' to look for adventures (www.fleetweeknewyork.com). For non-swabby visitors, this is a chance to take free tours of ships that have arrived from various corners of the globe. See them docked off Manhattan (around Midtown) and Brooklyn (just south of Brooklyn Bridge Park's pier 6).

June

Summer's definitely here and locals crawl out of their offices to relax in the city's green spaces. Parades roll down the big streets and portable movie screens are strung up in several parks.

June–August
☆ SummerStage
Central Park's SummerStage (www.summerstage.org) features an incredible lineup of music and dance throughout the summer. Django Django, Femi Kuti, Shuggie Otis and the Martha Graham Dance Company are among recent standouts. Most events are free. There's also a Summer-Stage Kids program just in case you've got the little ones in tow. Other parks throughout the city also host events.

June–August
☆ Bryant Park
Summer Film Festival
June through August, Bryant Park (www.bryantpark.org) hosts free Monday-night outdoor screenings of classic Hollywood films, which kick off after sundown. Arrive early (the lawn area opens at 5pm and folks line up by 4pm).

June 20
☉ Night at the Museums
Lower Manhattan museums throw open their doors for free visits from 4pm to 8pm. Special events (including curated walks) are part of the appeal. Some activities require advance booking (www.mjhnyc.org/nightatthemuseums).

Mid- to Late June
☆ River to River Festival
Over 11 days in June, this arts-loving fest (www.lmcc.net/program/river-to-river) offers a combo of live music, dance and visual art at spaces on the waterfront, on Governors Island and in Lower Manhattan.

Late June
⚡ Mermaid Parade
Celebrating sand, sea and the beginning of summer is this wonderfully quirky afternoon parade. It's a flash of glitter and glamour, as elaborately costumed folks display their fishy finery along the Coney Island boardwalk (www.coneyisland.com). It's even more fun to take part (all in costume are welcome). The parade is typically held on the Saturday closest to the summer solstice.

June 25
⚡ NYC Pride
Gay Pride Month culminates in a major march down Fifth Ave on the last Sunday of the month. NYC Pride (www.nycpride.org) is a five-hour spectacle of dancers, drag queens, gay police officers, leathermen, lesbian soccer-moms and representatives of just about every other queer scene under the rainbow.

Plan Your Trip
This Year in New York City

July

As the city swelters, locals flee to beachside escapes on Long Island. It's a busy month for tourism, however, as holidaying North Americans and Europeans fill the city.

July 4
✿ Independence Day
America's Independence Day is celebrated on the 4th of July with dramatic fireworks (http://social.macys.com/fireworks) over the East River, starting at 9pm. Good viewing spots include the waterfronts of the Lower East Side and Williamsburg, Brooklyn, or any high rooftop or east-facing Manhattan apartment.

July 4
✗ Nathan's Famous Hot Dog Eating Contest
For rare skills not often celebrated on the sports pages, head to Surf Ave and Stillwell in Coney Island to see competitive eaters down ungodly numbers of hot dogs in just 10 minutes (www.nathansfamous.com/contest). The current record for men is 69 by long-time champ Joey Chestnut. For women, it's 45 – held by the 98lb Sonya Thomas.

Late July–Early August
☆ Lincoln Center Out of Doors
New York City's performing arts power-house stages a festive line up of concerts and dance parties at outdoor stages in the Lincoln Center complex (www.lcoutofdoors.org). Afrobeat, Latin jazz and country are all part of the lineup, and there are special events for families.

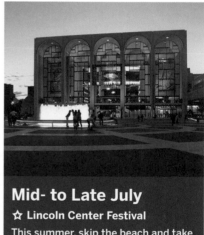

JOSEPH SOHM / SHUTTERSTOCK ©

Mid- to Late July
☆ Lincoln Center Festival
This summer, skip the beach and take advantage of the stellar lineup of drama, ballet, opera and new music hitting Lincoln Stages over three weeks in July (www.lincolncenter-festival.org). Expect high-quality and highly original fare.

August

Waves of summer heat slide between skyscrapers as everyone heads to the seashore or gulps cool blasts of air-conditioning when stuck in the city. Outdoor events add life to the languid urban heat.

Mid-August
☆ FringeNYC
The annual mid-August theater festival, FringeNYC (www.fringenyc.org), presents two weeks of performances by companies from all over the world. It's the best way to catch the edgiest, wackiest and most creative up-and comers around.

Mid-August
☆ Jazz Age Lawn Party
Don your best 1920s attire and head out to Governors Island for a day of big-band jazz, Charleston dancing and pre-Prohibition-era cocktails (www.jazzagelawnparty.com). Buy tickets as early as possible; this event always sells out. Also happens in June.

Late August
☆ Charlie Parker Jazz Festival
This open-air two-day fest (www.cityparks foundation.org) is a great day out for music fans. Incredible jazz talents take to the stage in Marcus Garvey Park in Harlem and in Tompkins Square Park in the East Village.

August 28–September 10
☆ US Open
In late August, Flushing Meadows Park in Queens takes center stage in sports as the world's top tennis players compete in the final Grand Slam tournament of the year (www.usopen.org). If you can't make it to the stadium, major sports bars will be showing it around town.

Michael Arenella and the Dreamland Orchestra perform at the Jazz Age Lawn Party

Plan Your Trip
This Year in New York City

September

Labor Day marks the end of the Hampton's share-house season as the blistering heat of summer fades to more tolerable levels. As locals return to work, the cultural calendar ramps up.

September 1–3

☆ Electric Zoo

Celebrated over the Labor Day weekend, Electric Zoo (www.electriczoofestival.com) is New York's electronic music festival (held in sprawling Randall's Island Park). Past headliners have included Moby, Afrojack, David Guetta, Martin Solveig and the Chemical Brothers.

September 4

✿ West Indian American Day Carnival

Brooklyn's biggest festival (www.wiadca carnival.org) draws some two million parade-goers to Crown Heights for a day of colorful costumes, steel-pan drumming and calypso bands. Go early to find a spot (and scout out food vendors!). The parade starts at 11am.

September–December

☆ BAM's Next Wave Festival

Celebrated for over 30 years, the Brooklyn Academy of Music's Next Wave Festival (www.bam.org) showcases world-class avant-garde theater, music and dance.

At BAM's Next Wave Festival, Japanese dance troupe Sankai Juku perform in Umusuna: Memories Before History, by Ushio Amagatsu

Late September

✿ Atlantic Antic

The best of New York's street festivals brings a medley of live bands, food and drink, and many craft and clothing vendors. You can also climb aboard vintage buses at the New York Transit Museum's display. It happens along Atlantic Ave (www.atlantic ave.org) between Fourth Ave and the waterfront.

October

Brilliant bursts of orange, red and gold fill the trees in Central and Prospect Parks as temperatures cool. Along with May, October is one of the most pleasant and scenic months to visit NYC.

October 1

🎐 Blessing of the Animals

In honor of the Feast Day of St Francis, which falls early in the month, pet owners flock to the grand Cathedral Church of St John the Divine for the annual Blessing of the Animals with their sidekicks – poodles, lizards, parrots, llamas, you name it – in tow. It's a wild and wonderful afternoon for participants and onlookers.

Early October

☆ Comic Con

Enthusiasts from near and far gather at this annual beacon of nerd-dom to dress up as their favorite characters and cavort with like-minded anime aficionados (www. newyorkcomiccon.com).

Mid-October

◉ Open House New York

The country's largest architecture and design event, Open House New York (www. ohny.org) features special architect-led tours, plus lectures, design workshops, studio visits and site-specific performances all over the city.

October 31

🎐 Village Halloween Parade

October 31 brings riotous fun to the city, as New Yorkers don their wildest costumes for a night of revelry. See the most outrageous displays at the Village Halloween Parade (www.halloween-nyc.com) that runs up Sixth Ave in the West Village. It's fun to watch, but even better to join in.

From left: Village Halloween Parade; Blessing of the Animals
LEV RADIN; A KATZ /SHUTTERSTOCK ©

Plan Your Trip
This Year in New York City

November

As the leaves tumble, light jackets are replaced by wool and down. A headliner marathon is tucked into the final days of prehibernation weather, then families gather to give thanks.

Early November

☆ New York Comedy Festival

Funny-makers take the city by storm during the New York Comedy Festival (www.nycomedyfestival.com), with stand-up sessions, improv nights and big-ticket shows hosted by the likes of Rosie O'Donnell and Ricky Gervais.

November 5

🏃 New York City Marathon

Held on the first Sunday of November, this annual 26-mile run (www.nycmarathon.org) draws thousands of athletes from around the world, and many more excited viewers line the streets to cheer the runners on.

November 23

🎈 Thanksgiving Day Parade

Massive helium-filled balloons soar overhead, high-school marching bands rattle their snares and millions of onlookers bundle up with scarves and coats to celebrate Thanksgiving (the fourth Thursday in November) with Macy's world-famous 2.5-mile-long parade (http://social.macys.com/parade).

November 29

⊙ Rockefeller Center Christmas Tree Lighting Ceremony

The flick of a switch ignites the massive Christmas tree in Rockefeller Center, officially ushering in the holiday season. Bedecked with over 25,000 lights, it is NYC's unofficial Yuletide headquarters and a must-see for anyone visiting the city during December.

STU99 / GETTY IMAGES ©

November–March

🏃 Ice Skating in New York

New Yorkers make the most of the winter by taking advantage of outdoor rinks across the city. These usually open in November and run through until late March, with top choices including Central Park, Prospect Park and Rockefeller Center.

2017

December

Winter's definitely here, but there's plenty of holiday cheer to warm the spirit. Fairy lights adorn most buildings, and Fifth Ave department stores create elaborate worlds within their windows.

November–January
☆ Radio City Christmas Spectacular
Radio City Music Hall stages this extravagant annual show (www.radiocitychristmas.com), featuring high-kicking Rockettes and even a visit from Santa Claus. Always a crowd-pleaser, especially with kids.

December 31
🎊 New Year's Eve
The ultimate place to ring in the New Year in the northern hemisphere, Times Square (www.timessquarenyc.org/nye) swarms with millions of revelers who come to stand squashed together like boxed sardines, swig booze, freeze in subarctic temperatures, witness the annual dropping of the ball made entirely of Waterford Crystal and chant the '10...9...8...' countdown in perfect unison.

December 31
🏃 NYRR Midnight Run
For a positive start to 2018, go for a 4-mile dash with other running fans through Central Park. The race starts at midnight, though the festivities and fireworks kick off beforehand. Sign up with New York Road Runners (www.nyrr.org).

JEREMY WALKER / GETTY IMAGES ©

December 1–24
🏠 Holiday Markets
In the lead-up to Christmas, New York becomes a wonderland of holiday markets, selling crafts, clothing and accessories, ceramics, toys and more. The big markets are at Union Square, Bryant Park and Grand Central Terminal.

Plan Your Trip
Need to Know

Daily Costs

**Budget:
less than $100**

- Dorm bed: $40–$70
- Slice of pizza: around $4
- Food-truck taco: from $3
- Bus or subway ride: $2.75

**Midrange:
$100–300**

- Double room in a mid-range hotel: from around $200
- Brunch for two at a mid-range restaurant: $70
- Dinner for two at a mid-range eatery: $130
- Craft cocktail at a lounge bar: $14–$18
- Discount TKTS ticket to a Broadway show: $80
- Brooklyn Academy of Music orchestra seats: from $84

**Top End:
more than $300**

- Luxury stay at the NoMad Hotel: $325–$850
- Tasting menu at a top-end restaurant: $85–$325
- A 1½-hour massage at the atmospheric Great Jones Spa: $200
- Metropolitan Opera orchestra seats: $100–$390

Advance Planning

Two months before Secure hotel reservations as soon as possible – prices increase the closer you get to your arrival date. Snag tickets to your favorite Broadway blockbuster.

Three weeks before If you haven't done so already, score a table at your top-choice high-end restaurant.

One week before Surf the web and scan blogs and Twitter for the latest restaurant and bar openings, plus upcoming art exhibitions.

Useful Websites

- **Lonely Planet** (www.lonelyplanet.com/usa/new-york-city) Destination information, hotel bookings, traveler forum and more.
- **NYC: The Official Guide** (www.nycgo.com) New York City's official tourism portal.
- **Explore Brooklyn** (www.explorebk.com) Brooklyn-specific events and listings.
- **New York Magazine** (www.nymag.com) Comprehensive, current listings for bars, restaurants, entertainment and shopping.
- **New York Times** (www.nytimes.com) Excellent local news coverage and theater listings.

Currency
US dollar (US$)

Language
English

Visas
The US Visa Waiver Program allows nationals of 38 countries to enter the US without a visa.

Money
ATMs widely available; credit cards accepted at most hotels, stores and restaurants.

Cell Phones
Most US cell (mobile) phones, besides the iPhone, operate on CDMA, not the European standard GSM – make sure you check compatibility with your phone service provider. There are stores (mostly run by T-Mobile, Verizon or AT&T) where you can buy a cheap phone and load it with prepaid minutes, to avoid long-term contract.

Time
Eastern Standard Time (GMT/UTC minus five hours)

Tourist Information
There are official NYC Visitor Information Centers throughout the city. The main office is in Midtown (p233).

When to Go

Summers can be scorching hot; winters cold and not without their blizzards. Spring or autumn are the best times to explore.

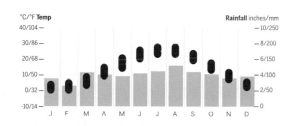

Arriving in New York

John F Kennedy International Airport (p234) The Air Train ($5) links to the Metropolitan Transportation Authority's subway ($2.75), which makes the one-hour journey into Manhattan. Express bus to Grand Central or Port Authority costs $16. Shared vans to Manhattan hotels run $20 to $25. Taxis cost a flat rate of $52 excluding tolls and tip.

LaGuardia Airport (p234) This is the closest airport to Manhattan, but the least accessible by public transit: take the Q70 express bus from the airport to the 74th St–Broadway subway station (7 line, or the E, F, M and R lines at the connecting Jackson Heights Roosevelt Ave station). Express bus to Midtown costs $13. Taxis range from $26 to $48 (excluding tolls and tip), depending on traffic.

Newark Liberty International Airport (p235) Take the Air Train to Newark Airport train station, and board any train bound for New York's Penn Station ($12.50). Express bus to Port Authority or Grand Central costs $16. Shared shuttle to Midtown costs $20 to $26. Taxis range from $60 to $80 (excluding the unavoidable $13 toll and tip). Allow 45 minutes to one hour of travel time.

Tipping

Tipping is *not* optional; only withhold tips in cases of outrageously bad service.

○ **Airport & hotel porters** $2 per bag, $5 per cart.

○ **Bartenders** 15%–20% per round, minimum $1 per standard drink and $2 per specialty cocktail.

○ **Hotel maids** $2–$4 per night, left in an envelope or under the card provided.

○ **Restaurant servers** 18%–20%, unless a gratuity is already charged on the bill (usually only for groups of five or more).

○ **Taxi drivers** 10%–15%, rounded up to the next dollar.

Sleeping

In general, accommodations prices in New York City do not abide by any high-season or low-season rules; wavering rates usually reflect availability. With over 50 million visitors descending upon the city every year, you can expect hotel rooms to fill up quickly – especially in summer. Accommodations options range from boxy cookie-culler rooms in Midtown high-rises to stylish boutique options downtown.

Useful Websites

○ **newyorkhotels.com** (www.newyorkhotels.com)

○ **NYC** (www.nycgo.com/hotels)

○ **Lonely Planet** (lonelyplanet.com/usa/new-york-city/hotels)

For more, see the Survival Guide, p229

Plan Your Trip
Top Days in New York City

MITCHELL FUNK / GETTY IMAGES ©

Midtown & Uptown Icons

Landmarks, highlights, big ticket items: on this itinerary you will experience the NYC of everyone's collective imagination, including the city's most famous museum and park. Take in the mythic landscape of Midtown's concrete and skyscrapers, from the street and from amid the clouds.

❶ Metropolitan Museum of Art (p70)

Start uptown at the big daddy of museums. Check out the Egyptian Wing and the European paintings on the 2nd floor.

➲ Metropolitan Museum of Art to Central Park

🏃 Walk into Central Park at the 79th St entrance.

❷ Central Park (p36)

Get some fresh air in Central Park, the city's spectacular public backyard. Walk south to the Conservatory Pond where toy boats ply the waters.

➲ Central Park to Times Square

🏃 Exit the park on Fifth Ave however far south you'd like, and grab a cab for Times Square.

Day
01

COCOZERO / SHUTTERSTOCK ©

❸ Times Square (p62)

Soak up the Vegas-like atmosphere of Times Square from the TKTS Booth and get discounted tickets for that night. Head to the stadium seating at the northern end where you can take in the dazzling tableau.

⭕ Times Square to Rockefeller Center

🏃 For more elbow room walk up Sixth Ave to 49th St.

❹ Top of the Rock (p84)

Ride to the open-air observation deck at the Top of the Rock in Rockefeller Center for stunning vistas.

⭕ Rockefeller Center to ViceVersa

🏃 It's a half-mile walk west along 51st (or the weary can grab a taxi).

❺ Dinner at ViceVersa (p133)

For Broadway-goers, do an early dinner at this polished Italian eatery with a relaxing back patio.

⭕ ViceVersa to Broadway Theater

🏃 Walk east to the theater for which you've already purchased your tickets

❻ Broadway Theater (p190)

Check out a blockbuster musical for an only-in-New-York spectacle. Afterwards, swig cocktails late into the night at the Edison Hotel's restored piano bar, Rum House (p175).

From left: Central Park (p36); Empire State Building as seen from Top of the Rock (p84)

Plan Your Trip
Top Days in New York City

TONY SHI PHOTOGRAPHY / GETTY IMAGES ©

Lower Manhattan

Surprisingly for this part of downtown dominated by the canyons of Wall St, this day takes in broad horizons and river views, not to mention an iconic historic sight. This itinerary requires a little planning: book your tickets in advance for the Statue of Liberty and Ellis Island, and reserve tickets for One World Trade Center.

❶ Statue of Liberty & Ellis Island (p42)

Time your arrival with your booked ferry's departure. Ellis Island will likely occupy most of the morning. Food options are poor on the islands, so bring snacks.

➲ Ellis Island to Hudson Eats

🏃 After arriving back in Battery Park, walk a mile north along the riverfront promenade to the marina.

❷ Lunch at Hudson Eats (p122)

Inside Brookfield Place, you'll find a sprawling food hall, where you can dine on a wide range of delicacies, including sushi, gourmet tacos and French onion soup.

➲ Hudson Eats to One World Trade Center

🏃 It's a short stroll up to Vesey St, where you can cross busy West St on a covered pedestrian overpass. This will put you at the foot of One World Trade Center.

❸ One World Trade Center (p94)

Step into NYC's tallest building and take a ride up to the Observatory for the view over the metropolis. Reserve tickets in advance.

Day
02

One World Trade Center to the National September 11 Memorial

⚐ Make the 100-story descent and stroll over to the memorial located next to the building.

❹ National September 11 Memorial & Museum (p90)

One of New York's most powerful sites, this memorial pays moving tribute to the innocent victims of the 2001 terrorist attack. After strolling around the cascades, visit the adjoining museum to learn more about the tragic events that transpired on that day.

National September 11 Memorial to Brooklyn Bridge

⚐ Walk east on Vesey St Bowery and cut around City Hall Park after crossing Broadway. Walkway access to the bridge is across from the park (and City Hall).

❺ Brooklyn Bridge (p43)

Join the Brooklynites and hordes of other visitors making this magical pilgrimage over one of the city's most beautiful landmarks.

Brooklyn Bridge to Empire Fulton Ferry State Park

⚐ Walk over the bridge from Manhattan to Brooklyn. Take the stairs and turn left at the bottom. Walk downhill to the waterfront.

❻ Empire Fulton Ferry State Park (p108)

This lovely park has staggering views of Manhattan and the Brooklyn Bridge, and a fully restored 1922 carousel. The brick streets behind are sprinkled with cafes, shops and 19th-century warehouses.

Empire Fulton Ferry State Park to Juliana's

⚐ Walk up Old Fulton St to the corner of Front St.

❼ Dinner at Juliana's (p139)

Don't miss the thin-crust pies by famed pizza maestro Patsy Grimaldi. The classic margherita is one of New York's best.

From left: Statue of Liberty (p42) and Lower Manhattan skyline; Brooklyn Bridge (p48)

Plan Your Trip
Top Days in New York City

West Side Culture

A famed greenway, galleries, market adventures and one spectacular museum set the stage for a fun day's ramble on the West Side. Cap off the day at Lincoln Center, the stunning campus of some of the country's top performance spaces.

❶ The High Line (p54)

Take a taxi to the stroll-worthy High Line, an abandoned railway 30ft above the street, now one of New York's favorite downtown destinations. Enter at 30th St and walk the meandering path for views of the Hudson River and the city streets below.

○ The High Line to Chelsea Galleries

🏃 Exit at the 26th St stairway and explore the surrounding neighborhood on foot.

❷ Chelsea Galleries

One of the hubs of the city's art-gallery scene, here you can ogle works by up-and-comers and established artists alike, and maybe even take home an expensive souvenir. Some of the blue-chip galleries to check out are Gagosian, David Zwirner and Barbara Gladstone.

○ Chelsea Galleries to Chelsea Market

🏃 Walk to Ninth Ave and south to 15th St.

Day

03

JON HICKS / GETTY IMAGES ©

❸ Lunch at Chelsea Market (p127)

This building, a former cookie factory, has a huge concourse packed with food stalls slinging everything from Korean-style ramen to Aussie-style sausage rolls, plus shops selling fresh baked goods, wines, imported cheeses and other temptations

➲ Chelsea Market to American Museum of Natural History

🚇 Grab an uptown C train at Eighth Ave and 14th St and take it to 86th and Central Park West.

❹ American Museum of Natural History (p79)

No matter what your age, you'll experience childlike wonder at the exceptional American Museum of Natural History. Be sure to save time for the Rose Center for Earth & Space, a unique architectural gem in its own right.

➲ American Museum of Natural History to Barcibo Enoteca

🚶 Walk west to Amsterdam Ave and turn south; veer left on Broadway at 71st St.

❺ Drink at Barcibo Enoteca (p178)

Stop in for a pre-show glass of Italian wine, or go for some grub if you're seeing a full-length show.

➲ Barcibo Enoteca to Lincoln Center

🚶 Walk south on Broadway to 63rd St.

❻ Lincoln Center (p76)

Head to the Lincoln Center for opera at the Metropolitan Opera House (p193), the largest in the world, a symphony in Avery Fisher Hall, or a play at one of its two theaters. Don't miss the choreographed 'water shows' at the plaza fountain.

From left: Chelsea Market (p127); Mammoth skeletons in the American Museum of Natural History (p79)

Top Days in New York City

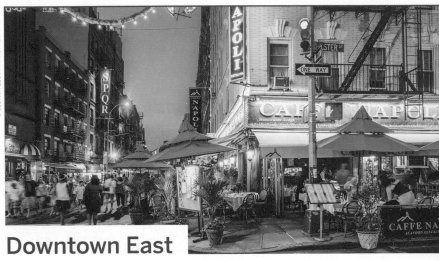

NAREMAGNUM / GETTY IMAGES ©

Downtown East

Gain insight into immigrant history, grab ethnic eats, check out cutting-edge art and theater (as well as cheap booze and live music), and walk up and down the tiny blocks to peek into stylish boutiques. As a general rule, the further east you go the looser things get.

Day

04

❶ Lower East Side Tenement Museum (p98)

Gain an insight into the life and cramped living conditions of immigrants during the 19th and early 20th centuries at this brilliantly curated museum.

➲ Lower East Side Tenement Museum to Little Italy

🚶 Walk west on Delancey St through Sara D Roosevelt Park to Mulberry St.

❷ Little Italy (p89)

Although it feels more like a theme park than an authentic Italian strip, Mulberry St is still the heart of the hood.

➲ Little Italy to the Butcher's Daughter

🚶 Walk two blocks north along Mulberry and turn right onto Kenmare; it's another two blocks further.

❸ Lunch at the Butcher's Daughter (p123)

Grab a bite at this delightful earth-friendly eatery in Nolita. The vegan cafe serves up creative, healthy dishes that also happen to

ROBERT K. CHIN / ALAMY STOCK PHOTO ©

be delicious. Add in craft beer and sidewalk dining, and you may find yourself whiling away the whole afternoon here.

🡒 Butcher's Daughter to New Museum of Contemporary Art

🏃 Walk several blocks east to Bowery and turn north.

❹ New Museum of Contemporary Art (p101)

Symbolic of the once-gritty Bowery's transformation, this ubercontemporary museum has a steady menu of edgy works in new forms. Stop by the bookstore with its eclectic mix of cutting-edge publications.

🡒 New Museum of Contemporary Art to St Marks Place

🏃 Turn right on Houston and then left up Second Ave until you reach 9th St.

❺ St Marks Place

Stroll this famous street past the cheesy T-shirt shops, tattoo parlors, punk-rock stores and sake bars, then head to the neighboring streets for a quieter round of nibbling and boutique-ing.

🡒 St Marks Place to New York Theater Workshop

🏃 Head to 4th St between Bowery and Second Ave.

❻ New York Theatre Workshop(p187)

A showcase for contemporary and cutting-edge fare, this much-lauded performance space is a great spot to see a show.

🡒 New York Theater Workshop to Babu Ji

🏃 It's a quick cab ride or a 15-minute walk. If walking, stroll up to 10th St and turn right. Walk three blocks to Ave C and turn left.

❼ Dinner at Babu Ji (p125)

Part of a new breed of innovative ethnic eateries downtown, Babu Ji serves upscale versions of Indian street food. Afterwards, you're well-placed for bar-hopping on lively Ave C.

From left: Mulberry St, Little Italy (p89); St Mark's Place

Plan Your Trip
Hotspots For...

CULTURE VULTURES

👁 **Metropolitan Museum of Art**
One of the greatest repositories of
art on the planet. (p70)

☆ **Lincoln Center** (pictured above)
Enchanting setting for world-renowned
opera, ballet and classical music.
(p76)

👁 **Guggenheim** The retrospectives
here are among the best anywhere in
the art world. (p80)

✕ **Degustation** Tiny East Village
spot where chefs bring high art to
the cooking. (p126)

🍷 **Rum House** All class, this candlelit Midtown spot has live acoustic
sessions and first-rate libations.
(p175)

GLITZ & GLAMOUR

👜 **Barneys** This fashionista's aspi-
rational closet spreads a staggering
array of temptations. (p115)

👜 **Tiffany & Co** Admire the diamonds
and sapphires at the famed Fifth Ave
jeweler. (p114)

✕ **SixtyFive** Take in the magical
views over Manhattan from this high-
up cocktail bar. (p175)

☆ **Chicago** One of the most scintillating shows on Broadway. (p191)

✕ **Le Bernardin** (pictured below)
With three Michelin stars, this fine-dining beauty serves unforgettable fare.
(p135)

ACTIVE OUTDOORS

☉ **Central Park** Free and open to all, the famous green space has lakes, meadows and forested paths. (p36)

☉ **High Line** A former railway turned greenway with wild plants and surprising vantage points. (p54)

🏄 **Downtown Boathouse** Manhattan views while kayaking on the Hudson. (p204)

✕ **Union Square Greenmarket** Assemble a picnic from the lovely produce and gourmet goodies at this outdoor market. (p131)

🍷 **Pier A Harbor House** A great outdoor spot for a drink or a bite after strolling the waterfront. (p167)

HISTORY BUFFS

☉ **Ellis Island** (pictured above) The gateway to a new life for so many of America's immigrants. (p43)

☉ **Lower East Side Tenement Museum** Fascinating insight into working-class life during the 19th and early 20th centuries. (p98)

☆ **Hamilton** An American history lesson set to urban rhythms. (p191)

✕ **Barney Greengrass** Still serving up some of NYC's best smoked fish after a century in the business. (p136)

🍷 **Dead Rabbit** Brilliantly reviving vintage cocktail recipes, many dating back to the 19th century. (p166)

CRAFTY CREATIVES

☉ **MoMA PS1** (pictured above) Former schoolhouse turned art museum with celebrated exhibitions. (p52)

✕ **Roosevelt Avenue Food Trucks** Sample the street foods of Latin America on a Queens food crawl.

☆ **Smalls** Catch brassy jazz shows at this atmospheric West Village music den. (p188)

✕ **Marlow & Sons** Great place to check out Brooklyn's craft food and drink scene. (p139)

Plan Your Trip
What's New

Whitney Museum of American Art

At the southern end of the High Line, the Whitney Museum (p57) has opened its brand new Renzo Piano–designed building. The gorgeous light-filled galleries bring more space and innovation to downtown's most impressive art center.

Market Madness

The love for food markets shows no signs of abating, with a number of sprawling new Manhattan foodie halls, including Gansevoort Market (p127). There's more ahead, including Anthony Bourdain's 155,000-sq-ft market opening in 2017, on a Hudson pier west of the Meatpacking District.

St Ann's Warehouse

Avant-garde performance company St Ann's Warehouse (p195) has opened its doors in its first-ever permanent location under the Brooklyn Bridge. Expect to see more cutting-edge programming, for which St Ann's is so well-known.

One World Trade Center

The tallest building in New York now looms high above Lower Manhattan. While you can admire its jewel-like facade from afar, the best view is up top from the magnificent observatory (p95) on the 102nd floor.

Uptown Allure

Downtown cool is finally arriving in both the Upper West and Upper East Sides, with a sprinkling of earth-friendly eateries, craft brew pubs (West End Hall, p178) and creative cocktail dens (The Daisy, p177).

Whitney Museum of American Art (p57)

Plan Your Trip
For Free

AL PERERA / GETTY IMAGES ©

Free New York City

The Big Apple isn't exactly the world's cheapest destination. Nevertheless, there are many ways to kick open the NYC treasure chest without spending a dime – free concerts, theater and film screenings, pay-what-you-wish nights at legendary museums, city festivals, free ferry rides and kayaking, plus loads of green space.

Summertime Events

In summer there are scores of free events around town. From June through early September, **SummerStage** (p11) features over 100 free performances at 17 parks around the city, including Central Park. You'll have to be tenacious to get tickets to **Shakespeare in the Park** (p10), also

held in Central Park, but it's well worth the effort. Top actors such as Meryl Streep and Al Pacino have taken the stage in years past. Prospect Park has its own open-air summer concert and events series: **Celebrate Brooklyn** (www.bricartsmedia.org).

Summertime also brings free film screenings and events to the water's edge during the **River to River Festival** (p11) at Hudson River Park in Manhattan and at Brooklyn Bridge Park. Another great option for film lovers is the free **Bryant Park Summer Film Festival** (p11) screenings on Monday nights.

On the Water

The free Staten Island Ferry (p237) provides great views of the Statue of Liberty, and you can

enjoy it with a cold beer (available on the boat). On summer weekends, you can also take a free ferry over to Governors Island (p109), a car-free oasis with priceless views.

For more adventure, take out a free kayak, in the Hudson River Park (p57), Brooklyn Bridge Park (p106) and Red Hook.

Best Free Museum Days

New Museum of Contemporary Art (p101) 7–9pm Thursday

MoMA (p50) 4–8pm Friday

Whitney Museum of American Art (p57) 7–10pm Friday

Guggenheim Museum (p80) 5:45–7:45pm Saturday

Frick Collection (p73) 11am–1pm Sunday

Above: Celebrate Brooklyn, held in Prospect Park

Plan Your Trip
Family Travel

MATTES RENĀÐ / HEMIS.FR / GETTY IMAGES ©

Need to Know

o **Change Facilities** Not common in bars and restaurants.

o **Strollers** Not allowed on buses unless folded up.

o **Transportation** Subway stairs can be challenging with strollers; taxis are exempt from car-seat laws.

o **Useful Website** Time Out New York Kids (www.timeout.com/new-york-kids) has helpful tips.

Sights & Activities

Museums, especially those geared toward kids, such as the Children's Museum of the Arts (www.cmany.org) and the American Museum of Natural History (p79), are always great places, as are children's theaters, movie theaters, book and toy stores, and aquariums. The city is dotted with vintage carousels; rides cost from $2 to $3.

The boat ride to the Statue of Liberty (p42) offers the opportunity to chug around New York Harbor and to get to know an icon that most kids only know from textbooks.

The city has a number of zoos. The best, by far, is the Bronx Zoo (www.bronxzoo. com); otherwise, if you're pressed for time, the Central Park Zoo (www.centralparkzoo. com) will keep the tots entertained.

Central Park (p36) also has more than 800 acres of green space, a lake that can be navigated by rowboat, a carousel and a massive statue of Alice in Wonderland. Heckscher playground, near Seventh Ave and Central Park South, is the biggest and best of its 21 playgrounds.

With hot dogs, vintage coasters and an open stretch of beach, Coney Island (www. coneyisland.com) is just what the doctor ordered if the family is in need of some fun in the sun.

FRANZ MARC FREY / GETTY IMAGES ©

Transportation

The biggest pitfalls tend to revolve around public transportation, as a startling lack of subway-station elevators will have you lugging strollers up and down flights of stairs (though you can avoid the turnstile by getting buzzed through an easy-access gate); visit http://web.mta.info/accessibility/stations.htm to find a guide to subway stations with elevators. Regarding fares, anyone over 44in is supposed to pay full fare, but the rule is rarely enforced.

Babysitting

While most major hotels (and a handful of boutique-style places) offer on-site babysitting services – or can at least provide you with referrals – you could also turn to a local childcare organization. The

Top Five Parks for Families

Central Park (p36)
Brooklyn Bridge Park (p106)
Hudson River Park (p57)
High Line (p54)

Baby Sitters' Guild (☎ 212-682-0227; www.babysittersguild.com), established in 1940 to serve travelers who are staying in hotels with children, has a stable of sitters who speak a range of 16 languages. All are carefully screened, most are CPR-certified and many have nursing backgrounds; they'll come to your hotel room and even bring games and arts-and-crafts projects. This will set you back about $22 per hour.

From left: Statue of Liberty (p42); Central Park (p36)

SYLVAIN SONNET / GETTY IMAGES ©

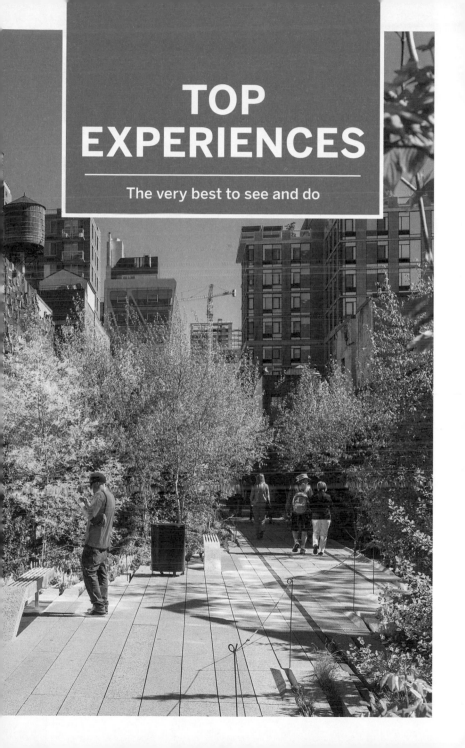

TOP
EXPERIENCES

The very best to see and do

Central Park

Lush lawns, cool forests, flowering gardens, glassy bodies of water and meandering, wooded paths provide a dose of serene nature amid the urban rush of New York City. Today, this 'people's park' is still one of the city's most popular attractions, beckoning throngs of New Yorkers with concerts, events and wildlife.

Great For...

🐦 🥾 👪

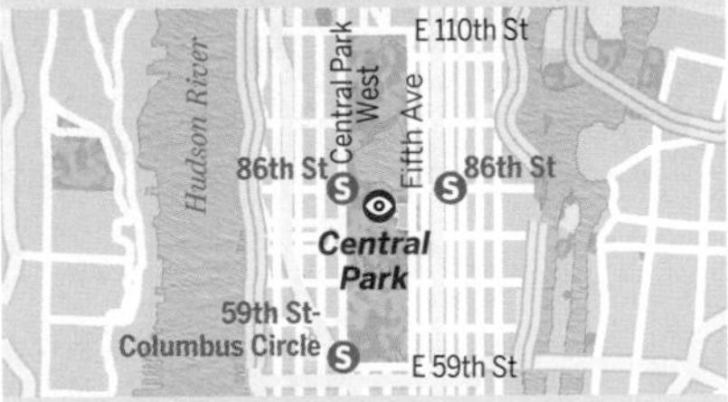
E 110th St
Central Park West
Fifth Ave
Hudson River
86th St
86th St
Central Park
59th St-Columbus Circle
E 59th St

Need to Know

Map p250; www.centralparknyc.org; 59th & 110th Sts, btwn Central Park West & Fifth Ave; 🕒6am-1am

★ **Top Tip**

To escape the crowds, try the North Meadow (north of 97th St) or the Harlem Meer.

Like the city's subway system, the vast and majestic Central Park, an 843-acre rectangle of open space in the middle of Manhattan, is a great class leveler – which is exactly what it was envisioned to be. Created in the 1860s and '70s by Frederick Law Olmsted and Calvert Vaux on the marshy northern fringe of the city, the immense park was designed as a leisure space for all New Yorkers, regardless of color, class or creed.

Olmsted and Vaux (who also created Prospect Park in Brooklyn) were determined to keep foot and road traffic separate and cleverly designed the crosstown transverses under elevated roads to do so.

Throughout the year, visitors find free outdoor concerts at the Great Lawn, precious animals at the Central Park Wildlife Center and top-notch drama at the annual Shakespeare in the Park productions. While parts of the park swarm with joggers, in-line skaters, musicians and tourists on warm weekends, it's quieter on weekday afternoons – but especially in less well-trodden spots above 72nd St such as the Harlem Meer and the North Meadow (north of 97th St).

Folks flock to the park even in winter, when snowstorms can inspire cross-country skiing and sledding or a simple stroll through the white wonderland, and crowds turn out every New Year's Eve for a midnight run. The **Central Park Conservancy** (Map p250; 212-310-6600; www.centralparknyc.org/tours; 14 E 60th St; S N/Q/R to 5th Ave-59th St) offers ever-changing guided tours of the park, including those that focus on public art, wildlife, and places of interest to kids.

Strawberry Fields

This tear-shaped garden serves as a memorial to Beatle John Lennon. It is composed of a grove of stately elms and a tiled mosaic that reads, 'Imagine.' Find it at the level of 72nd St on the park's west side.

Bethesda Terrace & Mall

The arched walkways of Bethesda Terrace, crowned by the magnificent Bethesda Fountain, have long been a gathering area for New Yorkers of all flavors. To the south is the Mall (featured in countless movies), a promenade shrouded in mature North American elms. The southern stretch, known as Literary Walk, is flanked by statues of famous authors.

☑ Don't Miss

Tours with the Central Park Conservancy; many are free, others cost $15.

STUART MONK / SHUTTERSTOCK ©

Conservatory Water & Around

North of the zoo at the level of 74th St is the Conservatory Water, where model sailboats drift lazily and kids scramble about on a statue of Alice in Wonderland. There are Saturday story hours at the Hans Christian Andersen statue to the west of the water.

Great Lawn & Around

The Great Lawn is a massive emerald carpet at the center of the park – between 79th and 86th Sts – and is surrounded by ball fields and London plane trees. Immediately to the southeast is the Delacorte Theater, home to the annual Shakespeare in the Park festival, as well as Belvedere Castle, a lookout. Further south, between 72nd and 79th Sts, is the leafy Ramble, a popular birding destination. On the southeastern end is the Loeb Boathouse, home to a waterside restaurant that offers rowboat and bicycle rentals.

What's Nearby?

American Folk Art Museum Museum

(Map p250; ☎212-595-9533; www.folkartmuseum.org; 2 Lincoln Sq, Columbus Ave, at 66th St; 🕒11:30am-7pm Tue-Thu & Sat, noon-7:30pm Fri, noon-6pm Sun; [S]1 to 66th St Lincoln Center) [FREE] This tiny institution contains a couple of centuries' worth of folk and outsider art treasures, including pieces by Henry Darger (known for his girl-filled battlescapes) and Martín Ramírez (producer of hallucinatory caballeros on horseback). There is also an array of wood carvings, paintings, hand-tinted photographs and decorative objects.

🍴 Take a Break

Class things up with an afternoon martini at the **Loeb Boathouse** (Map p250; ☎212-517-2233; www.thecentralparkboathouse.com; Central Park Lake, at 74th St; mains $25-36; 🕒hours vary; [S]A/C, B to 72nd St, 6 to 77th St).

Central Park

THE LUNGS OF NEW YORK

The rectangular patch of green that occupies Manhattan's heart began life in the mid-19th century as a swampy piece of land that was carefully bulldozed into the idyllic naturescape you see today. Since officially becoming Central Park, it has brought New Yorkers of all stripes together in interesting and unexpected ways. The park has served as a place for the rich to show off their fancy carriages (1860s), for the poor to enjoy free Sunday concerts (1880s) and for activists to hold be-ins against the Vietnam War (1960s).

Since then, legions of locals – not to mention travelers from all kinds of faraway places – have poured in to stroll, picnic, sunbathe, play ball and catch free concerts and performances of works by Shakespeare.

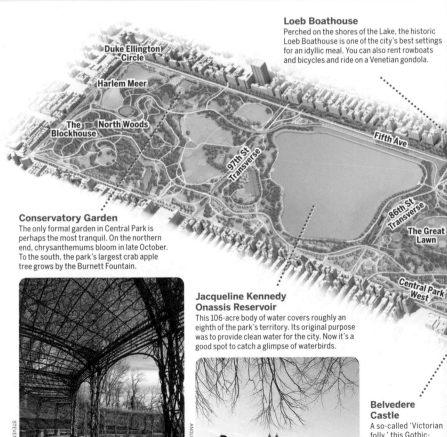

Loeb Boathouse
Perched on the shores of the Lake, the historic Loeb Boathouse is one of the city's best settings for an idyllic meal. You can also rent rowboats and bicycles and ride on a Venetian gondola.

Duke Ellington Circle

Harlem Meer

The Blockhouse

North Woods

97th St Transverse

Fifth Ave

86th St Transverse

The Great Lawn

Central Park West

Conservatory Garden
The only formal garden in Central Park is perhaps the most tranquil. On the northern end, chrysanthemums bloom in late October. To the south, the park's largest crab apple tree grows by the Burnett Fountain.

Jacqueline Kennedy Onassis Reservoir
This 106-acre body of water covers roughly an eighth of the park's territory. Its original purpose was to provide clean water for the city. Now it's a good spot to catch a glimpse of waterbirds.

Belvedere Castle
A so-called 'Victorian folly,' this Gothic-Romanesque castle serves no other purpose than to be a very dramatic lookout point. It was built by Central Park co-designer Calvert Vaux in 1869.

The park's varied terrain offers a wonderland of experiences. There are quiet, woodsy knolls in the north. To the south is the reservoir, crowded with joggers. There are European gardens, a zoo and various bodies of water. For maximum flamboyance, hit the Sheep Meadow on a sunny day, when all of New York shows up to lounge.

Central Park is more than just a green space. It is New York City's backyard.

FACTS & FIGURES

» **Landscape architects** Frederick Law Olmsted and Calvert Vaux

» **Year that construction began** 1858

» **Acres** 843

» **On film** Hundreds of movies have been shot on location, from Depression-era blockbusters such as *Gold Diggers* (1933) to the monster-attack flick *Cloverfield* (2008).

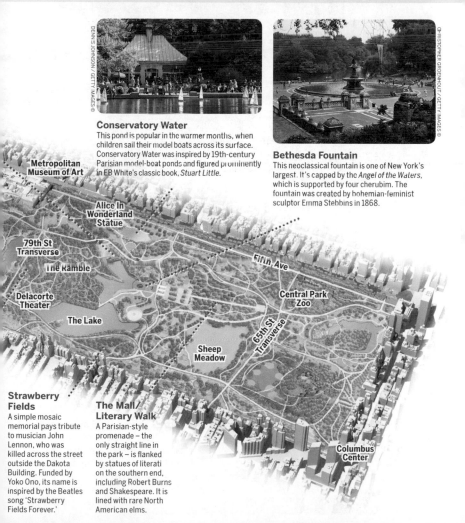

Conservatory Water
This pond is popular in the warmer months, when children sail their model boats across its surface. Conservatory Water was inspired by 19th-century Parisian model-boat ponds and figured prominently in EB White's classic book, *Stuart Little*.

Bethesda Fountain
This neoclassical fountain is one of New York's largest. It's capped by the *Angel of the Waters*, which is supported by four cherubim. The fountain was created by bohemian-feminist sculptor Emma Stebbins in 1868.

Metropolitan Museum of Art

Alice In Wonderland Statue

79th St Transverse

The Ramble

Delacorte Theater

The Lake

Fifth Ave

Central Park Zoo

65th St Transverse

Sheep Meadow

Strawberry Fields
A simple mosaic memorial pays tribute to musician John Lennon, who was killed across the street outside the Dakota Building. Funded by Yoko Ono, its name is inspired by the Beatles song 'Strawberry Fields Forever.'

The Mall/ Literary Walk
A Parisian-style promenade – the only straight line in the park – is flanked by statues of literati on the southern end, including Robert Burns and Shakespeare. It is lined with rare North American elms.

Columbus Center

KTSFOTOS / GETTY IMAGES ©

Statue of Liberty & Ellis Island

Stellar skyline views, a scenic ferry ride, a lookout from Lady Liberty's crown, and a moving tribute to America's immigrants at Ellis Island — unmissable is an understatement.

Great For...

☑ **Don't Miss**

The breathtaking views from Lady Liberty's crown (remember to reserve tickets well in advance).

Statue of Liberty

A Powerful Symbol

Lady Liberty has been gazing sternly toward 'unenlightened Europe' since 1886. Dubbed the 'Mother of Exiles,' the statue symbolically admonishes the rigid social structures of the old world. 'Give me your tired, your poor, your huddled masses yearning to breathe free, the wretched refuse of your teeming shore,' she declares in Emma Lazarus' 1883 poem 'The New Colossus.'

History of the Statue

Conceived as early as 1865 by French intellectual Edouard Laboulaye as a monument to the republican principals shared by France and the USA, the Statue of Liberty is still generally recognized by many as a symbol for at least the ideals of opportunity

A & L SINIBALDI / GETTY IMAGES ©

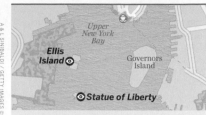

Upper New York Bay

Ellis Island ⊚

Governors Island

⊚ **Statue of Liberty**

❶ Need to Know

☎212-363-3200, tickets 877-523-9849; www. nps.gov/stli; Liberty Island; adult/child incl Ellis Island $18/9, incl crown $21/12; ⊙8:30am-5:30pm, check website for seasonal changes; Ⓢ1 to South Ferry, 4/5 to Bowling Green, then 🚢to Liberty Island

✕ Take a Break

Pack a picnic or chow beforehand at the Hudson Eats (p122) food hall.

★ Top Tip

Pick up a free audioguide when you reach Liberty island; there's even a version for kids.

and freedom. French sculptor Frédéric-Auguste Bartholdi traveled to New York in 1871 to select the site, then spent more than 10 years in Paris designing and making the 151ft-tall figure Liberty Enlightening the World. It was then shipped to New York, erected on a small island in the harbor and unveiled in 1886. Structurally, it consists of an iron skeleton (designed by Gustave Eiffel) with a copper skin attached to it by stiff but flexible metal bars.

Visiting the Statue of Liberty

Access to the crown is limited, so reservations are required. Book as far in advance as possible (additional $3). Pedestal access is also limited, so reserve in advance (no additional fee). Keep in mind, there's no elevator and the climb from the base is equal to a 22-story building. Otherwise, a visit means you can wander the grounds

and enjoy the view of Lady Liberty from all sides (plus the great views of Manhattan). A free audioguide provides historical details and little-known facts about the statue.

The trip to Liberty island, via ferry, is usually made in conjunction with nearby Ellis Island. Ferries leave from Battery Park and tickets include admission to both sights. Reserve in advance to cut down on long wait times.

Ellis Island

Ellis Island (☎212-363-3200, tickets 877-523-9849; www.nps.gov/elis; Ellis Island; ferry incl Statue of Liberty adult/child $18/9; ⊙8:30am-5:30pm, check website for seasonal changes; Ⓢ1 to South Ferry, 4/5 to Bowling Green, then 🚢to Ellis Island) **FREE** is America's most famous and historically important gateway – the very spot where Old World despair met New World promise. Between 1892 and 1924, over 12 million immigrants passed through this processing station, their dreams in tow. An estimated 40% of Americans today have at least one ancestor who was processed here, confirming the major role this tiny harbor island has played in the making of modern America.

Main Building Architecture

With their Main Building, architects Edward Lippincott Tilton and William A Boring created a suitably impressive and imposing 'prologue' to America. The designing duo won the contract after the original wooden building burnt down in 1897. Having attended the Ecole des Beaux Arts in Paris, it's not surprising that they opted for a beaux-arts aesthetic for the project. The building evokes a grand train station, with majestic triple-arched entrances, decorative Flemish bond brickwork, and granite quoins (cornerstones) and belvederes.

Inside, it's the 2nd-floor, 338ft-long Registry Room (also known as the Great Hall) that takes the breath away. It was under its beautiful vaulted ceiling that the newly arrived lined up to have their documents checked, and that the polygamists, paupers, criminals and anarchists were turned back. The original plaster ceiling was severely damaged by an explosion of munition barges at nearby Black Tom Wharf. It was a blessing in disguise; the rebuilt version was adorned with striking, herringbone-patterned tiles by Rafael Guastavino. The Catalan-born engineer is also behind the beautiful tiled ceiling at the Grand Central Oyster Bar & Restaurant at Grand Central Terminal.

Main Building Restoration

After a $160-million restoration, the Main Building was reopened to the public as the Ellis Island Immigration Museum in 1990. Now anybody who rides the ferry to the island can experience a cleaned-up, modern version of the historic new-arrival experience, the museum's interactive exhibits paying homage to the hope, jubilation and sometimes-bitter disappointment of the millions who came here in search of a new beginning. Among them were Hungarian Erik Weisz (Harry Houdini), Italian Rodolfo Guglielmi (Rudolph Valentino) and Brit Archibald Alexander Leach (Cary Grant).

★ Did You Know?

The Statue of Liberty weighs 225 tonnes and stretches 93m from ground to tip.

Immigration Museum Exhibits

The museum's exhibits are spread over three levels. To get the most out of your visit, opt for the 50-minute self-guided audio tour (free with ferry ticket, available from the museum lobby). Featuring narratives from a number of sources, including historians, architects and the immigrants themselves, the tour brings to life the museum's hefty collection of personal objects, official documents, photographs and film footage. It's an evocative experience to relive personal memories – both good and bad – in the very halls and corridors in which they occurred.

The collection itself is divided into a number of permanent and temporary exhibitions. If you're very short on time, skip the 'Journeys: The Peopling of America 1550–1890' exhibit on the 1st floor and focus on 2nd floor. It's here that you'll find the two most fascinating exhibitions. The first, 'Through America's Gate,' examines the step-by-step process faced by the newly arrived, including the chalk-marking of those suspected of illness, a wince-inducing eye examination, and 29 questions in the beautiful, vaulted Registry Room. The second, 'Peak Immigration Years,' explores the motives behind the immigrants' journeys and the challenges they faced once free to begin their new American lives. Particularly interesting is the collection of old photographs, which offers intimate glimpses into the daily lives of these courageous new Americans.

For a history of the rise, fall and resurrection of the building itself, make time for the 'Restoring a Landmark' exhibition on the 3rd floor; its tableaux of trashed desks, chairs and other abandoned possessions are strangely haunting. Best of all, the audio tour offers optional, in-depth coverage for those wanting to delve deeper into the collections and the island's history. If you don't feel like opting for the audio tour, you can always pick up one of the phones in each display area and listen to the recorded, yet affecting memories of real Ellis Island immigrants, taped in the 1980s.

Another option is the free, 45-minute guided tour with a park ranger. If booked three weeks in advance by phone, the tour is also available in American sign language.

American Immigrant Wall of Honor & Fort Gibson Ruins

Accessible from the 1st-floor 'Journeys: The Peopling of America 1550–1890' exhibit is the outdoor American Immigrant Wall of Honor, inscribed with the names of over 700,000 immigrants. Believed to be the world's longest wall of names, it's a fund-raising project, allowing any American to have an immigrant relative's name recorded for the cost of a donation. Construction of the wall in the 1990s uncovered the remains of the island's original structure, Fort Gibson – you can see the ruins at the southwestern corner of the memorial. Built in 1808, the fortification was part of a harbor-defense system against the British that also included Castle Clinton in Battery Park and Castle Williams on Governors Island. During this time, Ellis Island measured a modest 3.3 acres of sand and slush. Between 1892 and 1934, the island expanded dramatically thanks to landfill brought in from the ballast of ships and construction of the city's subway system.

What's Nearby?

Ferries depart from Battery Park. Nearby attractions include the following museums.

Museum of Jewish Heritage   Museum

(Map p246; ☏646-437-4202; www.mjhnyc.org; 36 Battery Pl; adult/child $12/free, 4-8pm Wed free; ◷10am-5:45pm Sun-Tue & Thu, to 8pm Wed, to 5pm Fri mid-Mar–mid-Nov, to 3pm Fri rest of year; 🚻; 🚇4/5 to Bowling Green; R to Whitehall St) An evocative waterfront museum exploring all aspects of modern Jewish identity and culture, from religious traditions to artistic accomplishments. The museum's core exhibition includes a detailed exploration of the Holocaust, with personal artifacts, photographs and documentary films providing a personal,

moving experience. Outdoors is the Garden of Stones installation. Created by artist Andy Goldsworthy and dedicated to those who lost loved ones in the Holocaust, its 18 boulders form a narrow pathway for contemplating the fragility of life.

The building itself consists of six sides and three tiers to symbolize the Star of David and the six million Jews who perished in WWII. Exhibitions aside, the venue also hosts films, music concerts, ongoing lecture series and special holiday performances. Frequent, free workshops for families with children are also on offer, while the on-site, kosher cafe serves light food.

National Museum of the American Indian   Museum

(Map p246; ☏212-514-3700; www.nmai.si.edu; 1 Bowling Green; ◷10am-5pm Fri-Wed, to 8pm Thu;

American Immigrant Wall of Honor at Ellis Island

§4/5 to Bowling Green; R to Whitehall St) `FREE`
An affiliate of the Smithsonian Institution, this elegant tribute to Native American culture is set in Cass Gilbert's spectacular 1907 Custom House, one of NYC's finest beaux-arts buildings. Beyond a vast elliptical rotunda, sleek galleries play host to changing exhibitions documenting Native American art, culture, life and beliefs. The museum's permanent collection includes stunning decorative arts, textiles and ceremonial objects that document the diverse native cultures across the Americas.

The four giant female sculptures outside the building are the work of Daniel Chester French, who would go on to sculpt the seated Abraham Lincoln at Washington, DC's Lincoln Memorial. Representing (from left to right) Asia, North America, Europe and Africa, the figures offer a revealing look at America's world view at the beginning of the 20th century; Asia 'bound' by its religions, America 'youthful and virile,' Europe 'wise yet decaying' and Africa 'asleep and barbaric.' The museum also hosts a range of cultural programs, including dance and music performances, readings for children, craft demonstrations, films and workshops. The museum shop is well stocked with cultural souvenir items, cush as Native American jewelry, books, CDs and crafts.

★ Hospital of All Nations

At the turn of the 20th century, the now-defunct hospital on Ellis Island was one of the world's largest. Consisting of 22 buildings and dubbed the 'Hospital of all Nations,' it was America's front line in the fight against 'imported' diseases.

MATT MUNRO / LONELY PLANET ©

Brooklyn Bridge

Marianne Moore's description of the world's first suspension bridge as a 'climactic ornament, a double rainbow' is perhaps most evocative.

Great For...

☑ **Don't Miss**

Empire Fulton Ferry (p108), part of Brooklyn Bridge Park located just past the span, for its dramatic bridge and skyscraper views.

A New York icon, the Brooklyn Bridge was the world's first steel suspension bridge. Indeed, when it opened in 1883, the 1596ft span between its two support towers was the longest in history. Although its construction was fraught with disaster, the bridge became a magnificent example of urban design, inspiring poets, writers and painters.

Today, its pedestrian walkway – which begins just east of City Hall – delivers a soul-stirring view of Lower Manhattan.

Construction

Ironically, one man deprived of this view was the bridge's very designer, John Roebling. The Prussian-born engineer was knocked off a pier in Fulton Landing in June 1869, dying of tetanus poisoning before construction of the Brooklyn Bridge even began. Consequently, his son, Washington

RAFAEL PAULUCCI / GETTY IMAGES ©

Chambers St/
Brooklyn Bridge-
City Hall
Ⓢ

Franklin D Roosevelt Dr

East River

**Brooklyn
Bridge**
◉

Fulton St
Ⓢ

ℹ️ Need to Know

Map p246; Ⓢ4/5/6 to Brooklyn Bridge-City Hall; J/Z to Chambers St; R to City Hall

✕ Take a Break

For drinks with a view, you can't beat Brooklyn Bridge Garden Bar (p109).

★ Top Tip

To beat the crowds, visit the bridge early in the morning.

Roebling, supervised its construction, which lasted 14 years and managed to survive budget overruns and the deaths of 20 workers. The younger Roebling himself suffered from the bends while helping to excavate the riverbed for the bridge's western tower and remained bedridden for much of the project; his wife, Emily, oversaw construction in his stead. There was one final tragedy to come in June 1883, when the bridge opened to pedestrian traffic. Someone in the crowd shouted, perhaps as a joke, that the bridge was collapsing into the river, setting off a mad rush in which 12 people were trampled to death.

Crossing the Bridge

Walking across the grand Brooklyn Bridge is a rite of passage for New Yorkers and visitors alike – with this in mind, walk no more than two abreast or else you're in danger of colliding with runners and speeding cyclists. And take care to stay on the side of the walkway marked for folks on foot, and not in the bike lane.

The bridge walk is 1.3 miles (2km), but allow around an hour in either direction to stop and soak up the views.

What's Nearby?

Just north of the Manhattan-side access to the bridge lies Chinatown (p54). On the Brooklyn side, you're a short stroll from Dumbo and Brooklyn Bridge Park (p74).

Dumbo Neighborhood
Dumbo's nickname is an acronym for its location: 'Down Under the Manhattan Bridge Overpass,' and while this north Brooklyn slice of waterfront used to be strictly for industry, it's now the domain of high-end condos, furniture shops and art galleries. Several highly regarded performing-arts spaces are located in the cobblestone streets and the Empire-Fulton Ferry State Park (p108) hugs the waterfront and offers picture-postcard Manhattan views.

MoMA

Quite possibly the greatest hoarder of modern masterpieces on earth, the Museum of Modern Art (MoMA) is a cultural promised land.

Great For...

☑ Don't Miss

- Van Gogh's *Starry Night.*
- Edward Hopper's *House by the Railroad.*
- Andy Warhol's *Gold Marilyn Monroe.*

Since its founding in 1929, MoMA has amassed over 150,000 artworks, documenting the emerging creative ideas and movements of the late 19th century through to those that dominate today. For art buffs, it's Valhalla. For the uninitiated, it's a thrilling crash course in all that is beautiful and addictive about art.

Visiting MoMA

It's easy to get lost in MoMA's vast collection. To maximize your time and create a plan of attack, download the museum's free smartphone app from the website beforehand. MoMA's permanent collection spans four levels, with prints, illustrated books and the unmissable Contemporary Galleries on level two; architecture, design, drawings and photography on level three; and painting and sculpture on levels four and five. Many of the big hitters are on

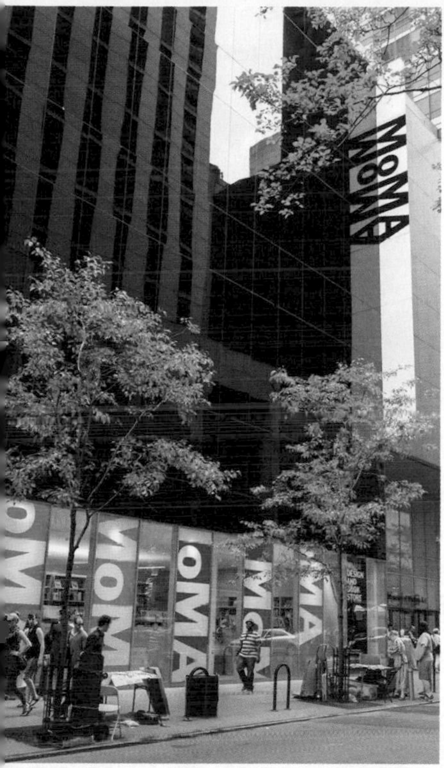

MIKECPHOTO / SHUTTERSTOCK ©

these last two levels, so tackle the museum from the top down before fatigue sets in. Must-sees include Van Gogh's *Starry Night*, Cézanne's *The Bather*, Picasso's *Les Demoiselles d'Avignon*, and Henri Rousseau's *The Sleeping Gypsy*, not to mention iconic American works such as Warhol's *Campbell's Soup Cans* and *Gold Marilyn Monroe*, Lichtenstein's equally poptastic *Girl With Ball*, and Hopper's haunting *House by the Railroad*.

Lunchtime Talks

To delve a little deeper into MoMA's collection, join one of the museum's lunchtime talks and readings, which see writers, artists, curators and designers offering expert insight into specific works and exhibitions on view. The talks take place daily at 11.30am and 1.30pm. To check upcoming topics, click the 'Learn' link on the MoMA website, followed by the 'Lectures & Events' and 'Gallery Sessions' links.

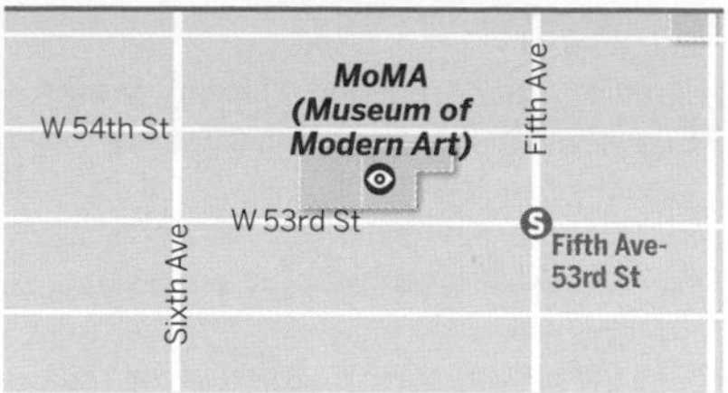

ℹ Need to Know

Museum of Modern Art; Map p252; ☎212-708-9400; www.moma.org; 11 W 53rd St, btwn Fifth & Sixth Aves; adult/child $25/free, 4-8pm Fri free; 🕒10:30am-5:30pm Sat-Thu, to 8pm Fri, to 8pm Thu Jul-Aug; 👪; [S] E, M to 5th Ave 53rd St

🍴 Take a Break

For a casual vibe, nosh on Italian-inspired fare at MoMA's **Cafe 2** (Map p252; ☎212-333 1299; www.moma.org; Museum of Modern Art, 11 W 53rd St, btwn Fifth & Sixth Aves; sandwiches & salads $12-14, mains $19; 🕒11am-5pm, to 7:30pm Fri; 📶; [S] E, M to 5th Ave-53rd St).

★ Top Tip

Keep your museum ticket handy, as it also provides free entry to film screenings and MoMA PS1.

Film Screenings

Not only a palace of visual art, MoMA screens an incredibly well-rounded selection of celluloid gems from its collection of over 22,000 films, including the works of the Maysles Brothers and every Pixar animation film ever produced. Expect anything from Academy Award–nominated documentary shorts and Hollywood classics to experimental works and international retrospectives. Best of all, your museum ticket will get you in for free.

MoMA PS1

A smaller, hipper relative of MoMA, **MoMA PS1** (☎718-784-2084; www.momaps1.org; 22-25 Jackson Ave, Long Island City; suggested donation adult/child $10/free, admission with MoMA ticket free, Warm Up party admission online/at venue $18/20; 🕒noon-6pm Thu-Mon, Warm Up parties 3-9pm Sat Jul-Aug; [S]E, M to 23rd St-Court Sq; G, 7 to Court Sq) is a master at hunting down fresh, bold contemporary art and serving it up in a Berlin-esque, ex-school locale. Forget about pretty lily ponds in gilded frames. Here you'll be peering at videos through floorboards, schmoozing at DJ-pimped parties, and debating the meaning of nonstatic structures while staring through a hole in the wall. Best of all, admission is free with your MoMA ticket – so hold on tight!

What's Nearby?

St Patrick's Cathedral Church

(Map p252; www.saintpatrickscathedral.org; Fifth Ave, btwn 50th & 51st Sts; 🕒6:30am-8:45pm; [S]B/D/F/M to 47th-50th Sts-Rockefeller Center; E/M to 5th Ave-53rd St) Fresh from a major restoration, America's largest Catholic cathedral graces Fifth Ave with its Gothic Revival splendor. Built at a cost of nearly $2 million during the Civil War, the building did not originally include the two front spires; those were added in 1888. Step inside to appreciate the Louis Tiffany–designed altar and Charles Connick's stunning Rose Window, the latter gleaming above a 7000-pipe church organ.

A basement crypt behind the altar contains the coffins of every New York cardinal and the remains of Pierre Touissant, a champion of the poor and the first African American up for sainthood.

St Patrick's Cathedral

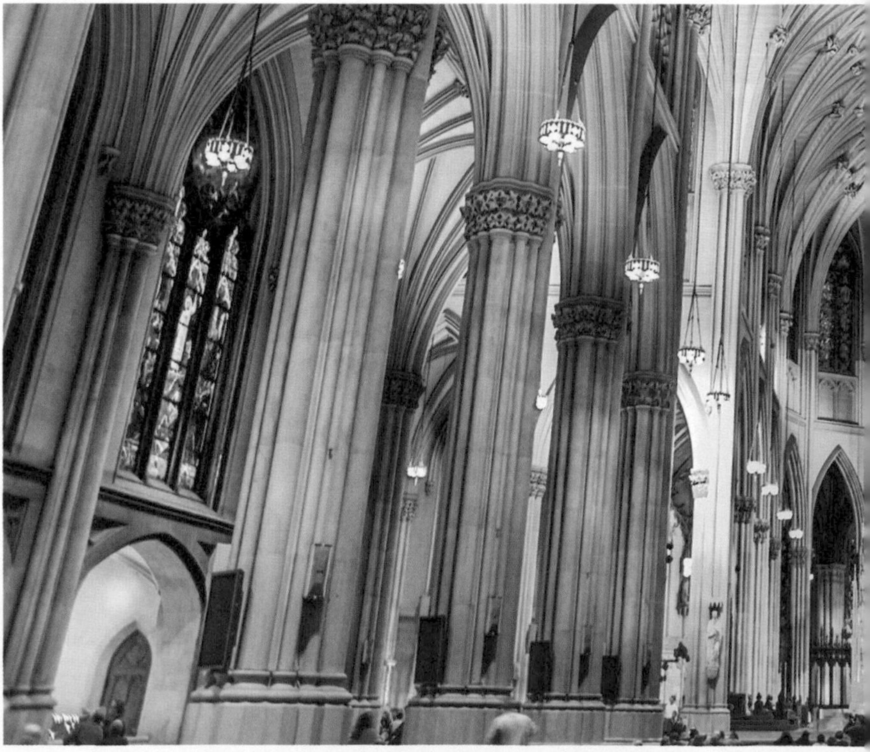

Radio City
Music Hall
Historic Building

(Map p252; www.radiocity.com; 1260 Sixth
Ave, at 51st St; tours adult/child $26.95/19.95;
⏰tours 10am-5pm; 🚻; Ⓢ B/D/F/M to 47th-50th
Sts-Rockefeller Center) This spectacular
moderne movie palace was the brainchild
of vaudeville producer Samuel Lionel 'Roxy'
Rothafel. Never one for understatement,
Roxy launched his venue on 23 December
1932 with an over-the-top extravaganza
that included camp dance troupe the Roxy-
ettes (mercifully renamed the Rockettes).
Guided tours (75 minutes) of the sumptuous interiors include the glorious auditorium, Witold Gordon's classically inspired
mural *History of Cosmetics* in the Women's
Downstairs Lounge, and the *très* exclusive
VIP Roxy Suite.

As far as catching a show here goes, be
warned: the vibe doesn't quite match the

theater's glamor these days. That said,
there are often some fabulous talents in
the lineup, with past performers including
Rufus Wainwright, Aretha Franklin and Dolly
Parton. And while the word 'Rockettes'
provokes eye rolling from most cynical New
Yorkers, fans of glitz and kitsch might just
get a thrill from the troupe's annual Christmas Spectacular.

Same-day tickets are available at the
candy store beside the Sixth Ave entrance,
though it's worth considering paying the
extra $5 to book your ticket online given
that tours can sell out quickly, particularly
on rainy days.

☑ Don't Miss
The outdoor sculpture garden; it's free
to visit from 9:30am to 10:15am daily.

ARNAB GUHA PHOTOGRAPHY / GETTY IMAGES ©

The High Line

A resounding triumph of urban renewal, the High Line is a remarkable linear public park built along a disused elevated rail line. This aerial greenway attracts millions of visitors each year.

Great For...

🖼 🔭 🚶

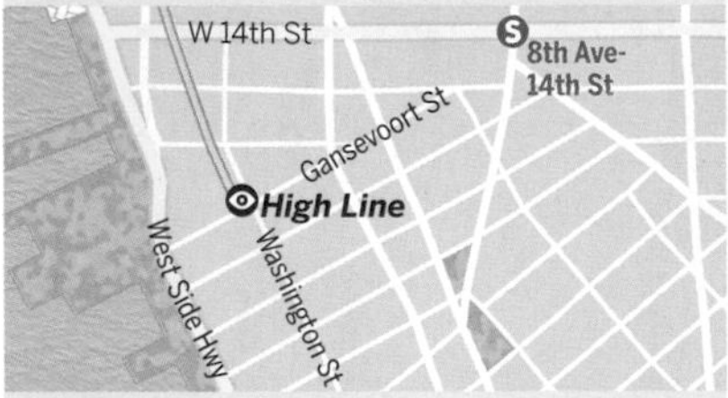

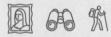

Need to Know

Map p246; www.thehighline.org; Gansevoort St; 🕒7am-11pm Jun-Sep, to 10pm Apr, May, Oct & Nov, to 7pm Dec-Mar; 🚌M11 to Washington St; M11, M14 to 9th Ave; M23, M34 to 10th Ave, [S]L, A/C/E to 14th St-8th Ave; C/E to 23rd St-8th Ave; [FREE]

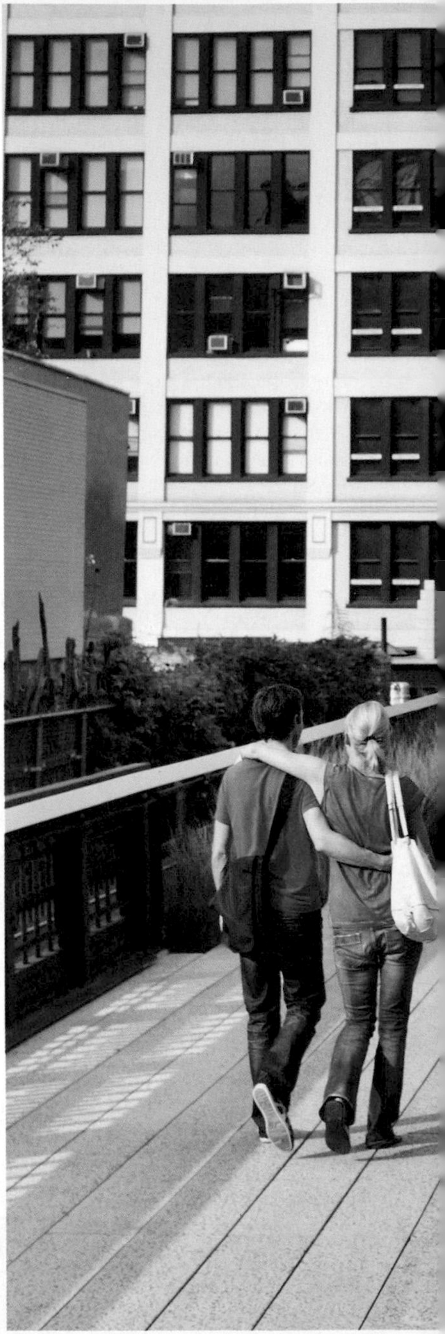

★ **Top Tip**

Entrances are at Gansevoort, 14th, 16th, 18th, 20th and 30th Sts.

History

It's hard to believe that the   was once a disused railway that anchored a rather unsavory district of ramshackle domestic dwellings and slaughterhouses. The tracks that would one day become the High Line were commissioned in the 1930s when the municipal government decided to raise the street-level tracks after years of deadly accidents.

By the 1980s, the rails became obsolete (thanks to a rise in truck transportation). Petitions were signed by local residents to remove the eyesores, but in 1999 a committee called the Friends of the High Line was formed to save the tracks and to transform them into a public open space. Community support grew, and on June 9, 2009 part one of the celebrated project opened with much ado.

Along the Way

The main things to do on the High Line are stroll, sit and picnic in a park 30ft above the city. Along the park's length you'll encounter stunning vistas of the Hudson River, public art installations, fat lounge chairs for soaking up some sun, willowy stretches of native-inspired landscaping and a thoroughly unique perspective on the neighborhood streets below – especially at the cool Gansevoort Overlook, where bleacher-like seating faces a huge pane of glass that allows you to view the traffic, buildings and pedestrians beyond as living works of urban art.

Information, Tours, Events & Eats

As you walk along the High Line you'll find staffers wearing shirts with the signature double-H logo who can point you in the right direction or offer you additional information about the converted rails. There are also myriad staffers behind the scenes organizing public art exhibitions and activity sessions, including warm-weather family events such as story time, and science and craft projects.

Free tours take place periodically and explore a variety of topics: history, horticulture, design, art and food. Check the event schedule on the website for the latest details.

To top it all off, the High Line also invites various gastronomic establishments from around the city to set up vending carts and stalls so that strollers can enjoy to-go items on the green. Expect a showing of the finest coffee and ice-cream establishments during the warmer months.

☑ **Don't Miss**

The third and final part of the High Line, which bends by the Hudson River at 34th St.

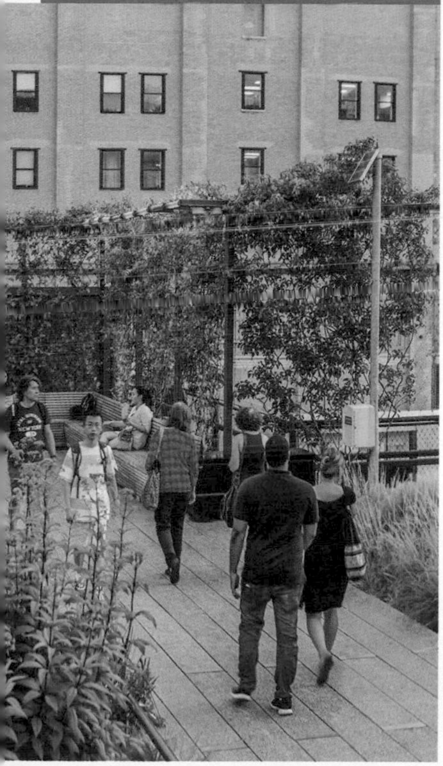

MAREMAGNUM / GETTY IMAGES ©

What's Nearby?

Whitney Museum of American Art — Museum

(Map p246; ☎212-570-3600; www.whitney.org; 99 Gansevoort St; adult/child $22/free; ⌚10:30am-6pm Mon, Wed & Sun, to 10pm Thu-Sat; [S] L to 8th Ave) After years of construction, the Whitney's new downtown location opened to much fanfare in 2015. Perched near the foot of the High Line, this architecturally stunning building – designed by Renzo Piano – makes a suitable introduction to the museum's superb collection. Inside the spacious, light-filled galleries, you'll find works by all the great American artists, including Edward Hopper, Jasper Johns, Georgia O'Keeffe and Mark Rothko.

Hudson River Park — Park

(Map p246; www.hudsonriverpark.org) The High Line may be all the rage these days, but one block away from that famous elevated green space, there stretches a 5-mile-long ribbon of green that has dramatically transformed the city over the past decade. Covering 550 acres, and running from Battery Park at Manhattan's southern tip to 59th St in Midtown, the Hudson River Park is Manhattan's wondrous backyard. The long riverside path is a great spot for cycling, running and strolling.

🍴 **Take a Break**

A cache of eateries is stashed within Chelsea Market (p127) at the 14th St exit.

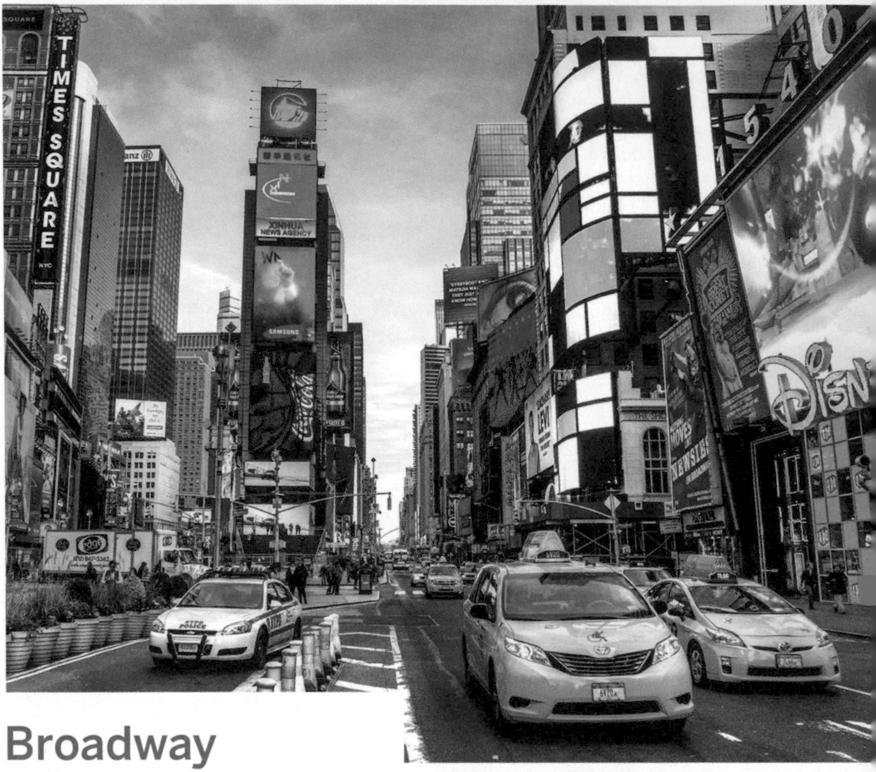

Broadway

Broadway is NYC's dream factory – a place where romance, betrayal, murder and triumph come with dazzling costumes, toe-tapping tunes and stirring scores.

Great For...

☑ Don't Miss

The famed **Brill Building** (Map p252; Broadway, at 49th St, Midtown West; [S]N/Q/R to 49th St; 1, C/E to 50th St); Carol King, Neil Diamond and Joni Mitchell are among the musicians who worked here.

Broadway Beginnings

The neighborhood's first playhouse was the long-gone Empire, opened in 1893 and located on Broadway between 40th and 41st Sts. Two years later, cigar manufacturer and part-time comedy scribe Oscar Hammerstein opened the Olympia, also on Broadway, before opening the Republic, now children's theater **New Victory** (Map p252; ☎646-223-3010; www.newvictory.org; 209 W 42nd St, btwn Seventh & Eighth Aves, Midtown West; 👪; [S]N/Q/R, S, 1/2/3, 7 to Times Sq-42nd St; A/C/E to 42nd St-Port Authority Bus Terminal), in 1900. This led to a string of new venues, among them the still-beating **New Amsterdam Theatre** (Map p252; ☎212-282-2900; www.new-amsterdam-theatre.com; 214 W 42nd St, btwn Seventh & Eighth Aves, Midtown West; 👪; [S]N/Q/R, S, 1/2/3, 7 to Times Sq-42nd St; A/C/E to 42nd St-Port Authority Bus

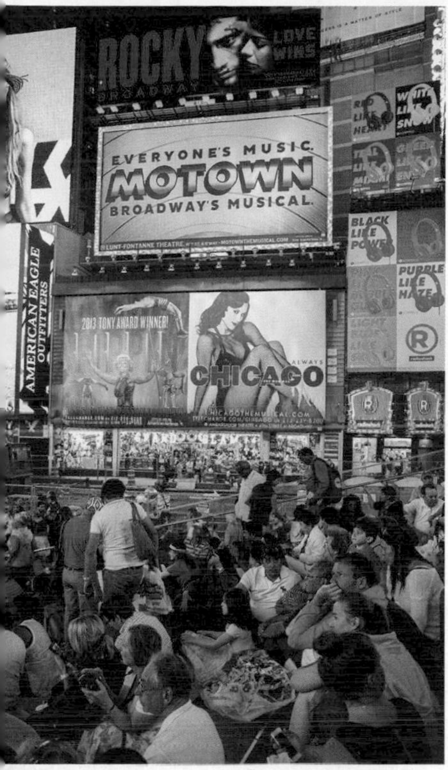

OZGUR DONMAZ / GETTY IMAGES ©

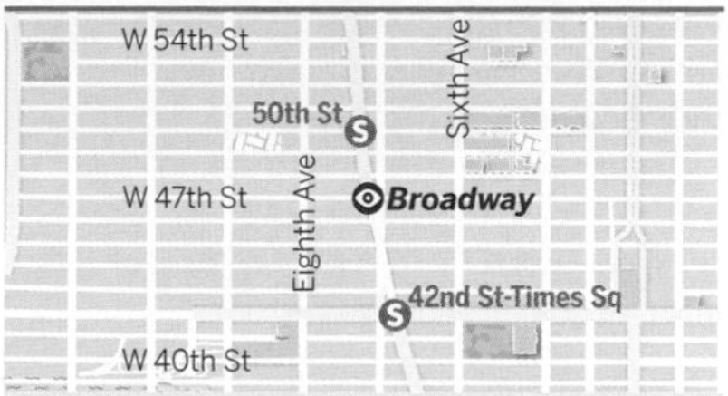

ⓘ Need to Know

Theatermania (www.theatermania.com) provides listings, reviews and ticketing for any form of theater.

🍴 Take a Break

Stiff drinks and a whiff of nostalgia await at the Jimmy's Corner (p177) bar.

★ Top Tip

Many shows offer discounted, day-of 'rush' tickets, available each morning when the box office opens; expect queues.

Terminal) and **Lyceum Theatre** (Map p252; www.shubert.nyc/theatres/lyceum; 149 W 45th St, btwn Sixth & Seventh Aves, Midtown West; [S]N/Q/R to 49th St).

The Broadway of the 1920s was well-known for its lighthearted musicals, commonly fusing vaudeville and music-hall traditions, and producing classic tunes like Cole Porter's *Let's Misbehave.* At the same time, Midtown's theater district was evolving as a platform for new American dramatists. One of the greatest was Eugene O'Neill. Born in Times Square at the long-gone Barrett Hotel (1500 Broadway) in 1888, the playwright debuted many of his works here, including Pulitzer Prize winners *Beyond the Horizon* and *Anna Christie*. O'Neill's success on Broadway paved the way for other American greats like Tennessee Williams, Arthur Miller and Edward Albee – a surge of serious talent that led to the establishment of the annual Tony Awards in 1947.

These days, New York's Theater District covers an area stretching roughly from 40th St to 54th St between Sixth and Eighth Aves, with dozens of Broadway and off-Broadway theaters spanning blockbuster musicals to new and classic drama.

Getting a Ticket

Unless there's a specific show you're after, the best – and cheapest – way to score tickets in the area is at the **TKTS Booth** (Map p252; www.tdf.org/tkts; Broadway, at W 47th St, Midtown West; ⏲3-8pm Mon & Wed-Sat, 2-8pm Tue, 3-7pm Sun, also 10am-2pm Tue-Sat & 11am-3pm Sun during matinee performances; [S]N/Q/R, S, 1/2/3, 7 to Times Sq-42nd St), where you can line up and get same-day discounted tickets for top Broadway and off-Broadway shows. Smartphone users can download the free TKTS app, which offers rundowns of both Broadway and off-Broadway shows, as well as real-time updates of what's available on that day.

Always have a back-up choice in case your first preference sells out, and never buy from scalpers on the street.

The TKTS Booth is an attraction in its own right, with its illuminated roof of 27 ruby-red steps rising a panoramic 16ft 1in above the 47th St sidewalk.

What's On?

Musicals rule the marquees on Broadway, with the hottest shows of the day blending song and dance in lavish productions.

Hamilton

Lin-Manuel Miranda's acclaimed new musical is Broadway's hottest ticket, using contemporary hip-hop beats to recount the story of America's founding father, Alexander Hamilton. Inspired by Ron Chernow's

biography *Alexander Hamilton*, the musical has won a swath of awards, including Outstanding Musical at the Drama Desk Awards and Best Musical at the New York Drama Critics' Circle Awards.

Book of Mormon

Subversive, obscene and ridiculously hilarious, this cutting musical satire is the work of *South Park* creators Trey Parker and Matt Stone and Avenue Q composer Robert Lopez. Winner of nine Tony Awards, it tells the story of two naive Mormons on a mission to 'save' a Ugandan village.

Kinky Boots

Adapted from a 2005 British indie film, Harvey Fierstein and Cyndi Lauper's smash hit tells the story of a doomed English shoe factory unexpectedly saved by Lola, a

Walter Kerr Theater, Broadway

business-savvy drag queen. Its solid characters and energy have not been lost on critics, the musical winning six Tony Awards, including Best Musical in 2013.

Matilda

Giddily subversive, this multi-award-winning musical is an adaptation of Roald Dahl's classic children's tale. Star of the

show is a precocious five-year-old who uses wit, intellect and a little telekinesis to tackle parental neglect, unjust punishment, and even the Russian mafia.

An American in Paris

Adapted from the 1951 film starring Gene Kelly, this critically acclaimed stage musical tells the story of an American ex-GI in post-WWII Paris, following his artistic dreams and falling head over heels for an alluring dancer. Packed with toe-tapping Gershwin tunes, it's directed by renowned English choreographer Christopher Wheeldon.

Lion King

A top choice for families with kids, Disney's blockbuster musical tells the tale of a lion cub's journey to adulthood and the throne of the animal kingdom. The spectacular sets, costumes and African chants are worth the ticket alone.

Chicago

A little easier to score tickets to than some of the newer Broadway musicals, this beloved Bob Fosse/Kander & Ebb classic tells the story of showgirl Velma Kelly, wannabe Roxie Hart, lawyer Billy Flynn and the fabulously sordid goings-on of the Chicago underworld. Revived by director Walter Bobbie, its sassy, infectious energy more than makes up for the theater's tight squeeze seating.

Wicked

An extravagant prequel to *The Wizard of Oz*, this long-running, pop-rock musical gives the story's witches a turn to tell the tale. The musical is based on Gregory Maguire's 1995 novel.

Aladdin

This witty dervish of a musical recounts the tale of a street urchin who falls in love with the daughter of a sultan. Based on the 1992 Disney animation, the stage version includes songs from the film, numerous numbers which didn't make the final cut, as well as new material written specifically for the live production.

★ The Logest-Running Shows

Following are the district's longest-running shows - the first three are still playing!

Phantom of the Opera
Chicago
The Lion King
Cats
Les Misérables

BARRY WINKER / GETTY IMAGES ©

Times Square

Love it or hate it, the intersection of Broadway and Seventh Ave – better known as Times Square – is New York City's hyperactive heart; a restless, hypnotic torrent of glittering lights, bombastic billboards and raw urban energy.

Great For...

Need to Know

Map p252; www.timessquarenyc.org; Broadway, at Seventh Ave; [S]N/Q/R, S, 1/2/3, 7 to Times Sq-42nd St

★ **Top Tip**

In the museum, write your dreams onto a piece of ready-to-flutter New Year's Eve confetti.

NYC Icons

Times Square is not hip, fashionable or in the know, and it couldn't care less. It's too busy pumping out iconic, mass-marketed NYC – yellow cabs, golden arches, soaring skyscrapers and razzle-dazzle Broadway marquees. This is the New York of collective fantasies – the place where Al Jolson 'makes it' in the 1927 film *The Jazz Singer*, where photojournalist Alfred Eisenstaedt famously captured a lip-locked sailor and nurse on VJ Day in 1945, and where Alicia Keys and Jay-Z waxed lyrically about this 'concrete jungle where dreams are made.'

For several decades, the dream here was a sordid, wet one. The economic crash of the early 1970s led to a mass exodus of corporations from Times Square. Billboard niches went dark, stores shut and once-grand hotels were converted into

single-room occupancy (SRO) dives. While the adjoining Theater District survived, its respectable playhouses shared the streets with porn cinemas and strip clubs. That all changed with tough-talking Mayor Rudolph Giuliani, who, in the 1990s, boosted police numbers and lured a wave of 'respectable' retail chains, restaurants and attractions. By the new millennium, Times Square had gone from 'X-rated' to 'G-rated,' drawing almost 40 million visitors annually.

Top To-Dos

People-watch Times Square is often called the 'crossroads of the world' and you better believe you'll get an eyeful of more than shimmering neon here. All kinds of folks don costumes to make money posing for photographs. Keep an eye out for buffed topless cowboys, *Sesame Street* Elmos and a wide range of superheroes.

Artist JR's Inside Out New York City Project

Get a drink with a view For a panoramic overview of the square, order a drink at the Renaissance Hotel's **R Lounge** (Renaissance Hotel; Map p252; ☎212-261-5200; www.rlounge timessquare.com; Two Times Square, 714 Seventh Ave, at 48th St, Midtown West; 🕓5-11pm Mon, to 11:30pm Tue-Thu, to midnight Fri, 7:30am-midnight Sat, 7:30am-11pm Sun; [S]N/Q/R to 49th St), the floor-to-ceiling windows of which overlook the neon-lit spectacle.

A Subway & A Newspaper

At the start of the 20th century, Times Square was known as Longacre Sq, an unremarkable intersection far from the commercial epicenter of Lower Manhattan. This would change with a deal made between subway pioneer August Belmont and *New York Times* publisher Adolph Ochs.

Belmont approached Ochs, and convinced him that moving the *New York Times* to the intersection of Broadway and 42nd St would be a win-win – an in-house subway station meant faster newspaper distribution and the influx of commuters would also mean more sales right outside its headquarters. Belmont even convinced New York Mayor George B McClellan Jr to rename the square in honor of the broadsheet. It was an irresistible offer and, in the winter of 1904–05, both subway station and the *Times'* new headquarters at One Times Sq made their debut.

☑ Don't Miss

Seeing the Centennial Ball, weighing in at nearly 6 tons, descending at midnight on New Year's Eve.

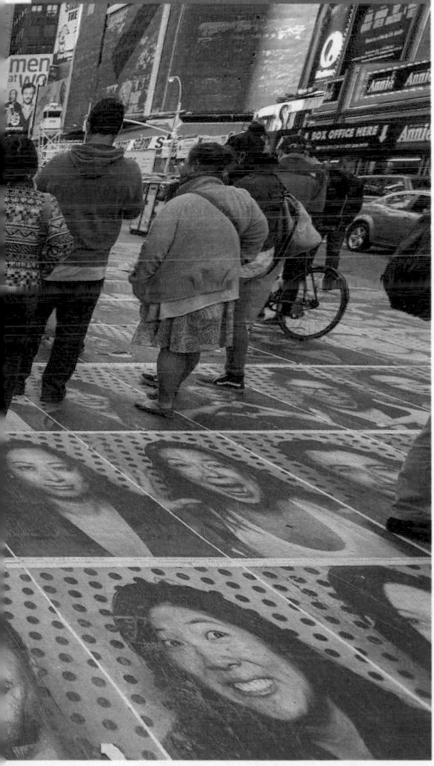

STEPHEN ALVAREZ / GETTY IMAGES ©

What's Nearby?

Museum of Arts & Design Museum

(MAD; Map p250; www.madmuseum.org; 2 Columbus Circle, btwn Eighth Ave & Broadway; adult/child $16/free, by donation 6-9pm Thu; 🕓10am-6pm Tue, Wed, Sat & Sun, to 9pm Thu & Fri; 👪; [S]A/C, B/D, 1 to 59th St-Columbus Circle) MAD offers four floors of superlative design and handicrafts, from blown glass and carved wood to elaborate metal jewelry. Its temporary exhibitions are top notch and innovative; one past show explored the art of scent. Usually on the first Sunday of the month, professional artists lead family-friendly explorations of the galleries, followed by hands-on workshops inspired by the current exhibitions. The museum gift shop sells some fantastic contemporary jewelry, while the 9th-floor restaurant-bar Robert is perfect for panoramic cocktails.

🍴 Take a Break

Grab a legendary cubano sandwich from **El Margon** (Map p252; ☎212-354-5013; www.margonnyc.com; 136 W 46th St, btwn Sixth & Seventh Aves, Midtown West; sandwiches $4-8, mains from $10; 🕓6am-5pm Mon-Fri, from 7am Sat; [S]B/D/F/M to 47th-50th Sts-Rockefeller Center), only a minute's walk from the square.

Empire State Building

The striking art-deco skyscraper has appeared in dozens of films and still provides one of the best views in town – particularly around sunset when the twinkling lights of the city switch on.

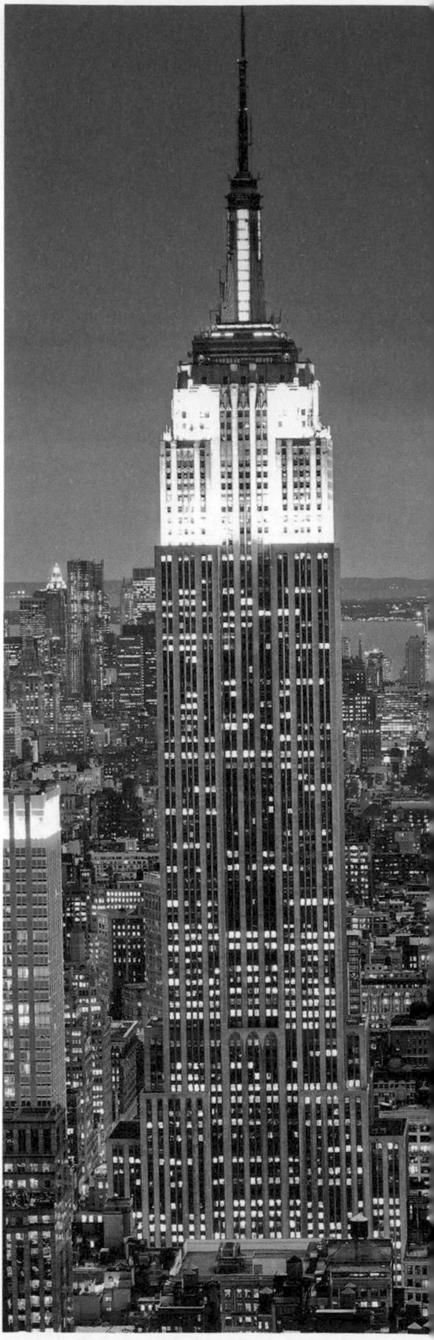

Great For...

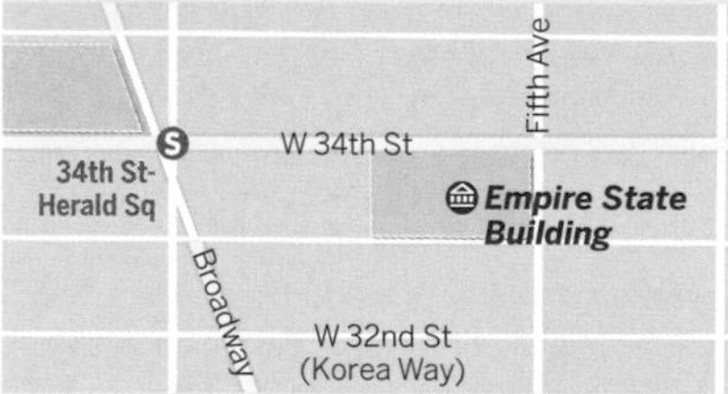

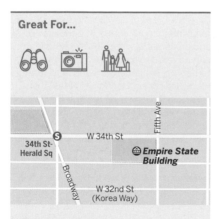

Need to Know

Map p252; www.esbnyc.com; 350 Fifth Ave, at 34th St; 86th-fl observation deck adult/child $32/26, incl 102nd-fl observation deck $52/46; ⏰8am-2am, last elevators up 1:15am; [S]B/D/F/M, N/Q/R to 34th St-Herald Sq

★ Top Tip

To beat the crowds, buy tickets online (well worth the extra $2 convenience fee).

PAWEL GAUL / GETTY IMAGES ©

The Chrysler Building may be prettier and One World Trade Center and 432 Park Avenue may be taller, but the Queen Bee of the New York skyline remains the Empire State Building. NYC's tallest star, it has enjoyed close-ups in around 100 films, from *King Kong* to *Independence Day*. Heading up to the top is a quintessential NYC experience.

Observation Decks

There are two observation decks. The open-air 86th-floor deck offers an alfresco experience, with coin-operated telescopes for close-up glimpses of the metropolis in action. Further up, the enclosed 102nd-floor deck is New York's second-highest observation deck, trumped only by the observation deck at One World Trade Center. Needless to say, the views over the city's five boroughs (and five neighboring states, weather permitting) are spectacular. Particularly memorable are the views at sunset, when the city dons its nighttime cloak in dusk's afterglow. For a little of that Burt Bacharach magic, head to the 86th floor between 9pm and 1am from Thursday to Saturday, when the twinkling sea of lights is accompanied by a soundtrack of live jazz (yes, requests are taken). Alas, the passage to heaven will involve a trip through purgatory: the queues to the top are notorious. Getting here very early or very late will help you avoid delays – as will buying your tickets online, ahead of time.

By the Numbers

The statistics are astonishing: 10 million bricks, 60,000 tons of steel, 6400 windows and 328,000 sq ft of marble. Built on the original site of the Waldorf-Astoria,

The Empire State Building overlooks Bryant Park

construction took a record-setting 410 days, using seven million hours of labor and costing a mere $41 million. It might sound like a lot, but it fell well below its $50 million budget (just as well, given it went up during the Great Depression). Coming in at 102 stories and 1472ft from bottom to top, the limestone monolith opened for business on May 1, 1931.

Language of Light

Since 1976, the building's top 30 floors have been floodlit in a spectrum of colors each night, reflecting seasonal and holiday hues. Famous combos include orange, white and green for St Patrick's Day; blue and white for Chanukah; white, red and green for Christmas; and the rainbow colors for Gay Pride weekend in June. For a full rundown of the color schemes, check the website.

☑ **Don't Miss**

Live jazz held on Thursday to Saturday nights from 9pm to 1am.

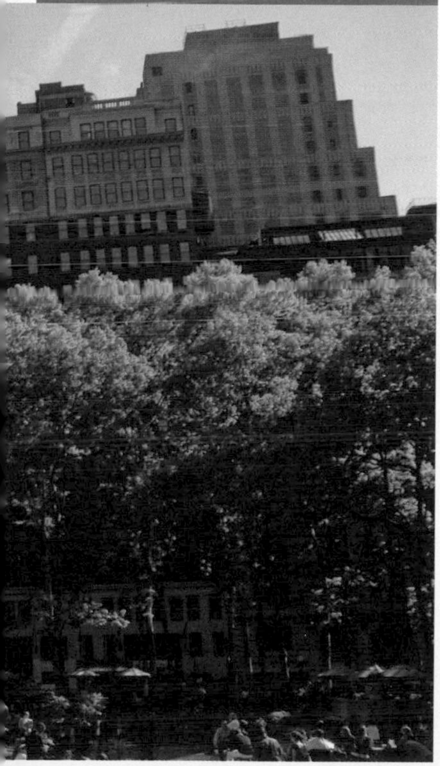

CURTIS HAMILTON / GETTY IMAGES ©

What's Nearby?

Madison Square Park Park

(Map p252; ☎212-520-7600; www.madisonsquarepark.org; 23rd to 26th Sts, btwn Fifth & Madison Aves; ⏰6am-midnight; 👪; [S]N/R, F/M, 6 to 23rd St) This park defined the northern reaches of Manhattan until the island's population exploded after the Civil War. These days it's a much-welcome oasis from Manhattan's relentless pace, with a popular children's playground, dog-run area and **Shake Shack** (Map p252; ☎646-747-2606; www.shakeshack.com; Madison Square Park, cnr 23rd St & Madison Ave; burgers $4.20-9.50; ⏰11am-11pm; [S]N/R, F/M, 6 to 23rd St) burger joint. It's also one of the city's most cultured parks, with specially commissioned art installations and (in the warmer months) activities ranging from literary discussions to live music gigs. See the website for more information.

The park is also the perfect spot from which to gaze up at the landmarks that surround it, including the Flatiron Building to the southwest, the moderne Metropolitan Life Tower to the southeast and the New York Life Insurance Building, topped with a gilded spire, to the northeast.

Between 1876 and 1882 the torch-bearing arm of the Statue of Liberty was on display here, and in 1879 the first Madison Square Garden arena was constructed at Madison Ave and 26th St. At the southeastern corner of the park, you'll find one of the city's few self-cleaning, coin-operated toilets.

🍴 **Take a Break**

Feast on dumplings, barbecue and kimchi in nearby restaurant-lined Koreatown (32nd St between Fifth & Sixth Aves).

The Colonial Andes
Tapestries and Silverwork
1530–1830

THE
DRESDEN
COURT

china

dawn of a golden age 200–750 AD

The
Pierre and
Maria-Gaetana
Matisse
Collection

WILD
Fashion Untam

Metropolitan Museum of Art

This museum of encyclopedic proportions has over two million objects in its permanent collection, and many of its treasures are showcased in no less than 17 acres' worth of galleries.

Great For...

☑ Don't Miss

The hieroglyphic-covered Temple of Dendur, complete with reflecting pond and Central Park views.

This sprawling museum, founded in 1870, houses one of the biggest art collections in the world. Its permanent collection has everything from Egyptian temples to American paintings. Known colloquially as 'The Met,' the museum draws over six million visitors a year to its galleries – making it the largest single-site attraction in New York City. In other words, plan on spending some time here.

Egyptian Art

The museum has an unrivaled collection of ancient Egyptian art, some of which dates back to the Paleolithic era. Located to the north of the Great Hall, the 39 Egyptian galleries open dramatically with one of the Met's prized pieces: the Mastaba Tomb of Perneb (c 2300 BC), an Old Kingdom burial chamber crafted from limestone. From here, a web of rooms is cluttered with fu-

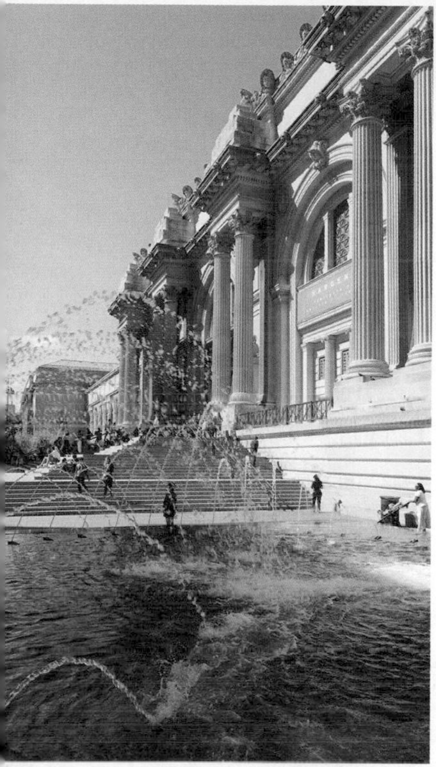

ANTON HAVELAAR / SHUTTERSTOCK ©

nerary stelae, carved reliefs and fragments of pyramids. (Don't miss the intriguing Models of Meketre, clay figurines meant to help in the afterlife, in Gallery 105.) These eventually lead to the Temple of Dendur (Gallery 131), a sandstone temple to the goddess Isis that resides in a sunny atrium gallery with a reflecting pool.

Greek & Roman Art

The 27 galleries devoted to classical antiquity are another Met doozy. From the Great Hall, a passageway takes viewers through a barrel-vaulted room flanked by the chiseled torsos of Greek figures. This spills right into one of the Met's loveliest spaces: the airy Roman sculpture court (Gallery 162), full of marble carvings of gods and historical figures. The statue of a bearded Hercules from AD 68–98, with a lion's skin draped about him, is particularly awe-inspiring.

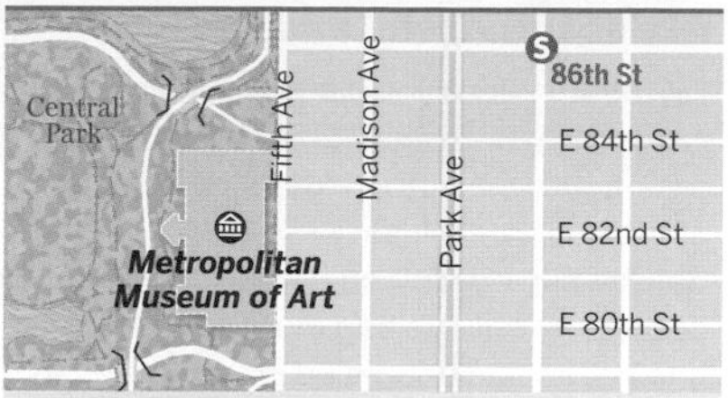
Central Park
Fifth Ave
Madison Ave
Park Ave
86th St
E 84th St
E 82nd St
E 80th St
Metropolitan Museum of Art

Need to Know

Map p250; ☎212-535-7710; www.metmuseum.org; 1000 Fifth Ave, at 82nd St; suggested donation adult/child $25/free; ⏰10am-5.30pm Sun-Thu, to 9pm Fri & Sat; 👪; [S]4/5/6 to 86th St

🍴 Take a Break

The casual Petrie Court Cafe serves good lunch and drink options in a pretty setting.

★ Top Tip

Docents offer free guided tours of specific galleries. Check the website or information desk for details.

European Paintings

Want Renaissance? The Met's got it. On the museum's 2nd floor, the European Paintings' galleries display a stunning collection of masterworks. This includes more than 1700 canvases from the roughly 500-year-period starting in the 13th century, with works by every important painter from Duccio to Rembrandt. In fact, everything here is, literally, a masterpiece. In Gallery 621 are several Caravaggios, including the masterfully painted *The Denial of St Peter.* Gallery 611, to the west, is packed with Spanish treasures, including El Greco's famed *View of Toledo*. Continue south to Gallery 632 to see various Vermeers, including the *Young Woman with a Water Pitcher*. Nearby, in Gallery 634, gaze at several Rembrandts, including a 1660 *Self-Portrait*. And that's just the beginning. You could spend hours exploring these many powerful works.

Art of the Arab Lands

On the 2nd floor you'll find the Islamic galleries, with 15 incredible rooms showcasing the museum's extensive collection of art from the Middle East and Central and South Asia. In addition to garments, secular decorative objects and manuscripts, you'll find gilded and enameled glassware (Gallery 452) and a magnificent 14th-century *mihrab* (prayer niche) lined with elaborately patterned polychrome tile-work (Gallery 455). There is also a superb array of Ottoman textiles (Gallery 459), a medieval-style Moroccan court (Gallery 456) and an 18th-century room from Damascus (Gallery 461).

American Wing

In the northwestern corner, the American galleries showcase a wide variety of decorative and fine art from throughout US history. These include everything from colonial portraiture to Hudson River School masterpieces to John Singer Sargent's unbearably sexy *Madame X* (Gallery 771) – not to mention Emanuel Leutze's massive canvas of *Washington Crossing the Delaware* (Gallery 760).

The Roof Garden

One of the best spots in the entire museum is the roof garden, which features rotating sculpture installations by contemporary and 20th-century artists (Jeff Koons, Andy Goldsworthy and Imran Qureshi have all shown here). But its best feature are the views it offers of the city and Central Park. It's also home to the **Roof Garden Café & Martini Bar** (Map p250; ☏212-535-7710; www.metmuseum.org; 1000 Fifth Ave, at 82nd

Inside the Great Hall foyer of the Met

St; ⊘10am-4:30pm Sun-Thu, to 8:15pm Fri & Sat May-Oct; 👶; 🚇4/5/6 to 86th St), an ideal spot for a drink – especially at sunset. The roof garden is open from April to October.

For Kids

The Met hosts plenty of kid-centric happenings in the museum (check the website) and distributes a special museum brochure and map that are created specifically for the little tykes.

★ Kids at the Met

The most popular galleries with children are generally the Egyptian, African and Oceania galleries (great masks) and the collection of medieval arms and armor.

HIROYUKI MATSUMOTO / GETTY IMAGES ©

What's Nearby?

Frick Collection   Gallery

(Map p250; ☎212-288-0700; www.frick.org; 1 E 70th St, at Fifth Ave; admission $20, by donation 11am-1pm Sun, children under 10 not admitted; ⊘10am-6pm Tue-Sat, 11am-5pm Sun; 🚇6 to 68th St-Hunter College) This spectacular art collection sits in a mansion built by prickly steel magnate Henry Clay Frick, one of the many such residences that made up Millionaires' Row. The museum has splendid rooms that display masterpieces by Titian, Vermeer, Gilbert Stuart, El Greco and Goya.

The museum is a treat for a number of reasons. One, it resides in a lovely, rambling beaux arts structure built from 1913–14 by Carrère and Hastings. Two, it's generally not crowded (one exception being during popular shows). And, three, it feels refreshingly intimate, with a trickling indoor courtyard fountain and gardens that can be explored on warmer days. A demure Portico Gallery displays decorative works and sculpture.

A worthwhile audio tour (available in several languages) is included in the price of admission. Classical-music fans will enjoy the frequent piano and violin concerts that take place on Sunday.

Neue Galerie   Museum

(Map p250; ☎212-628-6200; www.neuegalerie. org; 1048 Fifth Ave, cnr E 86th St; admission $20, 6-8pm 1st Fri of the month free, children under 12 not admitted; ⊘11am-6pm Thu-Mon; 🚇4/5/6 to 86th St) This restored Carrère and Hastings mansion from 1914 is a resplendent showcase for German and Austrian art, featuring works by Paul Klee, Ernst Ludwig Kirchner and Egon Schiele. In pride of place on the 2nd floor is Gustav Klimt's golden 1907 portrait of Adele Bloch-Bauer – which was acquired for the museum by cosmetics magnate Ronald Lauder for $135 million.

This is a small but beautiful place with winding staircases and wrought-iron banisters. It also boasts a lovely, street-level eatery, Café Sabarsky (p135). Avoid weekends (and the free first Friday of the month) if you don't want to deal with gallery-clogging crowds.

Iconic Architecture

Midtown is home to some of New York's grandest monuments, with works of architecture soaring above. This walk provides a mix of perspectives – with godlike views from up high and street-side exploring amid the raw energy of the whirling city.

Start: Grand Central Terminal
Distance: 2 miles
Duration: 3 hours

7 Nearby is the **Rockefeller Center** (p74), a magnificent complex of art-deco skyscrapers and sculptures.

8 Head to the GE Building's 70th-floor for an unforgettable vista at the **Top of the Rock** (p74).

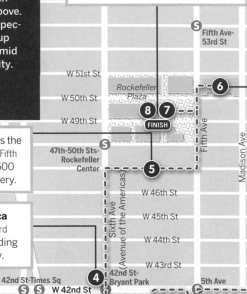

5 Between Sixth and Fifth Aves is the **Diamond District** (47th St, btwn Fifth & Sixth Aves), where more than 2600 businesses sell gems and jewellery.

4 The soaring **Bank of America Tower** (Sixth Ave, btwn 42nd & 43rd Sts) is NYC's fourth-tallest building and one of its most ecofriendly.

✕ Take a Break

In Bryant Park, stop in for a tasty snack or meal at the Bryant Park Grill (p115).

3 Step inside the **New York Public Library** (Fifth Ave, at 42nd St; ☺10am-6pm Mon & Thu-Sat, to 8pm Tue & Wed, 1-5pm Sun)

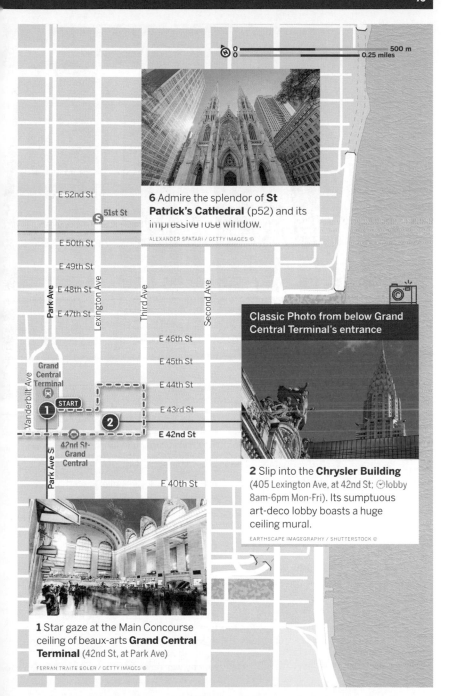

6 Admire the splendor of **St Patrick's Cathedral** (p52) and its impressive rose window.

ALEXANDER SPATARI / GETTY IMAGES ©

E 52nd St

51st St

E 50th St

E 49th St

E 48th St

E 47th St

Park Ave

Lexington Ave

Third Ave

Second Ave

E 46th St

E 45th St

E 44th St

E 43rd St

E 42nd St

E 40th St

Grand Central Terminal

Vanderbilt Ave

START

Park Ave S

42nd St-Grand Central

500 m
0.25 miles

Classic Photo from below Grand Central Terminal's entrance

2 Slip into the **Chrysler Building** (405 Lexington Ave, at 42nd St; ⊙lobby 8am-6pm Mon-Fri). Its sumptuous art-deco lobby boasts a huge ceiling mural.

EARTHSCAPE IMAGEGRAPHY / SHUTTERSTOCK ©

1 Star gaze at the Main Concourse ceiling of beaux-arts **Grand Central Terminal** (42nd St, at Park Ave)

FERRAN TRAITE SOLER / GETTY IMAGES ©

ROBERT CICCHETTI / SHUTTERSTOCK ©

Lincoln Center

This vast cultural complex is the epicenter of high art in Manhattan. Famed venues spread around the 16-acre campus include concert halls, an opera house, film-screening centers and the renowned Julliard School.

Great For...

☑ Don't Miss

A lush production at the world-famous Metropolitan Opera House.

This stark arrangement of gleaming modernist temples contains some of Manhattan's most important performance spaces: Avery Fisher Hall (home to the New York Philharmonic), David H Koch Theater (site of the New York City ballet) and the iconic Metropolitan Opera House, the interior walls of which are dressed with brightly saturated murals by painter Marc Chagall.

A History of Building & Rebuilding

Built in the 1960s, this imposing campus replaced a group of tenements called San Juan Hill, a predominantly African American neighborhood where the exterior shots for the movie *West Side Story* were filmed. In addition to being a controversial urban-planning move, Lincoln Center wasn't exactly well received at an architectural level – it was relentlessly criticized for its

The Center's orchestra pit sits below a striking ceiling design

BARRY WINKER / GETTY IMAGES ©

❶ Need to Know

Map p250; ☏212-875-5456, tours 212-875-5350; www.lincolncenter.org; Columbus Ave btwn 62nd & 66th Sts; public plazas free, tours adult/student $18/15; ♿; ⓢ1 to 66th St-Lincoln Center

✕ Take a Break

Across the street from Lincoln Center, the **Smith** (Map p250; ☏212-496-5700; thesmithrestaurant.com; 1900 Broadway, btwn 63rd & 64th Sts; mains $17-44; ⏰7:30am-midnight Mon-Fri, from 9am Sat & Sun; ⓢ1, A/C, B/D to 59th-St-Columbus Circle) serves high-end comfort fare.

★ Top Tip

Daily tours are a great way to get acquainted with the many facets of Lincoln Center.

conservative design, fortresslike aspect and poor acoustics. For the center's 50th anniversary (2009–10), Diller Scofidio + Renfro and other architects gave the complex a much-needed and critically acclaimed freshening up.

Highlights

A survey of the three classic buildings surrounding Revson Fountain is a must. These include the Metropolitan Opera, Avery Fisher Hall and the David H Koch Theater, the latter designed by Philip Johnson. (These are all located on the main plaza at Columbus Ave, between 62nd and 65th Sts.) The fountain is spectacular in the evenings when it puts on Las Vegas–like light shows.

Of the refurbished structures, there are a number that are worth examining, including Alice Tully Hall, now displaying a very

contemporary translucent, angled facade, and the David Rubenstein Atrium, a public space offering a lounge area, a cafe, an information desk and a ticket vendor plying day-of discount tickets to Lincoln Center performances. Free events are held here on Thursday evenings, with a wide-ranging roster including eclectic global sounds (such as Indian classical music or Afro-Cuban jazz), prog rock, chamber music, opera and ballet.

Performances & Screenings

On any given night, there are at least 10 performances happening throughout Lincoln Center – and even more in summer, when Lincoln Center Out of Doors (dance and music concerts) and Midsummer Night

Swing (ballroom dancing under the stars) lure those who love parks and culture. For details on seasons, tickets and programming – which runs the gamut from opera to dance to theater to ballet – check the website.

Metropolitan Opera House

The Metropolitan Opera is the place to see classics such as *Carmen, Madame Butterfly* and *Macbeth,* not to mention Wagner's *Ring Cycle*. The Opera also hosts premieres and revivals of more contemporary works, such as Peter Sellars' *Nixon in China*. The season runs from September to April.

Ticket prices start at $25 and can get close to $500. Note that the box seats can be a bargain, but unless you're in boxes right over the stage, the views are dreadful.

Seeing the stage requires sitting with your head cocked over a handrail – a literal pain in the neck.

For last-minute ticket-buyers there are other deals. You can get bargain-priced standing-room tickets ($20 to $25) starting at 10am on the day of the performance. (You won't see much, but you'll hear everything.) Monday through Friday at noon and Saturdays at 2pm, a number of rush tickets are put on sale for starving-artist types – just $25 for a seat. These are available online only. Matinee tickets go on sale four hours before curtain.

For a behind-the-scenes look at the Opera House, tours ($25) are offered weekdays at 3pm and Sundays at 10:30am and 1:30pm during the performance season.

The New York City Ballet performs *The Nutcracker Suite*

New York City Ballet

This prestigious ballet company was first directed by renowned Russian-born choreographer George Balanchine back in the 1940s. Today, the company has 90 dancers and is the largest ballet organization in the US, performing 23 weeks a year at Lincoln Center's David H Koch Theater. During the holidays the troop is best known for its annual production of *The Nutcracker*.

Depending on the ballet, ticket prices can range from $30 to $170. Rush tickets for those under age 30 are available for $29. There are also select one-hour Family Saturday performances, appropriate for young audiences ($22 per ticket).

> **☑ Don't Miss**
> The gift shop is full of operatic bric-a-brac, including Met curtain cuff links and Rhinemaidens soap. (Seriously.)

KELLY/MOONEY PHOTOGRAPHY / GETTY IMAGES ©

New York Philharmonic

The oldest professional orchestra in the US (dating back to 1842) holds its season every year at Avery Fisher Hall. Directed by Alan Gilbert, the son of two Philharmonic musicians, the orchestra plays a mix of classics (Tchaikovsky, Mahler, Haydn) and contemporary works, as well as concerts geared toward children.

Tickets run in the $29 to $125 range. If you're on a budget, check out its open rehearsals held several times a month (starting at 9:45am) on the day of the concert for only $20. In addition, students with a valid school ID can pick up rush tickets for $16 up to 10 days before an event.

What's Nearby?

American Museum of Natural History — Museum

(Map p250; ☎212-769-5100; www.amnh.org; Central Park West, at 79th St; suggested donation adult/child $22/12.50; ⏰10am-5:45pm, Rose Center to 8:45pm Fri; 👪; [S]B, C to 81st St-Museum of Natural History, 1 to 79th St) Founded in 1869, this museum contains a wonderland of more than 30 million artifacts, including lots of menacing dinosaur skeletons, as well as the Rose Center for Earth & Space, with its cutting-edge planetarium. From September through May, the museum is home to the Butterfly Conservatory, a glasshouse featuring 500-plus butterflies from all over the world.

On the natural-history side, the museum is perhaps best known for its Fossil Halls containing nearly 600 specimens, including the skeletons of a massive mammoth and a fearsome Tyrannosaurus rex.

There are also plentiful animal exhibits, galleries devoted to gems and an IMAX theater. The Milstein Hall of Ocean Life contains dioramas devoted to ecologies, weather and conservation, as well as a beloved 94ft replica of a blue whale.

Guggenheim Museum

A sculpture in its own right, architect Frank Lloyd Wright's swirling white building is a worthy match for the booty of 20th-century art housed inside.

Great For...

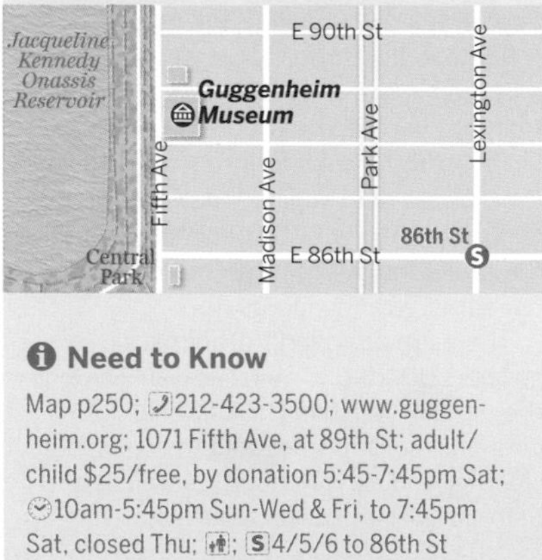

Need to Know

Map p250; ☎212-423-3500; www.guggenheim.org; 1071 Fifth Ave, at 89th St; adult/child $25/free, by donation 5:45-7:45pm Sat; 🕒10am-5:45pm Sun-Wed & Fri, to 7:45pm Sat, closed Thu; 👪; [S]4/5/6 to 86th St

★ **Top Tip**

Entrance lines can be brutal; save time by purchasing tickets online in advance.

Frank Lloyd Wright's building almost overshadows the collection of 20th-century art that it houses. Completed in 1959, the inverted ziggurat structure was derided by some critics but hailed by others, who welcomed it as an architectural icon. Since it first opened, this unusual structure has appeared on countless postcards, TV programs and films.

Abstract Roots

The Guggenheim came out of the collection of Solomon R Guggenheim, a New York mining magnate who began acquiring abstract art in his 60s at the behest of his art adviser, an eccentric German baroness named Hilla Rebay. In 1939, with Rebay serving as director, Guggenheim opened a temporary museum on 54th St titled the Museum of Non-Objective Painting. (Incredibly, it had grey velour walls, piped-in classical music and burning incense.) Four years later, the pair commissioned Wright to construct a permanent home for the collection.

Years in the Making

Like any development in New York City, the project took forever to come to fruition. Construction was delayed for almost 13 years due to budget constraints, the outbreak of WWII and outraged neighbors who weren't all that excited to see an architectural spaceship land in their midst. Construction was completed in 1959, after both Wright and Guggenheim had passed away.

When the Guggenheim finally opened its doors in October 1959, the ticket price was 50¢ and the works on view included pieces by Wassily Kandinsky, Alexander Calder and abstract expressionists Franz Kline and Willem de Kooning.

GUGGENHEIM

Visiting Today

A renovation in the early 1990s added an eight-story tower to the east, which provided an extra 50,000 sq ft of exhibition space. These galleries show the permanent collection and other exhibits, while the museum's ascending ramps are occupied by rotating exhibitions of modern and contemporary art. Though Wright intended visitors to go to the top and wind their way down, the cramped single elevator doesn't allow for this. Exhibitions, therefore, are installed from bottom to top.

Alongside works by Picasso and Jackson Pollock, the museum's permanent holdings include paintings by Monet, Van Gogh and Degas, photographs by Robert Mapplethorpe, and key surrealist works donated by Guggenheim's niece Peggy.

☑ Don't Miss

The view of the instantly recognizable facade from Fifth Ave and 88th St.

EXTERIOR OF THE SOLOMON R. GUGGENHEIM MUSEUM, NEW YORK. ©SRGF, NY /KORD.COM / GETTY IMAGES ©

What's Nearby?

National Academy Museum Gallery

(Map p250; ☎212-369-4880; www.nationalacademy.org; 1083 Fifth Ave, at 89th St; admission by donation; 🕒11am-6pm Wed-Sun; [S]4/5/6 to 86th St) Co-founded by painter/inventor Samuel Morse in 1825, the National Academy Museum comprises an incredible permanent collection of paintings by figures such as Will Barnet, Thomas Hart Benton and George Bellows. (This includes some highly compelling self-portraits.) It's housed in a beaux arts structure designed by Ogden Codman Jr and featuring a marble foyer and spiral staircase.

Cooper-Hewitt National Design Museum Museum

(Map p250; ☎212-849-8400; www.cooperhewitt.org; 2 E 91st St, at Fifth Ave; adult/student/child $18/9/free, by donation 6-9pm Sat; 🕒10am-6pm Sun-Fri, to 9pm Sat; [S]4/5/6 to 86th St) Part of the Smithsonian Institution in Washington, DC, this house of culture is the only museum in the country that's dedicated to both historic and contemporary design. The collection is housed in the 64-room mansion built by billionaire Andrew Carnegie in 1901. The 210,000-piece collection is exquisite, with artful displays spanning 3000 years spread across four floors of the building. An extensive three-year renovation, completed in 2014, brings novelty to its exhibitions with interactive touch screens and wild technology.

🍴 Take a Break

The **Wright** (☎212-427-5690; www.thewrightrestaurant.com; Guggenheim Museum, 1071 Fifth Ave, at 89th St; mains $18-26; 🕒11:30am-3:30pm Fri-Wed; [S]4/5/6 to 86th St), at ground level, is a space-age eatery serving modern American brunch and lunch dishes.

Art deco bronze figure of *Atlas*

SONGQUAN DENG / SHUTTERSTOCK ©

Rockefeller Center

Always a hive of activity, Rockefeller Center has wide-ranging appeal, with art-deco towers, a sky-high viewing platform and a famed ice rink in winter.

Great For...

☑ Don't Miss

Drinks with panoramic views at Sixty-Five (p175).

This 22-acre 'city within a city' debuted at the height of the Great Depression. Taking nine years to build, it was America's first multiuse retail, entertainment and office space – a modernist sprawl of 19 buildings (14 of which are the original art-deco structures), outdoor plazas and big-name tenants. Developer John D Rockefeller Jr may have sweated over the cost (a mere $100 million), but it was all worth it; the Center was declared a National Landmark in 1987.

Top of the Rock

There are views, and then there's *the* view from the **Top of the Rock** (Map p252; ☎212-698-2000; www.topoftherocknyc.com; 30 Rockefeller Plaza, at 49th St, entrance on W 50th St btwn Fifth & Sixth Aves; adult/child $32/26, sunrise/sunset combo $47/36; ⏰8am-midnight, last elevator at 11pm; [S]B/D/F/M to 47th-50th Sts-Rockefeller Center). Crowning the GE

Ice skating rink (p205) in front of *Prometheus* statue

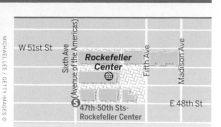

❶ Need to Know

Map p252; www.rockefellercenter.com; Fifth to Sixth Aves & 48th to 51st Sts; [S] B/D/F/M to 47th-50th Sts-Rockefeller Center

✗ Take a Break

Grab a bite at Burger Joint (p133), inside Le Parker Meridien Hotel.

★ Top Tip

To beat the wintertime ice-skating crowds, come at the first skating period (8.30am) to avoid a long wait.

Building, 70 stories above Midtown, its blockbuster vista includes one icon that you won't see from atop the Empire State Building – the Empire State Building. If possible, head up just before sunset to see the city transform from day to glittering night (if you're already in the area and the queues aren't long, purchase your tickets in advance to avoid the late-afternoon rush). Alternatively, if you don't have under-21s in tow, ditch Top of the Rock for the 65th-floor cocktail bar (p175), where the same spectacular views come with well-mixed drinks...at a cheaper price than the Top of the Rock admission.

Public Artworks

Rockefeller Center features the work of 30 great artists, commissioned around the theme 'Man at the Crossroads Looks Uncertainly But Hopefully at the Future.'

Paul Manship contributed *Prometheus*, overlooking the sunken plaza, and *Atlas*, in front of the International Building (630 Fifth Ave). Isamu Noguchi's *News* sits above the entrance to the Associated Press Building (50 Rockefeller Plaza), while José Maria Sert's oil *American Progress* awaits in the lobby of the GE Building. The latter work replaced Mexican artist Diego Rivera's original painting, rejected by the Rockefellers for containing 'communist imagery.'

Rockefeller Plaza

Come the festive season, Rockefeller Plaza is where you'll find New York's most famous Christmas tree. Ceremoniously lit just after Thanksgiving, it's a tradition that dates back to the 1930s, when construction workers set up a small tree on the site. In its shadow, Rink at Rockefeller Center (p205) is the city's most famous (and infamously crowded) ice-skating rink.

What's Nearby?

Radio City Music Hall (p53)

Lunar (Chinese) New Year parade (p6)

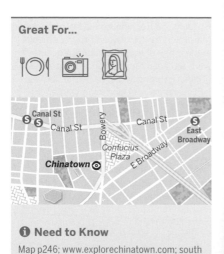

Chinatown

Take a trip to Asia without leaving the US mainland on a wander through the narrow lanes of Chinatown. It's pure sensory overload amid fast-talking street vendors, neon-lit noodle parlors and colorful storefronts packed with eye candy from the Far East.

Great For...

ℹ Need to Know

Map p246; www.explorechinatown.com; south of Canal St & east of Broadway; ⓢ N/Q/R, J/Z, 6 to Canal St; B/D to Grand St; F to East Broadway

★ **Top Tip**
Don't forget to wander down the back alleys for a Technicolor assortment of spices and herbs to perfect your own Eastern dishes.

Endless exotic moments await in New York City's most colorfully cramped community, where a walk through the neighborhood is never the same, no matter how many times you pass through. Catch the whiff of fresh fish and ripe persimmons, hear the clacking of mah-jongg tiles on makeshift tables, and shop for everything imaginable, from rice-paper lanterns and embroidered slippers to tire irons and a pound of pressed nutmeg.

Museum of Chinese in America

In a space designed by architect Maya Lin, the **Museum of Chinese in America** (Map p246; ☎212-619-4785; www.mocanyc.org; 215 Centre St, btwn Grand & Howard Sts; adult/child $10/free, first Thu of month free; ☺11am-6pm Tue, Wed & Fri-Sun, to 9pm Thu; ⓢN/Q/R, J/Z, 6 to Canal St) is a multifaceted space with engaging permanent and temporary exhibitions that shed light on Chinese American life, both past and present. Browse through interactive multimedia exhibits, maps, timelines, photos, letters, films and artifacts. The museum's anchor exhibit, 'With a Single Step: Stories in the Making of America,' provides an often-intimate glimpse into topics including immigration, cultural identity and racial stereotyping.

Food Glorious Food

The most rewarding experience for Chinatown neophytes is to access this wild and wonderful world through their taste buds. More than any other area of Manhattan, Chinatown's menus sport wonderfully low prices, uninflated by ambience, hype or reputation. But more than cheap eats, the neighborhood is rife with family recipes

Red lanterns decorate East Broadway

passed across generations and continents. Food displays and preparation remain unchanged and untempered by American norms, and steaming street stalls clutter the sidewalk serving pork buns and other finger-friendly food.

Buddhist Temples

Chinatown is home to Buddhist temples large and small, public and obscure. They are easily stumbled upon during a full-on stroll of the neighborhood, and at least two such temples are considered landmarks. The **Eastern States Buddhist Temple** (Map p246; ☎212-966-6229; 64 Mott St, btwn Bayard & Canal Sts; ⏰8.30am-6pm; [S]J/Z, 6 to Canal St) is filled with hundreds of Buddhas, while the **Mahayana Temple** (Map p246; ☎212-925-8787; http://en.mahayana.us; 133 Canal St, at Manhattan Bridge Plaza; ⏰8.30am-6pm; [S]B/D to Grand St; J/Z, 6 to Canal St) holds one golden, 16ft-high Buddha, sitting on a lotus and edged with offerings of fresh oranges, apples and flowers. Mahayana is the largest Buddhist temple in Chinatown, and its entrance, which overlooks the frenzied vehicle entrance to the Manhattan Bridge, is guarded by two proud and handsome golden lions. Step inside and you'll find a simple interior of wooden floor and red paper lanterns, dramatically upstaged by the temple's magnificent Buddha.

☑ **Don't Miss**

A family-style meal at a bustling, back-alley dive.

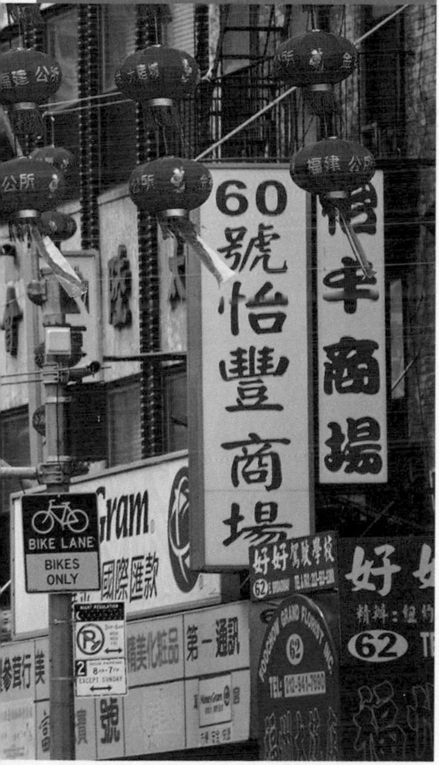

WIN-INITIATIVE / GETTY IMAGES ©

Canal Street

Walking down Canal St is like a game of Frogger played on the streets of Shanghai. This is Chinatown's spine, where you'll dodge oncoming human traffic as you scurry into side streets to scout treasures from the Far East. You'll pass stinky seafood stalls hawking slippery fish; mysterious herb shops peddling a witch's cauldron's worth of roots and potions; storefront bakeries with steamy windows and the tastiest 80¢ pork buns you've ever had; restaurants with whole roasted ducks hanging by their skinny necks in the windows; and produce markets piled high with fresh lychees, bok choy and Asian pears.

What's Nearby?

Little Italy Area

(Map p246; [S]N/Q/R, J/Z, 6 to Canal St; B/D to Grand St) This once-strong Italian neighborhood saw an exodus in the mid-20th century when many of its residents moved to more suburban neighborhoods in Brooklyn and beyond. Today, it's mostly concentrated on Mulberry St between Broome and Canal Sts, a stretch packed with checkerboard tablecloths and Italian fare.

🍴 **Take a Break**

Nyonya (p123) is a bustling temple to Chinese-Malay cuisine.

Reflecting pools the footprints of the fallen twin towers

CHRIS HEPBURN / GETTY IMAGES ©

National September 11 Memorial & Museum

An evocative museum and North America's largest humanmade waterfalls are as much a symbol of hope and renewal as they are a tribute to the victims of terrorism.

Great For...

☑ Don't Miss

The museum's 'Angel of 9/11' – the outline of a woman's anguished face on a twisted girder believed to originate from the point where American Airlines flight 11 slammed into the North Tower.

The National September 11 Memorial and Museum is a dignified tribute to the victims of the worst terrorist attack on American soil. Titled *Reflecting Absence,* the memorial's two massive reflecting pools are a symbol of renewal and commemorate the thousands who lost their lives. Beside them stands the Memorial Museum, a striking, solemn space documenting that horrific fall day in 2001.

Reflecting Pools

Surrounded by a plaza planted with 400 swamp white oak trees, theSeptember 11 Memorial's reflecting pools occupy the very footprints of the ill-fated twin towers. From their rim, a steady cascade of water pours 30ft down toward a central void. The flow of the water is richly symbolic, beginning as hundreds of smaller streams, merging into a massive torrent of collective confusion,

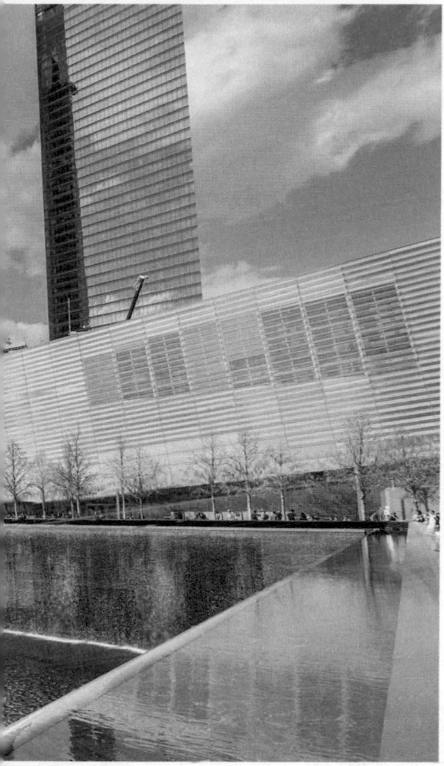

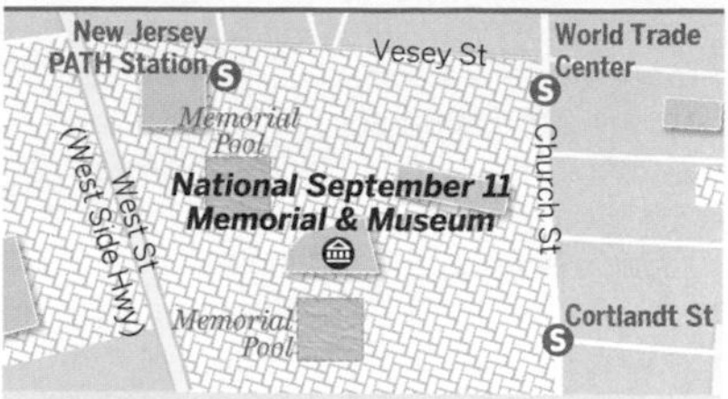

Need to Know

www.911memorial.org; 180 Greenwich St; ⏰7:30am-9pm; [S]E to World Trade Center; R to Cortlandt St; 2/3 to Park Pl [FREE]

🍴 Take a Break

Head up to Tribeca for great dining options such as Locanda Verde (p122).

★ Top Tip

It was the image of a child releasing a dove that inspired Santiago Calatrava's dramatic WTC Transportation Hub, located next to the museum.

and ending with a slow journey towards an abyss. Bronze panels frame the pools, inscribed with the names of those who died in the terrorist attacks of September 11, 2001, and in the World Trade Center car bombing on February 26, 1993. Designed by Michael Arad and Peter Walker, the pools are both striking and deeply poignant.

Memorial Museum

The contemplative energy of the monument is further enhanced by the National **September 11 Memorial Museum** (Map p246; www.911memorial.org/museum; 180 Greenwich St; memorial free, museum adult/child $24/15, 5-8pm Tue free; ⏰9am-8pm Sun-Thu, to 9pm Fri & Sat, last entry 2hr before close; [S]E to World Trade Center; R to Cortlandt St; 2/3 to Park Pl). Standing between the reflective pools, the museum's glass entrance pavilion eerily evokes a toppled tower. Inside the entrance, an escalator leads down to the museum's main subterranean lobby. On the descent, visitors stand in the shadow of two steel tridents, originally embedded in the bedrock at the base of the North Tower. Each standing over 80ft tall and weighing 50 tons, they once provided the structural support that allowed the towers to soar over 1360ft into the sky. In the subsequent sea of rubble, they remained standing, becoming immediate symbols of resilience.

The tridents are two of over 10,300 objects in the museum's collection. Among these are the Vesey Street Stairs; dubbed the 'survivors staircase,' they allowed hundreds of workers to flee the WTC site on the morning of September 11. At the bottom of these stairs is the moving In Memoriam gallery, its walls lined with the photographs and names of those who perished. Interactive touch screens and a central reflection room shed light on the victims' lives. Their humanity is further fleshed out by the numerous personal effects on display. Among these is a dust-covered wallet belonging to Robert Joseph Gschaar, an insurance underwriter working on level 92 of the South Tower. The wallet's contents include a photograph of Gschaar's wife, Myrta, and a $2 bill, twin to the one given to Myrta by Gschaar as a symbol of their second chance at happiness.

Around the corner from the In Memoriam gallery is the New York City Fire Department's Engine Company 21. One of the largest artifacts on display, its burnt-out cab is testament to the inferno faced by those at the scene. The fire engine stands at the entrance to the museum's main Historical Exhibition. Divided into three sections – Events of the Day, Before 9/11 and After 9/11 – its collection of videos, real-time audio recordings, images, objects and testimonies provide a rich, meditative exploration of the tragedy, the events that preceded it, and the stories of grief, resilience and hope that followed.

The Historical Exhibition spills into the monumental Foundation Hall, flanked by a massive section of the original slurry wall, built to hold back the waters of the Hudson River during the towers' construction.

What's Nearby?

Irish Hunger Memorial   Memorial
(Map p246; 290 Vesey St, at North End Ave; S 2/3 to Park Place; E to World Trade Center; A/C to Chambers St) FREE Artist Brian Tolle's compact labyrinth of low limestone walls and patches of grass pays tribute to the Great Irish Famine and Migration (1845–52), which prompted hundreds of thousands of immigrants to leave Ireland for better

Aerial view of the Ground Zero site

opportunities in the New World. Representing abandoned cottages, stone walls and potato fields, the work was created with stones from each of Ireland's 32 counties.

Trinity Church
Church

(Map p246; www.trinitywallstreet.org; Broadway, at Wall St; ☺church 7am-6pm Mon-Fri, 8am-4pm Sat, 7am-4pm Sun, churchyard 7am-4pm Mon-Fri, 8am-3pm Sat, 7am-3pm Sun; ⓢR to Rector St; 2/3, 4/5 to Wall St) New York City's tallest building upon completion in 1846, Trinity Church features a 280ft-high bell tower and a richly colored stained-glass window over the altar. Famous residents of its serene cemetery include founding father Alexander Hamilton, while its excellent music series includes Concerts at One (1pm Thursdays) and choir concerts, including a December rendition of Handel's *Messiah*.

The original Anglican parish church was founded by King William III in 1697 and once presided over several constituent chapels, including St Paul's Chapel at the corner of Fulton St and Broadway. Its huge landholdings in Lower Manhattan made it the country's wealthiest and most influential church throughout the 18th century. Burnt down in 1776, its second incarnation was demolished in 1839. The third and current church, designed by English architect Richard Upjohn, helped launch the picturesque neo-Gothic movement in America.

☑ **Don't Miss**

The museum houses the last steel column removed during the clean-up, adorned with the messages and mementos of recovery workers, responders and loved ones of the victims.

TONY SHI PHOTOGRAPHY / GETTY IMAGES ©

One World Trade Center

Soaring above the city skyline is this shimmering tower, a symbol of Lower Manhattan's rebirth. Its observation decks offer mesmerizing views over the vast metropolis (and surrounding states).

Great For...

☑ **Don't Miss**

The staggering view from the base of the tower looking skyward.

Filling what was a sore and glaring gap in the Lower Manhattan skyline, One World Trade Center symbolizes rebirth, determination and a city's resilience. More than just another supertall building, this tower is a richly symbolic giant, well aware of the past yet firmly focused on the future. For lovers of New York, it's also the hot new stop for dizzying, unforgettable urban views.

The Building

Leaping up from the northwest corner of the World Trade Center site, the 104-floor tower is architect David M Childs' redesign of Daniel Libeskind's original 2002 concept. Not only the loftiest building in America, this tapered giant is currently the tallest building in the western hemisphere, not to mention the fourth tallest in the world by pinnacle height. The tower soars skywards with chamfered edges. The result is a series

AMANDA HALL / ROBERTHARDING / GETTY IMAGES ©

ⓘ Need to Know

One WTC; Map p246; cnr West & Vesey Sts;
Ⓢ E to World Trade Center, 2/3 to Park Pl;
A/C, J/Z, 4/5 to Fulton St; R to Cortlandt St

✕ Take a Break

Inside Brookfield Place (p131), you'll
find a string of chef-driven dining spots
and a French food emporium.

★ Did You Know?

The building's most famous tenant
is Condé Nast Publications, which
made the move from 4 Times Square
in 2014.

One World Observatory

Not one to downplay its assets, the skyscraper is home to **One World Observatory** (Map p246; 844-696-1776; www.
oneworldobservatory.com; cnr West & Vesey Sts;
adult/child $32/26; 9am-8pm, last ticket sold
at 7:15pm; Ⓢ E to World Trade Center; 2/3 to Park
Pl; A/C, J/Z, 4/5 to Fulton St; R to Cortlandt St),
the city's loftiest observation deck. While
the observatory spans levels 100 to 102,
the experience begins at the ground-floor
Global Welcome Center, where an electronic world map highlights the homeland of
visitors (data relayed from ticket scans).
The bitter bickering that plagued much of
the project's development is all but forgot-
ten in the adjoining Voices exhibition, where
architects and construction workers wax
lyrically about the tower's formation on 144
video screens.

After a quick rundown of the site's geol-
ogy, the real thrills begin as you step inside
one of five Sky Pod elevators, among the

of isosceles triangles that, seen from the
building's base, reach to infinity.

Crowning the structure is a 408ft cable-
stayed spire. Co-designed by sculptor
Kenneth Snelson, it brings the building's
total height to 1776ft, a symbolic reference
to the year of American independence.
Indeed, symbolism feeds several aspects
of the building: the tower's footprint is
equal to those of the Twin Towers, while the
observation decks match the heights of
those in the old complex. Unlike the original
towers, however, One WTC was built with
a whole new level of safety in mind, its
precautionary features including a 200ft-
high blast-resistant base (clad in over 2000
pieces of glimmering prismatic glass) and
1m-thick concrete walls encasing all elevators, stairwells, and communication and
safety systems.

fastest in the world. As the elevators begin their 1250ft skyward journey, LED wall panels kick into action. Suddenly you're in a veritable time machine, watching Manhattan's evolution from forested island to teeming concrete jungle. Forty-seven seconds (and 500 years) later, you're on level 102, where another short presentation ends with a spectacular reveal.

Skip the overpriced eateries on level 101 and continue down to the real highlight: level 100. Waiting for you is an epic, 360-degree panorama guaranteed to keep your index finger busy pointing out landmarks, from the Brooklyn and Manhattan Bridges to Lady Liberty and the Woolworth, Empire State and Chrysler Buildings. If you need a hand, interactive mobile tablets are available for hire ($15). As expected, the view is extraordinary (choose a clear day!), taking in all five boroughs and adjoining states.

What's Nearby?

Woolworth Building Notable Building (Map p246; ☎203-966-9663; http://woolworthtours.com; 233 Broadway, at Park Pl; 30/60/90min tours $20/30/45; [S]R to City Hall; 2/3 to Park Pl; 4/5/6 to Brooklyn Bridge-City Hall) The world's tallest building upon completion in 1913, Cass Gilbert's 60-story, 792ft-tall Woolworth Building is a neo-Gothic marvel, elegantly clad in masonry and terracotta. Surpassed in height by the Chrysler Building in 1930, the building has a breathtaking lobby of dazzling, Byzantine-like mosaics. The lobby is only accessible on prebooked guided tours, which also offer insight into the building's more curious original

Breathtaking views from the One World Observatory

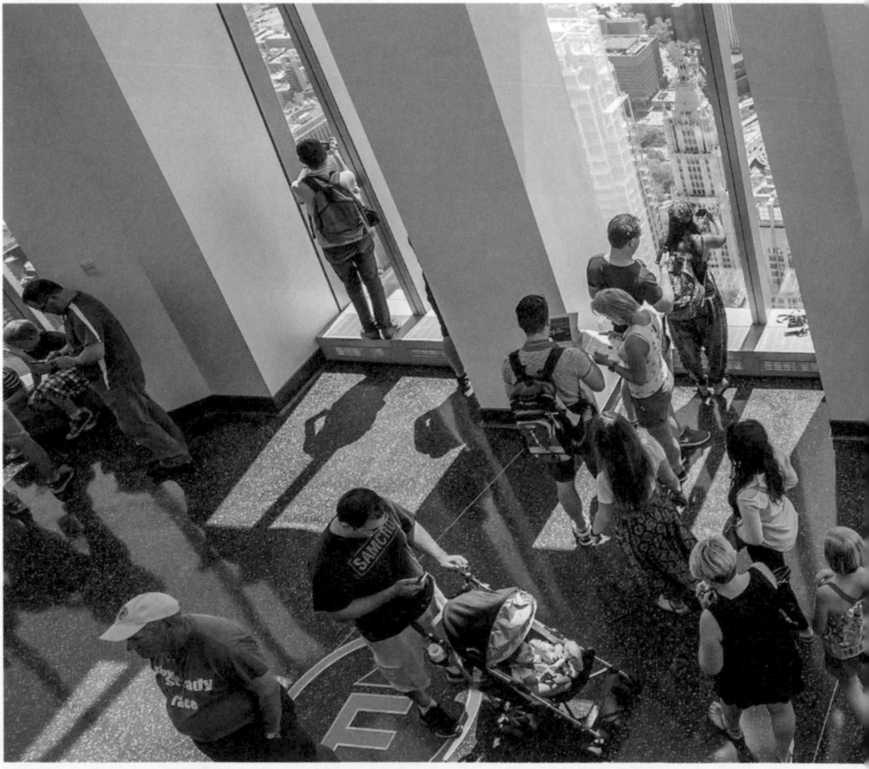

features, among them a dedicated subway entrance and a secret swimming pool.

At its dedication, the building was described as a 'cathedral of commerce'; though meant as an insult, FW Woolworth, head of the five-and-dime chain-store empire headquartered there, took the comment as a compliment and began throwing the term around himself.

St Paul's Chapel Church

(Map p246; ☎212-602-0800; www.trinitywallstreet.org; Broadway, at Fulton St; 🕐10am-6pm Mon-Sat, 7am-6pm Sun; [S]A/C, J/Z, 2/3, 4/5 to Fulton St; R to Cortlandt St; E to World Trade Center) After his inauguration in 1789, George Washington worshipped at this classic revival brownstone chapel, which found new fame in the aftermath of September 11. With the World Trade Center destruction occurring just a block away, the mighty structure became a spiritual support and volunteer center, movingly documented in its exhibition 'Unwavering Spirit: Hope & Healing at Ground Zero.'

Through photographs, personal objects and messages of support, the exhibition honors both the victims and the volunteers who worked round the clock, serving meals, setting up beds, doling out massages and counseling rescue workers.

★ Howling Spire

One thing not foreseen by the architects and engineers was the antenna's noisy disposition; the strong winds that race through its lattice design produce a haunting, howling sound that keeps some locals up at night.

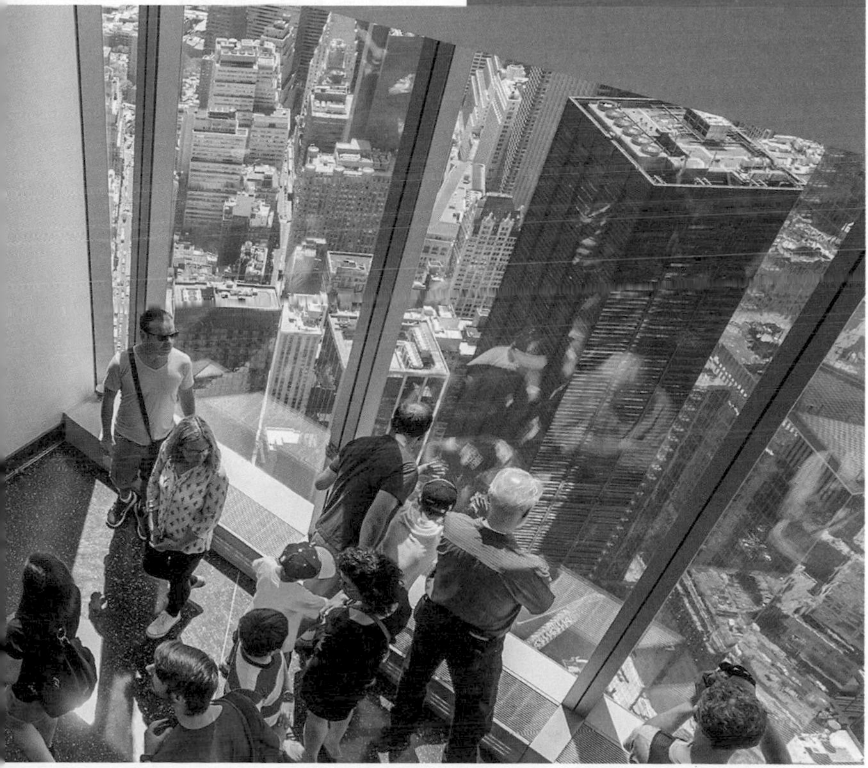

F11PHOTO / SHUTTERSTOCK ©

Lower East Side Tenement Museum

In a neighborhood once teeming with immigrants, this museum opens a window to the past via guided tours through meticulously preserved tenements. You'll learn all about real people who lived on these densely packed streets.

Great For...

ℹ Need to Know

Map p246; ☎877-975-3786; www.tenement. org; 103 Orchard St, btwn Broome & Delancey Sts; adult/student from $25/20; ⏱tours 10:15am-5pm Fri-Wed, to 6:30pm Thu; Ⓢ B/D to Grand St; J/M/Z to Essex St; F to Delancey St

★ **Top Tip**
Watch the free 30-minute film shown in the visitor center that gives an overview of immigrant life in NYC.

There's no museum in New York that humanizes the city's colorful past quite like the Lower East Side Tenement Museum, which puts the neighborhood's heartbreaking but inspiring heritage on full display in several re-creations of former tenements. Always evolving and expanding, the museum has a variety of tours and talks beyond the museum's walls – a must for anyone interested in old New York.

Inside the Tenement

A wide range of tenement tours lead visitors into the building where hundreds of immigrants lived and worked over the years. Hard Times, one of the most popular tours, visits apartments from two different time periods – the 1870s and the 1930s. There you'll see the squalid conditions tenants faced – in the early days there was a wretched communal outhouse, and no electricity or running water – and what life was like for the families who lived there. Other tours focus on Irish immigrants and the harsh discrimination they faced, sweatshop workers and 'shop life' (with a tour through a re-created 1870s German beer hall).

103 Orchard Street

The visitor center at 103 Orchard St has a museum shop and a small screening room that plays an original film. Several evenings a month, the museum hosts talks here, often relating to the present immigrant experience in America. The building itself was, naturally, a tenement too – ask the staff about the interesting families of Eastern European and Italian descent that once dwelled here.

Museum room depicting immigrant life in the tenements

Meet Victoria

Travel back to 1916 and meet Victoria Confino, a 14-year-old girl from a Greek Sephardic family. Played by a costumed interpreter, Victoria interacts with visitors, answering questions about what her life was like in those days. It's especially recommended for kids, as visitors are free to handle household objects. This one-hour tour is held on weekends year-round, and daily during the summer.

Neighborhood Tours

A great way to understand the immigrant experience is on a walking tour around the neighborhood. These tours, ranging from 75 minutes to two hours, explore a variety of topics. Foods of the Lower East Side looks at the ways traditional foods have shaped American cuisine; Then & Now explores the way the neighborhood has changed over the decades; and Outside the Home looks at life beyond the apartment – where immigrants stored (and lost) their life savings, and the churches and synagogues so integral to community life.

☑ Don't Miss

A peek into the 1870s and the 1930s on the Hard Times tour.

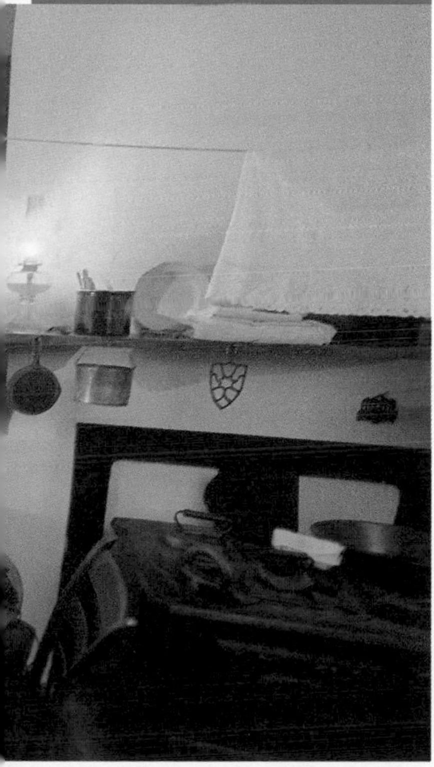

KEVIN FLEMING/CORBIS/VCG / GETTY IMAGES ©

What's Nearby?

Museum at Eldridge Street Synagogue — Museum

(Map p246; ☎212-219-0302; www.eldridgestreet.org; 12 Eldridge St, btwn Canal & Division Sts; adult/child $12/8, Mon free; ⏰10am-5pm Sun-Thu, 10am-3pm Fri; [S]F to East Broadway) This landmark house of worship, built in 1887, was once the center of Jewish life, before falling into squalor in the 1920s. Left to rot, the synagogue underwent a 20-year-long, $20-million restoration that was completed in 2007, and it now shines with original splendor.

New Museum of Contemporary Art — Museum

(Map p246; ☎212-219-1222; www.newmuseum.org; 235 Bowery, btwn Stanton & Rivington Sts; adult/child $16/free, 7-9pm Thu by donation; ⏰11am-6pm Wed & Fri-Sun, to 9pm Thu; [S]N/R to Prince St; F to 2nd Ave, J/Z to Bowery; 6 to Spring St) Rising above the neighborhood, the New Museum of Contemporary Art is a sight to behold: a seven-story stack of off-kilter, white, ethereal boxes designed by Tokyo-based architects Kazuyo Sejima and Ryue Nishizawa of Sanaa and the New York–based firm Gensler. The museum's mission statement is simple: 'New art, new ideas.' The city's sole museum dedicated to contemporary art brings a steady menu of edgy works in new forms.

🍴 Take a Break

Take a bite out of history at famed Jewish deli Russ & Daughters (p124), in business since 1914.

Audobon Center Boathouse (p105)

Prospect Park

Brooklyn's favorite green space is a grassy wonderland of rolling meadows, babbling brooks, hillside overlooks, flower strewn trails and an open lake. It's a fantastic place for running, walking, picnicking, skating or just getting a dose of the great outdoors.

Great For...

❶ Need to Know

☏718-965-8951; www.prospectpark.org; Grand Army Plaza; ⏱5am-1am; Ⓢ2/3 to Grand Army Plaza; F to 15th St-Prospect Park

★ **Top Tip**

One of the prettiest places for a park stroll is alongside the Lullwater, near the Boathouse.

The creators of the 585-acre Prospect Park, Calvert Vaux and Frederick Olmsted, considered this an improvement on their other New York project, Central Park. Created in 1866, Prospect Park has many of the same features: a gorgeous meadow, a scenic lake, forested pathways and rambling hills that are straddled with leafy walkways. It receives roughly 10 million visitors a year.

Grand Army Plaza

A large, landscaped traffic circle with a massive ceremonial arch sits at the intersection of Flatbush Ave and Prospect Park West. This marks the beginning of Eastern Parkway and the entrance to Prospect Park. The arch, which was built in the 1890s, is a memorial to Union soldiers who fought in the Civil War.

Long Meadow

The 90-acre Long Meadow, which is bigger than Central Park's Great Lawn, lies to the south of the park's formal entrance at Grand Army Plaza. It's a super strolling and lounging spot, filled with pick-up ball games and families flying kites. On the south end is the Picnic House, with a snack stand and public bathrooms.

Children's Corner

Near Flatbush Ave, the Children's Corner contains a terrific 1912 carousel, originally from Coney Island, and the **Prospect Park Zoo** (☎718-399-7339; www.prospectparkzoo.com; Prospect Park, at Lincoln Rd & Ocean Ave; adult/child $8/5; 🕒10am-5:30pm Apr-Oct, to 4:30pm Nov-Mar; [S]2/3 to Grand Army Plaza), featuring sea lions, baboons, wallabies and a small petting zoo. To the northeast of the

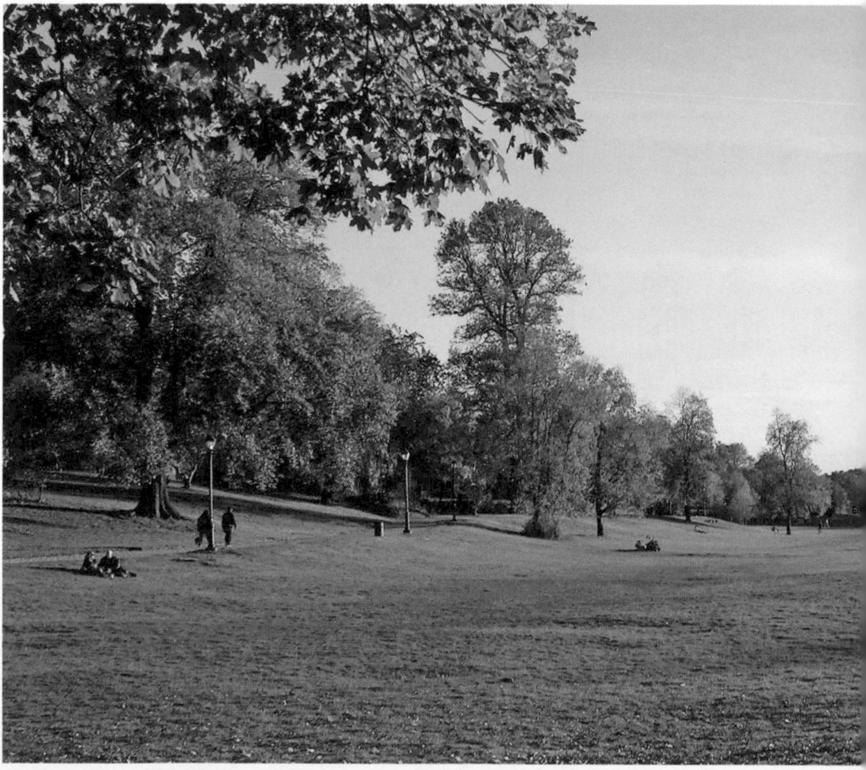

carousel is the 18th-century **Lefferts Historic House** (☎718-789-2822; www.prospectpark.org; Prospect Park, near Flatbush Ave & Empire Blvd; suggested donation $3; 🕒noon-5pm Thu-Sun May-Oct, noon-4pm Sat & Sun Nov-Apr; [S]B, Q to Prospect Park), which has plenty of old-fashioned toys to play with.

Audobon Center Boathouse

Sitting on a northern finger of Prospect Park Lake, the photogenic boathouse (aka Prospect Park Audubon Center) hosts a range of activities throughout the year (guided bird-watching sessions, free yoga classes, nature-themed art exhibitions, hands-on craft activities for kids). From here, there is a trailhead for 2.5 miles of woodsy nature trails. Check the website for downloadable maps or ask at the boathouse for details.

☑ Don't Miss

Free outdoor concerts in the summer at the Prospect Park Bandshell.

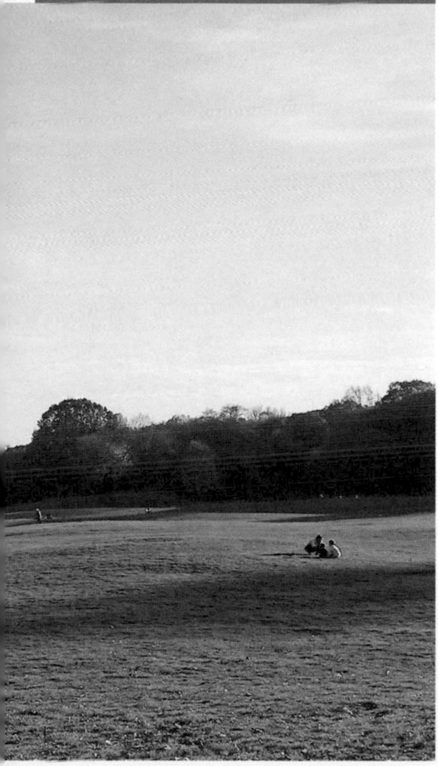

MARIO SAVOIA / SHUTTERSTOCK ©

Lakeside

Prospect Park's newest attraction continues to turn heads. The 26-acre Lakeside (p205) complex features rinks for ice skating and roller skating, as well as a cafe, new walking trails and a small concert space.

What's Nearby?

Brooklyn Botanic Garden Gardens

(www.bbg.org; 1000 Washington Ave, at Crown St; adult/child $12/free, Tue & 10am-noon Sat free; 🕒8am-6pm Tue-Fri, 10am-6pm Sat & Sun; 👪; [S]2/3 to Eastern Pkwy-Brooklyn Museum) This 52-acre garden is home to thousands of plants and trees, as well as a Japanese garden where river turtles swim alongside a Shinto shrine. The best time to visit is late April or early May, when the blooming cherry trees (a gift from Japan) are celebrated in Sakura Matsuri, the Cherry Blossom Festival.

Brooklyn Museum Museum

(☎718-638-5000; www.brooklynmuseum.org; 200 Eastern Pkwy; suggested donation $16; 🕒11am-6pm Wed & Fri-Sun, to 10pm Thu; [S]2/3 to Eastern Pkwy-Brooklyn Museum) This encyclopedic museum is housed in a five-story, 560,000-sq-ft beaux-arts building designed by McKim, Mead & White. Today, the building houses more than 1.5 million objects, including ancient artifacts, 19th-century period rooms, and sculptures and painting from across several centuries.

🍴 Take a Break

Near the park's north entrance, friendly **Cheryl's Global Soul** (☎347-529-2855; www.cherylsglobalsoul.com; 236 Underhill Ave, btwn Eastern Pkwy & St Johns Pl, Prospect Heights; sandwiches $8-14, mains $15-25; 🕒8am-4pm Mon, to 10pm Tue-Sun; vc; b2/3 to Eastern Pkwy-Brooklyn Museum) is a neighborhood favorite.

Brooklyn Bridge Park

The pride and joy of Brooklyn, this revitalized waterfront park offers loads of amusement, with playgrounds, walkways, and lawns with plenty of summertime outdoor entertainment, including live music and open-air cinema, not to mention grand views of Manhattan skyscrapers across the river.

Great For...

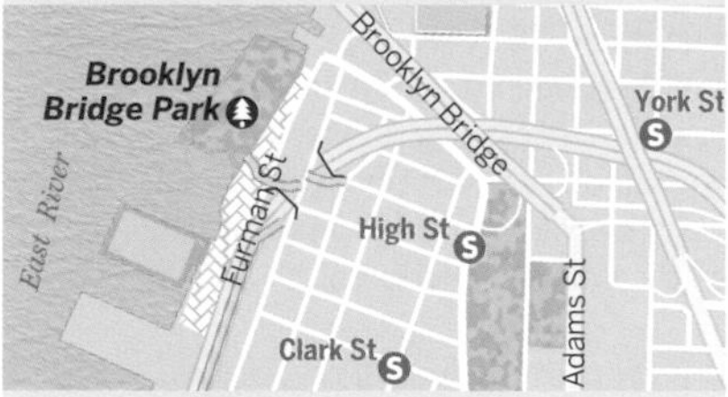

ⓘ Need to Know

Map p246; ☎718-802-0603; www.brooklyn bridgepark.org; East River Waterfront, btwn Atlantic Ave & Adams St; ⊘6am-1am; ⛹; ⑤A/C to High St; 2/3 to Clark St; F to York St; FREE

★ **Top Tip**

Be sure to check out what's on when you're in town: the website lists outdoor yoga and dance classes, theater and cinema, family activities and more.

This 85-acre park, nearing completion, is one of Brooklyn's most talked-about new sights. Wrapping around a bend on the East River, it runs for 1.3 miles from Jay St in Dumbo to the west end of Atlantic Ave in Cobble Hill. It has revitalized a once-barren stretch of shoreline, turning a series of abandoned piers into public parkland.

Empire Fulton Ferry State Park

Just east of the Brooklyn Bridge, in the northern section of Dumbo, you'll find a state park with a grassy lawn that faces the East River. Near the water is **Jane's Carousel** (Map p246; www.janescarousel. com; Brooklyn Bridge Park, Empire Fulton Ferry, Dumbo; tickets $2; ☻11am-7pm Wed-Mon mid-May–mid-Sep, 11am-6pm Thu-Sun mid-Sep–mid-May; ⚇; ⓈF to York St), a lovingly restored 1922 carousel set inside a glass pavilion

designed by Pritzker Prize–winning architect Jean Nouvel. The park is bordered on one side by the **Empire Stores & Tobacco Warehouse** (Map p246; Water St, near Main St; ⓈF to York St; A/C to High St), a series of Civil War–era structures that house restaurants, shops and a theater. Keep heading up to the Manhattan Bridge to find a new bouldering wall.

Pier 1

A 9-acre pier just south of the Empire Fulton Ferry is home to a stretch of park featuring a playground, walkways and the Harbor View and Bridge View Lawns, both of which overlook the river. On the Bridge View Lawn, you'll find artist Mark di Suvero's 30ft kinetic sculpture *Yoga* (1991). From July through August, free outdoor films are screened on the Harbor View

Jane's Carousel at the Empire Fulton Ferry State Park

Lawn against a stunning backdrop of Manhattan. Other free open-air events (outdoor dance parties, group yoga classes, history tours) happen throughout the summer. The seasonal **Brooklyn Bridge Garden Bar** (Map p246; http://brooklynbridgegardenbar.com; Pier 1, Brooklyn Bridge Park; 🕐noon-10pm Jun-Aug, to 6pm Apr, May, Sep & Oct; [S]A/C to High St) can be found on the pier's north end. You can also catch the East River Ferry (p237) from the north end of the pier.

Pier 2 & Pier 4

At Pier 2, you'll find courts for basketball, handball and boccie, plus a skating rink.

Nearby, there's a tiny beach at Pier 4. Though swimming is not allowed, you can hire stand-up paddleboards here. If you want to head up to Brooklyn Heights, you can take a bouncy pedestrian bridge (access near Pier 2).

Pier 5 & Pier 6

At the southern end of the park, off Atlantic Ave, Pier 6 has a fantastic playground and a small water-play area for tots (if you're bringing kids, pack swimsuits and towels). Neighboring Pier 5, just north, has walkways, sand volleyball courts, soccer fields and barbecue grills. There are also a few seasonal concessions (May to October), including wood-fired pizza, beer and Italian treats at **Fornino** (Map p246; ☎718-422-1107; www.fornino.com; Pier 6, Brooklyn Bridge Park; pizzas $12-25; 🕐10am-10pm Apr-Oct; 🚌B45 to Brooklyn Bridge Park/Pier 6, [S]2/3, 4/5 to Borough Hall), which has a rooftop deck. A free seasonal ferry runs on weekends from Pier 6 to **Governors Island** (www.govisland.com; 🕐10am-6pm Mon-Fri,to 7pm Sat & Sun; [S]4, 5 to Bowling Green; 1 to South Ferry) [FREE].

☑ Don't Miss

The views of Manhattan and the East River from Empire Fulton Ferry at sunset.

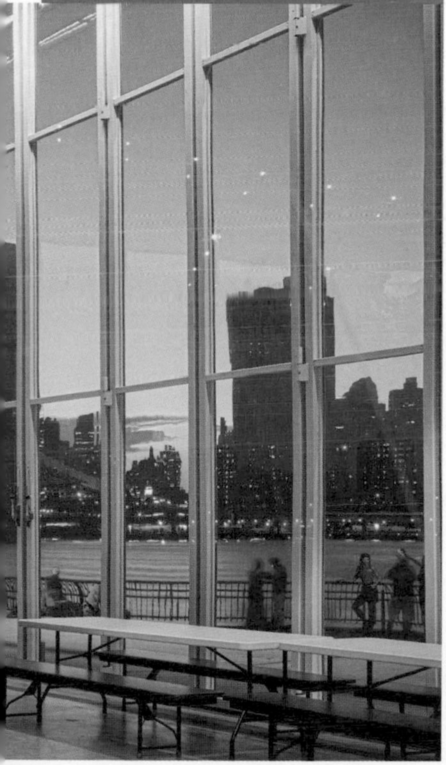

ANDRIA PATINO / GETTY IMAGES ©

What's Nearby?

Brooklyn Heights Promenade — Lookout

(Map p246; btwn Orange & Remsen Sts; 🕐24hr; 👪; [S]2/3 to Clark St) All of the east–west lanes of Brooklyn Heights (such as Clark and Pineapple Sts) lead to the neighborhood's number-one attraction: a narrow park with breathtaking views of Lower Manhattan and New York Harbor. Though it hangs over the busy Brooklyn–Queens Expressway (BQE), this little slice of urban beauty is a great spot for a sunset walk.

🍴 Take a Break

In the park at Pier 6, Fornino (see above) has wood-fired pizzas and rooftop dining at picnic tables with panoramic views.

West Village Wandering

Of all the neighborhoods in New York City, the West Village is easily the most walkable, its cobbled corners straying from the signature grid that unfurls across the rest of the island. An afternoon stroll is not to be missed; hidden landmarks and quaint cafes abound.

Start: Cherry Lane Theater, Commerce St
Distance: 1 mile
Duration: 1 hour

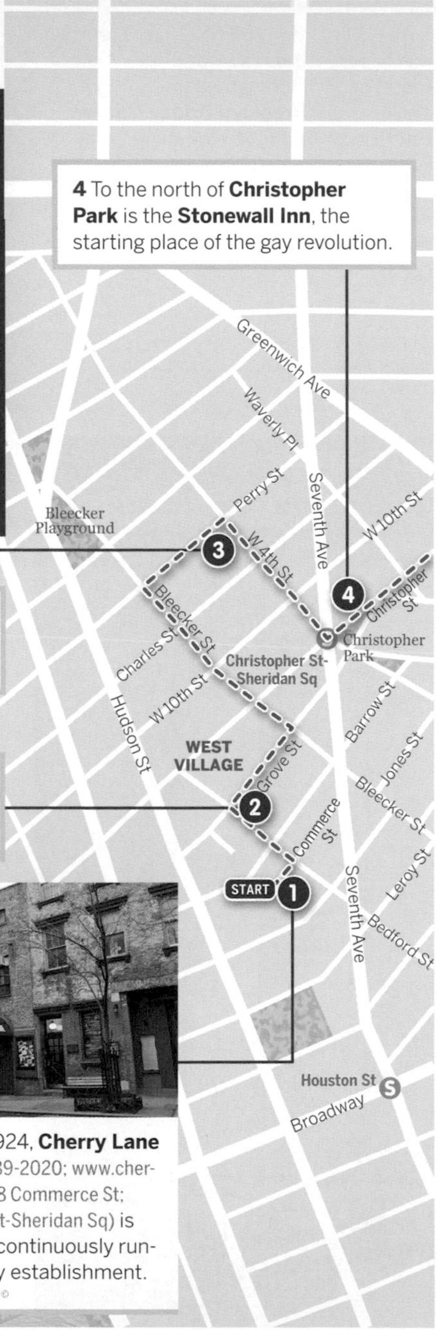

4 To the north of **Christopher Park** is the **Stonewall Inn**, the starting place of the gay revolution.

3 For another TV landmark, head to **66 Perry St**, Carrie Bradshaw's apartment in Sex and the City.

2 The apartment block at **90 Bedford** was the fictitious home of the cast of Friends.

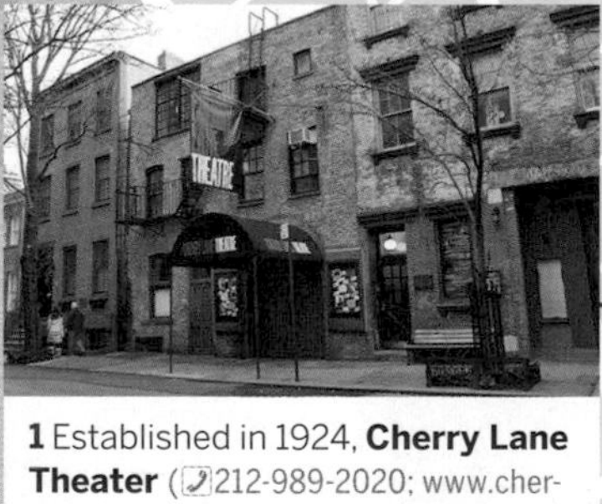

1 Established in 1924, **Cherry Lane Theater** (☎212-989-2020; www.cherrylanetheater.org; 38 Commerce St; [S]1 to Christopher St-Sheridan Sq) is the city's longest continuously running off-Broadway establishment.

B6GPYJ / ALAMY STOCK PHOTO©

5 The **Jefferson Market Library** building once served as a court-house and a fire-lookout tower.

RICK ELKINS/GETTY IMAGES ©

✕ **Take a Break**

Near Washington Square, Stump-town Coffee Roasters (30 W 8th St, at MacDougal St; ⊙7am-8pm) **serves some of NYC's best coffee.**

6th Ave-14th St

W 10th St

W 9th St

W 8th St

GREENWICH VILLAGE

Gay St

Sixth Ave (Avenue of the Americas)

Fifth Ave

Washington Sq W

Cornelia St

Washington Sq N

7 **FINISH**

Washington Sq S

W 4th St
W 4th St-Washington Sq

W 3rd St

Minetta La

Minetta St

6

New York University

📷

Classic Photo of street musicians at Washington Square Park

7 Washington Square Park (Fifth Ave at Washington Sq N; ʙA/C/F, B/D/F/M to W 4th St-Washington Sq; N/R to 8th St-NYU) is the Village's unofficial town square, which plays host to students, buskers and protestors.

DENNIS K. JOHNSON / GETTY IMAGES ©

6 Swing by **Cafe Wha?**, where many musicians and comedians – including Bob Dylan and Richard Pryor – got their start.

ANGUS OBORN / GETTY IMAGES ©

🧭 0 ⌁ 400 m
0 ⌁ 0.2 miles

Shopping on Fifth Avenue

New York's most celebrated shopping strip is studded with high-end department stores and glittering boutiques selling all manner of covetable goods. Fashionistas, designer-label bargain hunters and those who simply want to gawk at lavishly filled store windows all rub shoulders on Midtown's tony Fifth Avenue.

Great For...

ⓘ Need to Know

Map p252; 725 Fifth Ave, at 56th St; **S** E/M to 5th Ave-53rd St; N/Q/R to 5th Ave-59th St

BERGDORF GOODMAN
BERGDORF GOODMAN
NYU

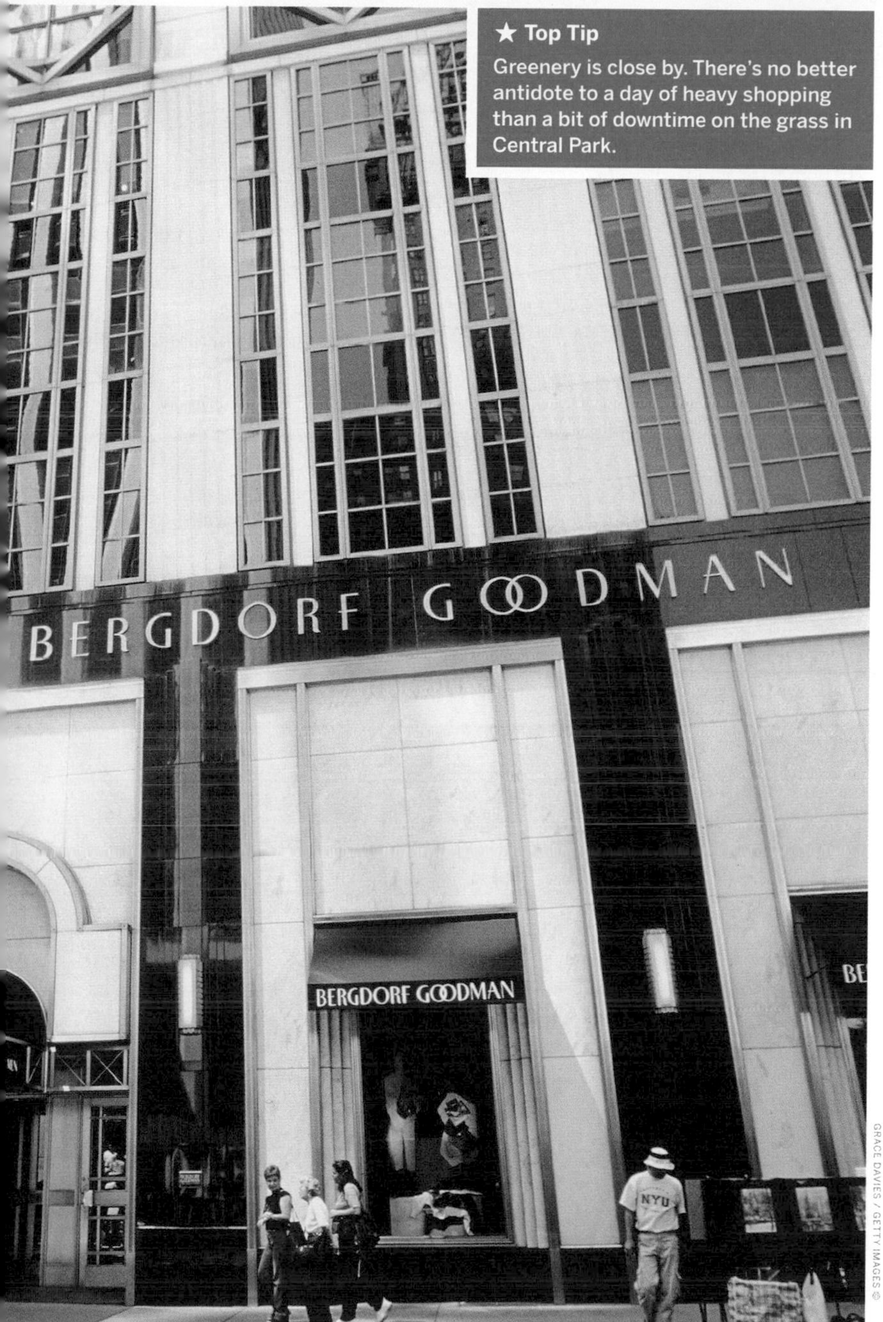

★ Top Tip

Greenery is close by. There's no better antidote to a day of heavy shopping than a bit of downtime on the grass in Central Park.

GRACE DAVIES / GETTY IMAGES ©

Immortalized in film and song, Fifth Ave first developed its high-class reputation in the early 20th century, when it was known for its 'country' air and open spaces. Today, despite a proliferation of ubiquitous chains, the avenue's Midtown stretch still glitters with upmarket establishments.

Bergdorf Goodman

Not merely loved for its Christmas windows (the city's best), plush BG (p155) leads the fashion race, its fashion director Linda Fargo considered an Anna Wintour of sorts. A mainstay of ladies who lunch, its drawcards include exclusive collections of Tom Ford and Chanel shoes and a coveted women's shoe department. The men's store is across the street.

Tiffany & Co

Ever since Audrey Hepburn gazed longingly through its windows, **Tiffany & Co** (Map p252; ✆212-755-8000; www.tiffany.com; 727 Fifth Ave, at 57th St; ⊙10am-7pm Mon-Sat, noon-6pm Sun; Ⓢ F to 57th St; N/Q/R to 5th Ave-59th St) has won countless hearts with its glittering diamond rings, watches, silver Elsa Peretti heart necklaces, crystal vases and glassware. But wait, there's more, including handbags and travel-friendly gifts such as letter openers. Swoon, drool, but whatever you do, don't harass the elevator attendants with tired 'Where's the breakfast?' jokes.

Saks Fifth Ave

Graced with vintage elevators, the 10-floor flagship store of **Saks** (Map p252; ✆212-753-4000; www.saksfifthavenue.com; 611 Fifth Ave,

Holiday-season shop window displays on Fifth Ave

at 50th St; ⏰10am-8:30pm Mon-Sat, 11am-7pm Sun; [S]B/D/F/M to 47th-50th Sts-Rockefeller Center; E/M to 5th Ave-53rd St) is home to the 'Shoe Salon,' NYC's biggest women's shoe department (complete with express elevator and zip code). Other fortes include the cosmetics and men's departments, the latter home to destination grooming salon John Allan's and a sharply edited offering of fashion-forward labels. The store's January sale is legendary.

Bloomingdale's

OK, so technically it's not on Fifth Avenue, but this shopping blockbuster two blocks east is such an icon of fashion that it would be heresy to exclude it. In fact, Bloomie's is something like the Metropolitan Museum of Art of the shopping world: historic, sprawling, overwhelming and packed with bodies, but you'd be sorry to miss it. Raid the racks for clothes and shoes from a who's who of US and global designers, including a number of 'new-blood' collections. Refuel pitstops include a branch of cupcake heaven Magnolia Bakery.

☑ Don't Miss

The store windows at Bergdorf Goodman. During Christmas, expect wildly enchanting designs in each one.

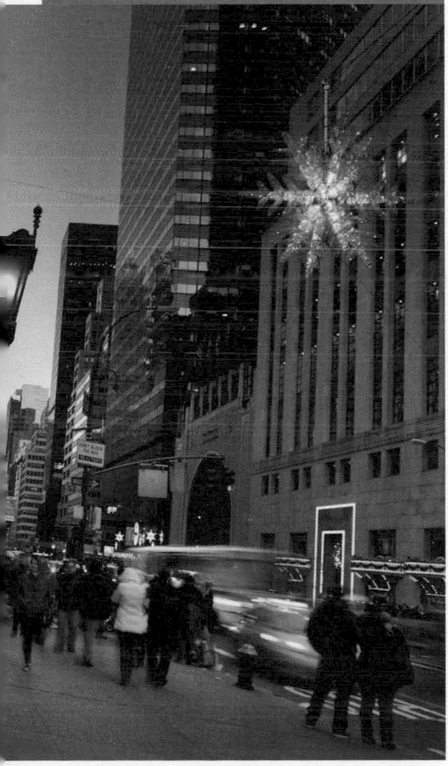

JON HICKS / GETTY IMAGES ©

Barneys

Like Bloomie's, Barneys is located a short stroll from Fifth Avenue, and draws equally veteran fashionistas. Barneys is respected for its spot-on collections of top-tier labels such as Isabel Marant Étoile, Mr & Mrs Italy and Lanvin. For (slightly) less expensive deals geared to a younger market, shop street-chic labels on the 8th floor. Gorgeous threads aside, other in-store highlights include a well-stocked basement cosmetics department and Genes, a futuristic cafe with touch-screen communal tables for online shopping.

Uniqlo

Uniqlo (Map p252; ☎877-486-4756; www.uniqlo.com; 666 Fifth Ave, at 53rd St; ⏰10am-9pm Mon-Sat, 11am-8pm Sun; [S]E, M to 5th Ave-53rd St) is Japan's answer to H&M and this is its showstopping 89,000-sq-ft flagship megastore. Grab a mesh bag at the entrance and let the elevators whoosh you up to the 3rd floor to begin your retail odyssey. Its strength is affordable, fashionable, quality basics, from T-shirts and undergarments to Japanese denim, cashmere sweaters and superlight, high-tech parkas.

🍴 Take a Break

Escape the shopping mayhem at the outdoor tables at the **Bryant Park Grill** (Map p252; ☎212-840-6500; www.arkrestaurants.com/bryant_park.html; Bryant Park, 25 W 40th St, btwn Fifth & Sixth Aves; mains $18.50-42; ⏰11:30am-11pm; [S]B/D/F/M to 42nd St-Bryant Park; 7 to 5th Ave).

RACHEL LEWIS / GETTY IMAGES ©

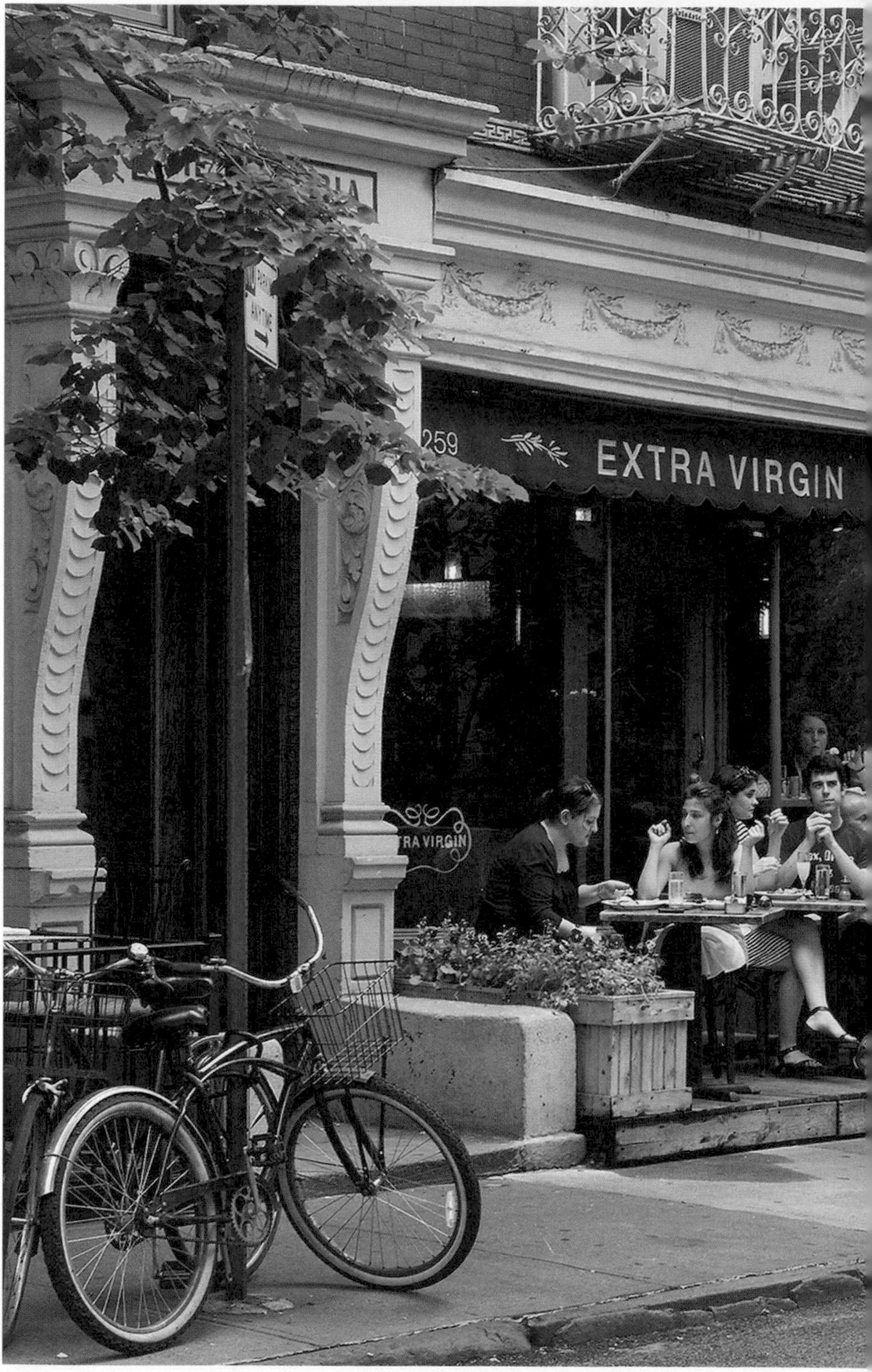

DINING OUT

Hot dogs, high-end cuisine
and a cup of joe

The Best...

Experience New York City's finest eating establishments

By Budget

$

Taïm (p128) Outstanding falafel sandwiches at downtown locations.

El Rey (p124) Daring combinations at a locavore haunt in the Lower East Side.

Moustache (p127) Tiny West Village gem serving satisfying Middle Eastern dishes.

$$

Upstate (p126) A seafood feast awaits in the East Village.

Jeffrey's Grocery (p128) Much-loved West Village neighborhood spot.

ViceVersa (p133) Elegant Italian in the shadow of the Theater District.

Babu Ji (p125) A celebration of Indian street food in a cheeky East Village dining room.

$$$

Eleven Madison Park (p132) Arresting, cutting-edge cuisine laced with unexpected whimsy.

Blue Hill (p130) A West Village classic using ingredients sourced straight from the associated farm upstate.

Degustation (p126) A tiny East Village eatery where you can watch the chefs create edible works of art.

Old-School NYC

Barney Greengrass (p136) Perfect plates of smoked salmon and sturgeon for over 100 years in the Upper West Side.

Russ & Daughters (pictured above; p124) A celebrated Jewish deli in the Lower East Side.

Zabar's (p134) Upper West Side store selling gourmet, kosher foods since the 1930s.

For Brunch

Estela (p123) Brilliant seasonal plates in a buzzing Nolita wine bar.

Rabbit Hole (p139) Excellent brunch plates served daily till 5pm at this Williamsburg gem.

Cookshop (p130) Great indoor-outdoor dining spot in west Chelsea.

Cafe Mogador (p125) An icon of the East Village brunch scene.

Upscale Market Groceries

Eataly (p132) A mecca for lovers of Italian food.

Union Square Greenmarket (pictured above; p131) Delicious vegies and bakery items from upstate producers.

Brookfield Place (p131) Sprawling food halls on the Hudson, including the Le District emporium packed with Gallic larder essentials.

By Cuisine

Asian

Uncle Boons (p122) Zesty, Michelin-starred Thai with a generous serve of fun in Nolita.

Zenkichi (p139) Candlelit culinary temple of exquisite sushi in Williamsburg.

Lan Larb (p122) Real-deal northeastern Thai in a cheap and cheery hole-in-the-wall on the edge of Chinatown.

Italian

Rosemary's (p130) A beautifully designed West Village spot with memorable cooking.

Roman's (p139) Changing seasonal menu of Italian invention in Fort Greene.

Morandi (p128) A West Village gem that invites lingering.

Vegetarian

Butcher's Daughter (p123) Inventive vegetarian menu in Nolita.

Hangawi (p135) Meat-free (and shoe-free) Korean restaurant in Koreatown.

Champs (p138) Comfort-food diner in East Williamsburg with outstanding vegan plates.

★ Lonely Planet's Top Choices

Gramercy Tavern (p132) Prime produce, culinary finesse and the choice of bustling tavern or fine-dining den.

RedFarm (p131) Savvy Sino-fusion dishes boast bold flavors, but it doesn't take itself too seriously.

Dovetail (p136) Simplicity is key at this Upper West Side stunner – vegetarians unite on Monday for a divine tasting menu.

Foragers City Table (p131) A triumph of farm-to-table cooking with flavorful sustainable recipes in Chelsea.

✖ Financial District & Lower Manhattan

Hudson Eats   Fast Food $
(Map p246; 📞212-417-2445; www.brookfield
placeny.com; Brookfield Place, 200 Vesey St;
dishes from $7; ⊗10am-9pm Mon-Sat, noon-7pm
Sun; 🛜; 🆂E to World Trade Center; 2/3 to Park
Place; R to Cortland St; A/C, 4/5, J/Z to Fulton
St) Renovated office and retail complex
Brookfield Place is home to Hudson Eats,
a slinky, new-school food hall. Decked out
in terrazzo floors, marble countertops and
floor-to-ceiling windows with Hudson and
Jersey City views, its string of chef-driven
eateries includes Blue Ribbon Sushi, Umani
Burger and Dos Toros Taqueria.

Seaport Smorgasburg   Market $
(Map p246; www.smorgasburg.com; Fulton St,
btwn Front & South Sts; dishes $6-19; ⊗11am-
8pm May-Sep; 🆂A/C, J/Z, 2/3, 4/5 to Fulton St)
Brooklyn's hipster food market has jumped
the East River, injecting touristy South
Street Seaport with some much-needed
local cred. Cooking up a storm from May to
late September, its offerings include anything from lobster rolls, ramen and pizza to
slow-smoked Texan-style brisket sandwiches. Add a splash of historic architecture and
you have one of downtown's coolest cheap
feeds.

Locanda Verde   Italian $$$
(Map p246; 📞212-925-3797; www.locanda
verdenyc.com; 377 Greenwich St, at Moore St;
mains lunch $19-29, dinner $29-36; ⊗7am-11pm
Mon-Thu, to 11:30pm Fri, 8am-11:30pm Sat,
8am-11pm Sun; 🆂A/C/E to Canal St; 1 to Franklin
St) Step through the velvet curtains into
a scene of loosened button-downs, black
dresses and slick barkeeps behind a long,
crowded bar. This celebrated brasserie
showcases modern, Italo-inspired fare like
house-made pappardelle with lamb bol-
ognese, mint and sheep's milk ricotta and
Sicilian-style halibut with heirloom squash
and almonds. Weekend brunch features no
less creative fare: try scampi and grits or
lemon ricotta pancakes with blueberries.

Bâtard   Modern American $$$
(Map p246; 📞212-219-2777; www.batardtribeca.
com; 239 W Broadway, btwn Walker & White Sts;
2-/3-/4-courses $55/69/79; ⊗5:30-10:30pm
Mon-Sat; 🆂1 to Franklin St; A/C/E to Canal St)
Austrian chef Markus Glocker heads this
warm, Michelin-starred hot spot, where a
pared-back interior puts the focus squarely
on the food. It's attention well deserved.
Glocker's dishes are beautifully balanced
and textured, whether it's sweet Maine
lobster paired with salsify and gritty potato
crisps, or tender venison wrapped in a skin
of Swiss chard and golden filo pastry for
added comfort.

✖ SoHo & Chinatown

Lan Larb   Thai $
(Map p246; 📞646-895-9264; 227 Centre St,
at Grand St; dishes $9-21; ⊗11:30am-10:15pm;
🆂N/Q/R, J/Z, 6 to Canal St) Food fiends
flock to Lan Larb's plastic tables for cheap,
flavor-packed Thai. The place specializes in
larb, a spicy, minced-meat salad from Thai-
land's northeast Isan region (opt for the
duck version). Other top choices include
sucker-punch *som tam* (green papaya
salad) and a delicate *kui teiw nam tok nuer*
(dark noodle soup with beef, morning glory,
scallion, cilantro and bean sprouts).

Uncle Boons   Thai $$
(Map p246; 📞646-370-6650; www.uncleboons.
com; 7 Spring St, btwn Elizabeth St & Bowery;
small plates $12-16, large plates $21-28; ⊗5:30-
11pm Mon-Thu, to midnight Fri & Sat, to 10pm
Sun; 🛜; 🆂J/Z to Bowery; 6 to Spring St) New
York's new favorite uncle, Boons serves up
Michelin-star Thai in a fun, tongue-in-cheek
combo of retro wood panels, Thai film
posters and old family snaps. Spanning the
old and the new, zesty, tangy dishes include
fantastically crunchy *mieng kum* (betel leaf
wrap with ginger, lime, toasted coconut,
dried shrimp, peanuts and chili), *kao pat
puu* (crab fried rice) and banana blossom
salad.

Little Italy (p89)

Butcher's Daughter   Vegetarian $$

(Map p246; ☏212-219-3434; www.thebutchers
daughter.com; 19 Kenmare St, at Elizabeth
St; salads & sandwiches $12-14, dinner mains
$16-18; ⊙8am-10pm Sun-Thu, to 11pm Fri &
Sat; ☏☏; ⓢ J to Bowery; 6 to Spring St) The
butcher's daughter certainly has rebelled,
peddling nothing but fresh herbivorous
fare in her whitewashed cafe. While healthy
it is, boring it's not: everything from the
soaked organic muesli, to the spicy kale
Caesar salad with almond Parmesan, to
the dinnertime Butcher's burger (vegetable
and black-bean patty with cashew cheddar
cheese) is devilishly delish.

Nyonya   Malaysian $$

(Map p246; ☏212-334-3669; www.ilovenyonya.
com; 199 Grand St, btwn Mott & Mulberry Sts;
mains $7-24; ⊙11am-11:30pm Mon-Thu & Sun,
to midnight Fri & Sat; ⓢN/Q/R, J/Z, 6 to Canal
Street; B/D to Grand St) Take your palate to
steamy Melaka at this bustling temple to
Chinese-Malay Nyonya cuisine. Savor the
sweet, the sour and the spicy in classics
such as tangy Assam fish-head casserole,
rich beef *rendang* (spicy dry curry) and re-

> *A stretch packed with
> checkerboard tablecloths
> and Italian fare*

freshing *rojak* (savory fruit salad tossed in
a piquant tamarind dressing). Vegetarians
should be warned: there's not much on the
menu for you. Cash only.

Amazing 66   Chinese $$

(Map p246; ☏212-334-0099; www.amazing66.
com; 66 Mott St, btwn Canal & Bayard Sts; mains
$9-27; ⊙11am-11pm; ⓢN/Q/R, J/Z, 6 to Canal
St) One of the best places to chomp on
Cantonese cuisine, bright, bustling Amaz-
ing 66 draws waves of local Chinese pining
for a taste of home. Join them for standout
dishes such as barbecued honey spare ribs
and shrimp with black-bean sauce.

Estela   Modern American $$$

(Map p246; ☏212-219-7693; www.estelanyc.
com; 47 E Houston St, btwn Mulberry & Mott Sts;
dishes $15-37; ⊙5:30-11pm Sun-Thu, to 11:30pm
Fri & Sat; ⓢB/D/F/M to Broadway-Lafayette St;
6 to Bleecker St) Estela might be hopeless

at hide-and-seek (its location up some nondescript stairs hardly tricks savvy gourmands), but this busy, skinny wine-bar kicks butt on the food and vino front. Graze from a competent string of market-driven sharing plates, from phenomenal beef tartare (spiked with beef heart for added complexity) to moreish mussels escabeche on toast, to an impossibly sexy endive salad with walnuts and anchovy.

Dutch   Modern American $$$

(Map p246; ☏212-677-6200; www.thedutchnyc. com; 131 Sullivan St, at Prince St; mains lunch $18-29, dinner $29-58; ☺11:30am-11pm Mon-Thu, 11:30am-11:30pm Fri, 10am-11:30pm Sat, 10am-11pm Sun; ⓢC/E to Spring St; N/R to Prince St; 1 to Houston St) Whether perched at the bar or dining snugly in the back room, you can always expect smart, farm-to-table comfort grub at this see-and-be-seen stalwart. Flavors traverse the globe, from sweet potato tempura with Thai basil and fermented chili sauce, to ricotta ravioli with Swiss chard and walnut pesto. Reservations are recommended, especially for dinner and all day on weekends.

✖ East Village & Lower East Side

Russ & Daughters   Deli $

(Map p246; www.russanddaughters.com; 179 E Houston St, btwn Orchard & Allen Sts; mains $10-14; ☺8am-7pm Mon-Sat, to 5:30pm Sun; ⓢF to 2nd Ave) In business since 1914, this landmark establishment serves up Eastern European Jewish delicacies such as caviar, herring and lox, and, of course, a smear of cream cheese on a bagel. There's nowhere to sit, so grab a number when you come in, order your salmon-topped bagel and other goodies, then retreat to a park bench around the corner.

El Rey   Cafe $

(Map p246; ☏212-260-3950; www.elreynyc. com; 100 Stanton St, btwn Orchard & Ludlow Sts; small plates $7-17; ☺7am-10:30pm Mon-Fri, from 8am Sat & Sun; ⌖; ⓢF to 2nd Ave) This white, minimalist space on Stanton feels more So-Cal than LES, and has earned a huge following for its delectably inventive (and fairly priced) farm-to-table plates with plenty of

vegan options. Stop by at lunchtime for a frittata with shaved fennel salad or roasted beets with granola and yogurt, or come at evening for octopus salad with black-bean puree.

Momofuku Noodle Bar   Noodles $$

(Map p246; ☎212-777-7773; www.momofuku. com; 171 First Ave, btwn 10th & 11th Sts; mains $17-28; ☺noon-11pm Sun-Thu, to 1am Fri & Sat; ⬛L to 1st Ave; 6 to Astor Pl) With just 30 stools and a no-reservations policy, you will always have to wait to cram into this tiny phenomenon. Queue up for the namesake special: homemade ramen noodles in broth, served with poached egg, pork belly and pork shoulder or some interesting combos. The menu changes daily and includes buns (such as brisket and horse-radish), snacks (smoked chicken wings) and desserts.

Cafe Mogador   Moroccan $$

(Map p246; ☎212-677-2226; www.cafemog-ador.com; 101 St Marks Pl; mains lunch $8-14, dinner $17-21; ☺9am-midnight; ⬛6 to Astor Pl) Family-run Mogador is a long-standing NYC classic serving fluffy piles of couscous,

char-grilled lamb and merguez sausage over basmati rice, as well as satisfying mixed platters of hummus and baba ghanoush. The standouts, however, are the tagines – traditionally spiced, long-simmered chicken or lamb dishes served up five different ways.

Babu Ji   Indian $$

(Map p246; ☎212-951-182; www.babujinyc. com; 175 Ave B, btwn 11th & 12 Sts; mains $16-25; ☺6pm-late Mon-Sat; ⬛L to 1st Ave) A playful spirit marks this excellent Australian-run Indian restaurant in Alphabet City. You can assemble a meal from street-food-style dishes such as *papadi chaat* (chickpeas, pomegranate and yogurt chutney) and potato croquettes stuffed with lobster, or feast on heartier dishes such as tandoori lamb chops or scallop coconut curry.

Dimes   Cafe $$

(Map p246; ☎212-925-1300; www.dimesnyc. com; 49 Canal St, btwn Orchard & Ludlow Sts; mains breakfast $8-13, dinner $14-23; ☺8am-11pm Mon-Fri, from 9am Sat & Sun; 🍽) This tiny, sun-drenched eatery has a strong local following for its friendly service and healthy,

★ Top Five Places for Pizza
Roberta's (p138)
Juliana's (p139)
Paulie Gee's (p139)
Luzzo's (p126)
Co (p130)

From left: Momofuku Noodle Bar; Juliana's (p139); Roberta's (p138)

good-value dishes. A design-minded group crowds in for spicy breakfast tacos (served till 4pm), bowls of granola with açaí (that strongly flavored, vitamin-rich Amazonian berry), creative salads (with sunchokes, anchovies, goat cheese) and heartier dishes for dinner (striped bass with green curry, pulled pork with jasmine rice).

Upstate   Seafood $$

(Map p246; ☎212-460-5293; www.upstatenyc. com; 95 First Ave, btwn 5th & 6th Sts; mains $15-30; ☉5-11pm; 🆂F to 2nd Ave) Upstate serves outstanding seafood dishes and craft beers. The small, always-changing menu features the likes of beer-steamed mussels, seafood stew, scallops over mushroom risotto, softshell crab and wondrous oyster selections. There's no freezer – seafood comes from the market each day, so you know you'll be getting only the freshest ingredients. Lines can be long, so go early.

Luzzo's   Pizza $$

(Map p246; ☎212-473-7447; www.luzzosgroup. com; 211 First Ave, btwn 12th & 13th Sts; pizzas $18-26; ☉noon-11pm Sun-Thu, to midnight Fri & Sat; 🆂L to 1st Ave) Fan-favorite Luzzo's occupies a thin sliver of real estate in the East Village, which gets stuffed to the gills each evening as discerning diners feast on thin-crust pies kissed with ripe tomatoes and cooked in a coal-fired stove.

Fung Tu   Fusion $$$

(Map p246; ☎212-219-8785; www.fungtu.com; 22 Orchard St, btwn Hester & Canal Sts; small plates $13-18, mains $24-32; ☉6pm-midnight Tue-Sat, 4pm-10pm Sun; 🆂F to East Broadway) Celebrated chef Jonathan Wu brilliantly blends Chinese cooking with global accents at this elegant little eatery on the edge of Chinatown. The complex sharing plates are superb (try scallion pancakes with cashew salad and smoked chicken or crepe roll stuffed with braised beef, pickled cucumbers and watercress) and pair nicely with creative cocktails like the Fung Tu Gibson.

Degustation   Modern European $$$

(Map p246; ☎212-979-1012; www.degustation-nyc.com; 239 E 5th St, btwn 2nd & 3rd Aves; small plates $12-22, tasting menu $85; ☉6-11:30pm Mon-Sat, to 10pm Sun; 🆂6 to Astor

Chelsea Market

Pl) Blending Iberian, French and New World recipes, Degustation does a beautiful array of tapas-style plates at this narrow 19-seat eatery. It's an intimate setting, with guests seated around a long wooden counter, with chef Nicholas Licata and team at center stage firing up crisp octopus, lamb belly with soft poached egg and paella with blue prawns and chorizo.

🍴 West Village, Chelsea & Meatpacking District

Chelsea Market Market $
(Map p252; www.chelseamarket.com; 75 9th Ave, btwn 15th & 16th Sts; 🕐7am-9pm Mon-Sat, 8am-8pm Sun; [S]A/C/E to 14th St) In a shining example of redevelopment and preservation, the Chelsea Market has taken a factory formerly owned by cookie giant Nabisco (creator of Oreo) and turned it into an 800ft-long shopping concourse that caters to foodies. Taking the place of the old factory ovens that churned out massive numbers of biscuits are eclectic eateries that fill the renovated hallways of this foodie haven.

Gansevoort Market Market $
(Map p246; www.gansmarket.com; 52 Gansevoort, btwn Greenwich & Washington Sts; mains $5-20; 🕐8am-8pm; [S]A/C/E to 14th St; L to 8th Ave) Inside a brick building in the heart of the Meatpacking District, this sprawling market is the latest and greatest food emporium to land in NYC. Inside a raw, industrial space lit by skylights, several dozen gourmet vendors sling tapas, arepas, tacos, pizzas, meat pies, ice cream, pastries and more.

Moustache Middle Eastern $
(Map p246; ☎212-229-2220; www.moustachepitzawest.com; 90 Bedford St, btwn Grove & Barrow Sts; mains $10-17; 🕐noon-midnight; [S]1 to Christopher St-Sheridan Sq) Small and delightful Moustache serves up rich, flavorful sandwiches (leg of lamb, merguez sausage, falafel), thin-crust pizzas, tangy salads and hearty specialties such as *ouzi* (filo stuffed

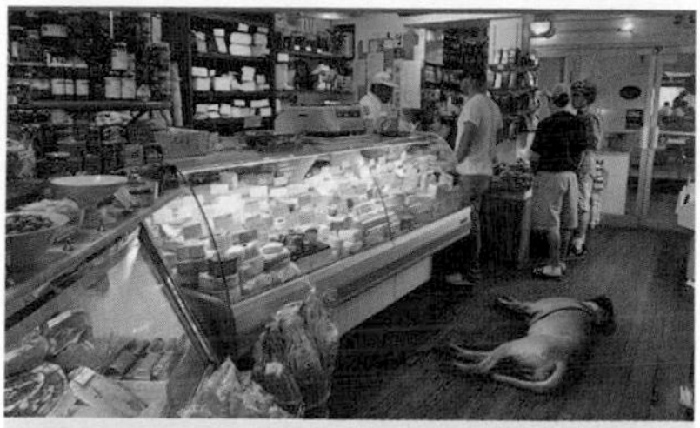

🍴 Urban Farm to Table

Whether it's upstate triple-cream Kunik at **Bedford Cheese Shop** (Map p252; ☎718-599-7588; www.bedfordcheeseshop.com; 67 Irving Pl, btwn 18th & 19th Sts; 🕐8am-9pm Mon-Sat, to 8pm Sun; [S]4/5/6, N/Q/R, L to 14th St-Union Sq) or Montauk Pearls oysters at fine-dining **Craft** (Map p252; ☎212-780-0880; www.craftrestaurantsinc.com; 43 E 19th St, btwn Broadway & Park Ave S; mains lunch $15-35, dinner $31-45; 🕐5:30-10pm Sun-Thu, to 11pm Fri & Sat; 📶; [S]4/5/6, N/Q/R, L to 14th St-Union Sq) 🌿, New York City's passion for all things local and artisanal continues unabated. The city itself has become an unlikely food bowl, with an ever-growing number of rooftops and community gardens finding new purpose as urban farms.

While you can expect to find anything from organic tomatoes atop Upper East Side delis to beehives on East Village tenement rooftops, the current queen of the crop is Brooklyn Grange (www.brooklyngrangefarm.com), an organic farm covering two rooftops in Long Island City and the Brooklyn Navy Yards. At 2.5 acres, it's purportedly the world's biggest rooftop farm, producing over 50,000lb of organically cultivated goodness annually, from eggs to carrots, chard and heirloom tomatoes. Collaborators include some of the city's top eateries, among them Marlow & Sons (p139) and Roberta's (p138) in Brooklyn, and Dutch (p124) in Manhattan.

Bedford Cheese Shop

with chicken, rice and spices) and moussaka. The best start to a meal: a platter of hummus or baba ghanoush, served with fluffy, piping hot pitas. It's an earthy space with copper-topped tables and brick walls.

Taïm   Israeli $

(Map p246; 📞212-691-1287; www.taimfalafel. com; 222 Waverly Pl, btwn Perry & W 11th Sts; sandwiches $7-8; ⏰11am-10pm; 🚇1/2/3, A/C/E to 14th St) This tiny joint whips up some of the best falafels in the city. You can order them Green (traditional style), Harissa (with Tunisian spices) or Red (with roasted peppers). Whichever you choose, you'll get them stuffed into pita bread with creamy tahini sauce and a generous dose of Israeli salad.

Jeffrey's Grocery   Modern American $$

(Map p246; 📞646-398-7630; www.jeffreysgrocery.com; 172 Waverly Pl, at Christopher St; mains $25-39; ⏰8am-11pm Mon-Fri, from 9:30am Sat & Sun; 🚇1 to Christopher St-Sheridan Sq) A West Village classic, Jeffrey's is a lively eating and drinking spot that hits all the right notes. Seafood is the focus: there's an oyster bar and beautifully executed seafood selections such as razor clams with caviar and dill, whole roasted dourade with curry, and seafood platters to share. Meat dishes come in the shape of roasted chicken with Jerusalem artichoke, and a humble but juicy pastrami burger.

Morandi   Italian $$

(Map p246; 📞212-627-7575; www.morandiny. com; 211 Waverly Pl, btwn Seventh Ave & Charles St; mains $18-38; ⏰8am-midnight Mon-Fri, from 10am Sat & Sun; 🚇1 to Christopher St-Sheridan Sq) Run by celebrated restaurateur Keith McNally, Morandi is a warmly lit space where the hubbub of garrulous diners resounds amid brick walls, wide plank floors and rustic chandeliers. Squeeze into a table for the full-meal experience – hand-rolled spaghetti with lemon and parmesan; meatballs with pine nuts and raisins; and grilled whole sea bream.

✕ NYC Restaurant Week

Bargain-savvy gastronomes love the biannual NYC Restaurant Week. Taking place from late January to early February and July to August, it sees many of the city's restaurants, including some of its very best, serve up three-course lunches for $25, or three-course dinners for $38. Check www.nycgo.com/restaurant-week for details and reservations.

Clockwise from top: Antipasto platters; Tacos with fresh cilantro; NYC Restaurant Week food truck

Cookshop Modern American $$

(Map p252; ☎212-924-4440; www.cookshopny.com; 156 Tenth Ave, btwn 19th & 20th Sts; mains brunch $14-20, lunch $16-24, dinner $22-38; 🕐8am-11:30pm Mon-Fri, from 10am Sat, 10am-10pm Sun; [S]L to 8th Ave; A/C/E to 23rd St) A brilliant brunching pit stop before (or after) tackling the verdant High Line across the street, Cookshop is a lively place that knows its niche and does it oh so well. Excellent service, eye-opening cocktails (good morning, bacon-infused BLT Mary!), a perfectly baked breadbasket and a selection of inventive egg mains make this a favorite in Chelsea on a Sunday afternoon.

Co Pizza $$

(Map p252; ☎212-243-1105; www.co-pane.com; 230 Ninth Ave, at 24th St; pizzas $17-21; 🕐5-11pm Mon, 11:30am-11pm Tue-Sat, 11am-10pm Sun; [S]C/E to 23rd St) Masterfully prepared pizza is served in trim wooden surrounds that have a Scandinavian farmhouse vibe. Expect a faithful reproduction of the trademark Neapolitan thin-crust pies topped with an assortment of fresh-from-the-farm items such as fennel and buffalo mozzarella. Salads of escarole, beet or radicchio – as well as global wines and a sprinkling of sweets – round out the offerings.

Rosemary's Italian $$

(Map p246; ☎212-647-1818; www.rosemarysnyc.com; 18 Greenwich Ave, at W 10th St; mains $15-32; 🕐8am-midnight Mon-Fri, from 10am Sat & Sun; [S]1 to Christopher St-Sheridan Sq) One of the West Village's hottest restaurants, Rosemary's serves high-end Italian fare that more than lives up to the hype. In a vaguely farmhouse-like setting, diners tuck into generous portions of housemade pastas, rich salads, and cheese and *salumi* (cured meat) boards. Current favorites include the *acqua pazza* (seafood stew) and smoked lamb with roasted vegetables.

Blue Hill American $$$

(Map p246; ☎212-539-1776; www.bluehillfarm.com; 75 Washington Pl, btwn Sixth Ave & Washington Sq W; prix-fixe menu $88-98; 🕐 5-11pm; [S]A/C/E, B/D/F/M to W 4th St-Washington Sq) A place for slow-food junkies with deep pockets, Blue Hill was an early crusader in the local-is-better movement. Gifted chef

Eataly (p132)

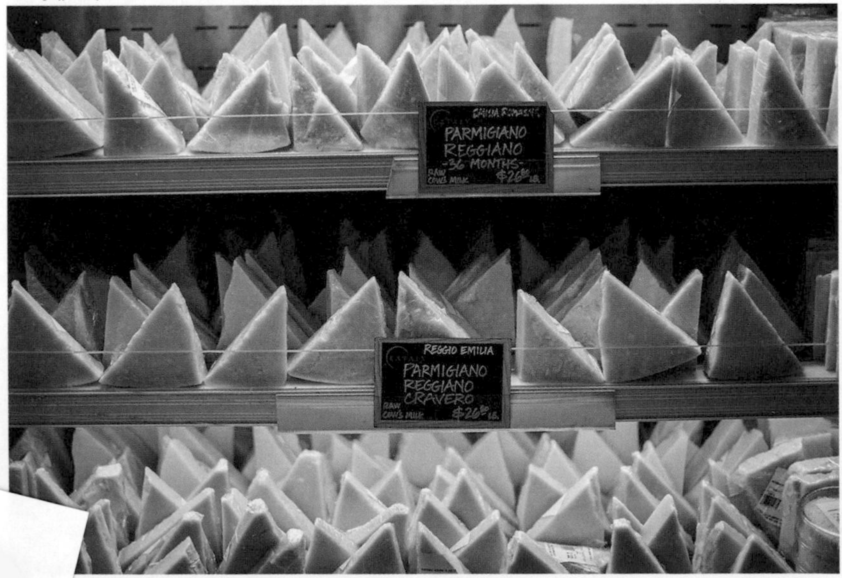

Dan Barber, who hails from a farm family in the Berkshires, Massachusetts, uses harvests from that land, as well as from farms in upstate New York, to create his widely praised fare.

RedFarm Fusion **$$$**

(Map p246; ☎212-792-9700; www.redfarmnyc.com; 529 Hudson St, btwn 10th & Charles Sts; mains $22-46, dim sum $10-16; 🕒11am-2:30pm Sat & Sun, 5pm-11pm daily; [S]A/C/E, B/D/F/M to W 4th St; 1 to Christopher St-Sheridan Sq) RedFarm transforms Chinese cooking into pure, delectable artistry at this small, buzzing space on Hudson St. Fresh crab and eggplant bruschetta, juicy rib steak (marinated overnight in papaya, ginger and soy) and pastrami egg rolls are among the many creative dishes that brilliantly blend East with West. Other hits include the spicy crispy beef, pan-fried lamb dumplings and the grilled jumbo shrimp red curry.

Foragers City Table Modern American **$$$**

(Map p252; ☎212-243-8888; www.foragerscitygrocer.com; 300 W 22nd St, cnr Eighth Ave; mains $25-36; 🕒10:30am-2:30pm Sat & Sun, 5:30-10pm daily; ✎; [S]C/E, 1 to 23rd St) Owners of this excellent restaurant in Chelsea run a 28-acre farm in the Hudson Valley, from which much of their menu is sourced. The menu, which showcases seasonal hits, changes frequently. Recent temptations include squash soup with Jerusalem artichokes and black truffles, roasted chicken with polenta, heritage pork loin, and the season's harvest with toasted quinoa and a flavorful mix of vegetables.

🍴 Union Square, Flatiron District & Gramercy

Tacombi Café El Presidente Mexican **$**

(Map p252; ☎212-242-3491; www.tacombi.com; 30 W 24th St, btwn Fifth & Sixth Aves; tacos $3.50-5.50, quesadillas $8-9; 🕒11am-midnight Mon-Sat, to 10:30pm Sun; [S]F/M, N/R to 23rd St) Channeling the cafes of Mexico City,

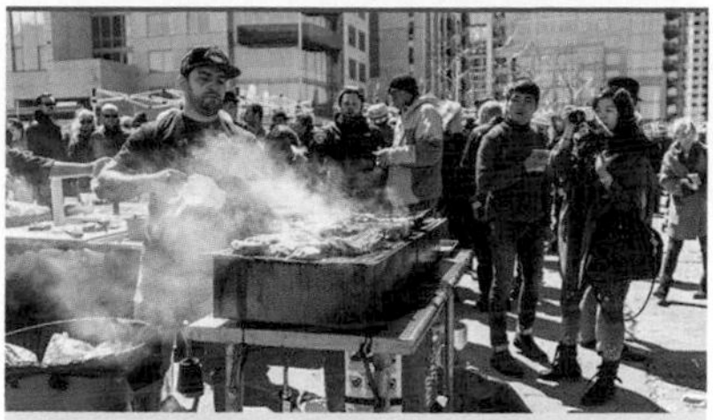

🍴 To Market, To Market

New York City has a thriving greens scene that comes in many shapes and sizes. At the top of your list should be the Chelsea Market (p127), which is packed with gourmet goodies of all kinds. Other food halls have opened in recent years, including Gansevoort Market (p127) in the Meatpacking District and a trio of food halls at **Brookfield Place** (Map p246; ☎212-417-7000; brookfieldplaceny.com; 200 Vesey St; 📶; [S]E to World Trade Center; 2/3 to Park Place; R to Cortland St; A/C, 4/5, J/Z to Fulton St), in Lower Manhattan.

Many neighborhoods in NYC have their own greenmarket. One of the biggest is the **Union Square Greenmarket** (Map p252; www.grownyc.org; Union Square, 17th St btwn Broadway & Park Ave S; 🕒8am-6pm Mon, Wed, Fri & Sat; [S]4/5/6, N/Q/R, L to 14th St-Union Sq), open four days a week throughout the year. Check Grow NYC (www.grownyc.org/greenmarket) for a list of the other 50-plus markets around the city.

Out in Brooklyn, the best weekend markets for noshers are **Smorgasburg** (www.smorgasburg.com; 🕒11am-6pm Sat & Sun), with over 100 craft food vendors (there's also a smaller seasonal Smorgasburg in the Southstreet Seaport), and the Brooklyn Flea Market (p151), which has several dozen stalls.

And, in recent market gossip, food-show host Anthony Bourdain will be opening a massive international market (with more than 100 stalls) on a pier facing the Hudson River. Look for it on Pier 57 (off W 15th St) in 2017.

Smorgasburg in Brooklyn

From left: Burger served with handcut potatoes and gherkin; Fruit stall under Empire State Building; Red shrimp with salsa verde at Eataly

pink-and-green Tacombi covers numerous bases, from juice and liquor bar to taco joint. Score a table, order a margarita and hop your way around a menu of Mexican street-food deliciousness. Top choices include *esquites* (grilled corn with *cotija* cheese and chipotle mayonnaise, served in a paper cup) and succulent *carnitas michoacan* (beer-marinated pork) tacos.

Eataly   Italian $$

(Map p252; www.eataly.com; 200 Fifth Ave, at 23rd St; ⊙8am-11pm; 🍴; 🆂N/R, F/M, 6 to 23rd St) Mario Batali's sleek, sprawling temple to Italian gastronomy is a veritable wonderland. Feast on everything from vibrant *crudo* (raw fish) and *fritto misto* (tempura-style vegetables) to steamy pasta and pizza at the emporium's string of sit-down eateries. Alternatively, guzzle espresso at the bar and scour the countless counters and shelves for a DIY picnic hamper *nonna* would approve of.

Eataly's other assets include its rooftop beer garden, **Birreria** (📞212-937-8910; mains $17-37; ⊙11:30am-11pm Sun-Thu, to midnight Fri & Sat), and a busy schedule of on-site

cooking and culinary appreciation classes. See the website for details.

Eleven Madison
Park   Modern American $$$

(Map p252; 📞212-889-0905; www.eleven madisonpark.com; 11 Madison Ave, btwn 24th & 25th Sts; tasting menu $225; ⊙noon-1pm Thu-Sat, 5.30-10pm daily; 🆂N/R, 6 to 23rd St) Fine-dining Eleven Madison Park came in at number five in the 2015 San Pellegrino World's 50 Best Restaurants list. Frankly, we're not surprised: this revamped poster child of modern, sustainable American cooking is also one of only six NYC restaurants sporting three Michelin stars.

Gramercy
Tavern   Modern American $$$

(Map p252; 📞212-477-0777; www.gramercytavern.com; 42 E 20th St, btwn Broadway & Park Ave S; tavern mains $19-24, dining room 3-course menu $98, tasting menus $105-120; ⊙tavern noon-11pm Sun-Thu, to midnight Fri & Sat, dining room noon-2pm & 5:30-10pm Mon-Thu, to 11pm Fri, noon-1:30pm & 5.30-11pm Sat, 5:30-10pm Sun; 🛜🍴; 🆂N/R, 6 to 23rd St) 🍴 Seasonal, local ingredients drive this perennial

favorite, a vibrant, country-chic institution aglow with copper sconces, murals and dramatic floral arrangements. Choose from two spaces: the walk-in-only tavern and its à la carte menu, or the swankier dining room and its fancier prix-fixe and degustation feasts. Tavern highlights include a show-stopping duck meatloaf with mushrooms, chestnuts and brussels sprouts.

✗ Midtown

Totto Ramen   Japanese $
(Map p252; ☑212-582-0052; www.tottoramen. com; 366 W 52nd St, btwn Eighth & Ninth Aves, Midtown West; ramen from $10; ⏱noon-4:30pm & 5:30pm-midnight Mon-Sat, 4-11pm Sun; ⓢC/E to 50th St) There might be another two branches in Midtown, but purists know that neither beats the tiny 20-seat original. Write your name and the number of guests on the clipboard and wait your turn. Your reward: extraordinary ramen. Skip the chicken and go for the pork, which sings in dishes like miso ramen (with fermented

soybean paste, egg, scallion, bean sprouts, onion and homemade chili paste).

Burger Joint   Burgers $
(Map p252; ☑212-708-7414; www.burgerjointny. com; Le Parker Meridien, 119 W 56th St, btwn Sixth & Seventh Aves, Midtown West; burgers from $8.50; ⏱11am-11:30pm Sun-Thu, to midnight Fri & Sat; ⓢF to 57th St) With only a small neon burger as your clue, this speakeasy-style burger hut lurks behind the lobby curtain in Le Parker Meridien hotel. Though it might not be as 'hip' or as 'secret' as it once was, it still delivers the same winning formula of graffiti-strewn walls, retro booths and attitude-loaded staff slapping up beef 'n' patty brilliance.

ViceVersa   Italian $$
(Map p252; ☑212-399-9291; www.viceversanyc. com; 325 W 51st St, btwn Eighth & Ninth Aves, Midtown West; 2-course lunch $25, dinner mains $24-32; ⏱noon-2:30pm & 4:30-11pm Mon-Fri, 4:30-11pm Sat, 11:30am-3pm & 4:30-10pm Sun; ⓢC/E to 50th St) ViceVersa is the quintessential Italian: suave and sophisticated, affable and scrumptious. Scan the menu for refined, cross-regional dishes like arancini

New York City on a Plate

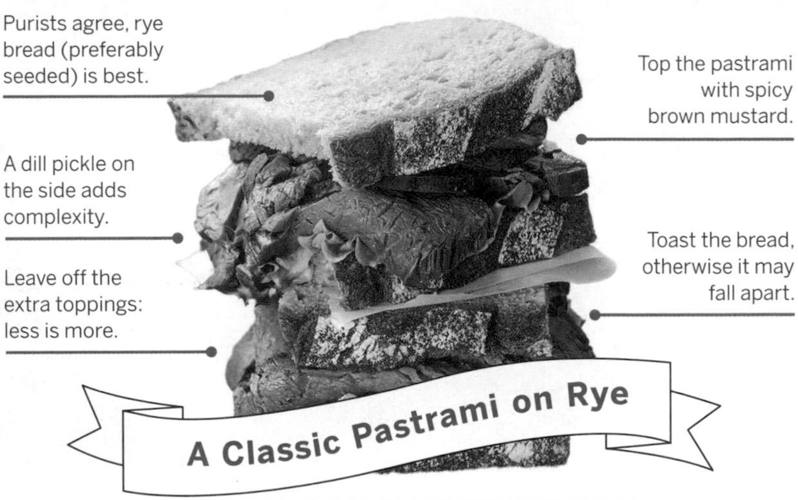
Purists agree, rye bread (preferably seeded) is best.
A dill pickle on the side adds complexity.
Leave off the extra toppings: less is more.
Top the pastrami with spicy brown mustard.
Toast the bread, otherwise it may fall apart.
A Classic Pastrami on Rye

LISOVSKAYA NATALIA / SHUTTERSTSOCK ©

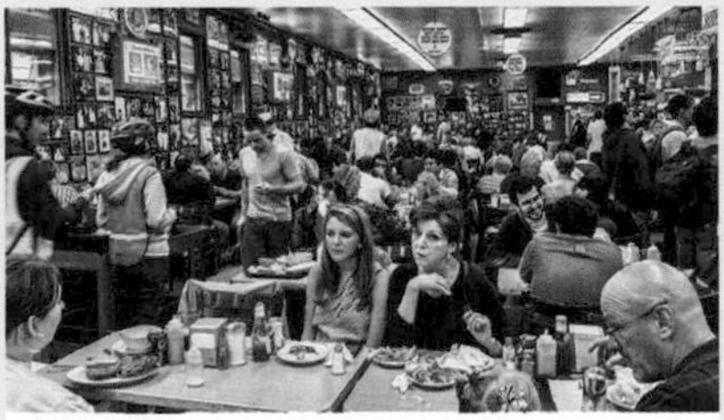

The Pastrami Sandwich Experience

Biting into a pastrami sandwich is a classic New York City experience. It's best eaten in one of the city's old-school Jewish delis – the kind with neon lights, counter seating, and gruff but kind-hearted staff. The sandwich comes piled high with tender, juicy slices of lightly spiced pastrami contrasting with the crunch of toasted rye, and the zing of mustard binding it all together: a delectable work of art.

Katz's Delicatessen
CRISTINAMURACA / SHUTTERSTOCK ©

Top Five Pastrami Joints

Katz's Delicatessen (Map p246; ☎212-254-2246; www.katzsdelicatessen.com; 205 E Houston St, at Ludlow St; sandwiches $15-22; 🕐8am-10:45pm Mon-Wed & Sun, to 2:45am Thu, all night Fri & Sat; [S]F to 2nd Ave)

Dickson Farmstand Meats (www.chelseamarket.com; inside Chelsea Market; Map p252; 75 9th Ave, btwn 15th & 16th Sts; 🕐7am-9pm Mon-Sat, 8am-8pm Sun; [S]A/C/E to 14th St)

Zabar's (Map p250; ☎212-787-2000; www.zabars.com; 2245 Broadway, at 80th St; 🕐8am-7:30pm Mon-Fri, to 8pm Sat, 9am-6pm Sun; [S]1 to 79th St)

Eisenberg's (Map p252; www.eisenbergsnyc.com; 174 Fifth Ave, at 22nd St; sandwiches $7-12; 🕐6:30am-8pm Mon-Fri, 9am-6pm Sat, to 5pm Sun)

Barney Greengrass (p136)

with black truffle and fontina cheese. For a celebrated classic, order the *casoncelli alla bergamasca* (ravioli-like pasta filled with minced veal, raisins and amaretto cookies and seasoned with sage, butter, pancetta and Grana Padano), a nod to chef Stefano Terzi's Lombard heritage.

The bar seating is perfect for solo diners, while the leafy courtyard is a fun spot for a see-and-be-seen Sunday brunch.

Hangawi Korean **$$**

(Map p252; ☎212-213-0077; www.hangawirestaurant.com; 12 E 32nd St, btwn Fifth & Madison Aves; mains lunch $11-30, dinner $19-30; 🕒noon-2:30pm & 5:30-10:15pm Mon-Fri, 1-10:30pm Sat, 5-9:30pm Sun; 🌶; [S]B/D/F/M, N/Q/R to 34th St-Herald Sq) Meat-free Korean is the draw at high-achieving Hangawi. Leave your shoes at the entrance and slip into a soothing, Zen-like space of meditative music, soft low seating and clean, complex dishes. Show-stoppers include the leek pancakes and a seductively smooth tofu claypot in ginger sauce.

Le Bernardin Seafood **$$$**

(Map p252; ☎212-554-1515; www.le-bernardin.com; 155 W 51st St, btwn Sixth & Seventh Aves, Midtown West; prix fixe lunch/dinner $80/140, tasting menus $170-205; 🕒noon-2:30pm & 5:15-10:30pm Mon-Thu, to 11pm Fri, 5:15-11pm Sat; [S]1 to 50th St; B/D, E to 7th Ave) The interiors may have been subtly sexed-up for a 'younger clientele' (the stunning storm-themed triptych was created by Brooklyn artist Ran Ortner), but triple Michelin-starred Le Bernardin remains a luxe, fine-dining holy grail. At the helm is French-born celebrity chef Éric Ripert, whose deceptively simple-looking seafood often borders on the transcendental.

Artisanal French **$$$**

(Map p252; ☎212-725-8585; www.artisanalbistro.com; 2 Park Ave S, btwn 32nd & 33rd Sts, Midtown East; mains $24-50 ; 🕒10am-midnight Mon-Fri, from 9am Sat & Sun; 🌶; [S]6 to 33rd St) Artisanazl is Valhalla for *fromage* fiends. From spicy Italian Canestrato to pungent French Livarot, you'll find over 200 varieties of cheese at what is a modern take on an old Parisian bistro. Experiment with a cheese-and-wine flight or throw caution to the wind with one of a string of fondues. Beyond them is a cast of bistro standbys, from onion soup *gratinée* (with a three-cheese blend, naturally) to bouillabaisse.

🍴 Upper East Side

Café Sabarsky Austrian **$$**

(Map p250; ☎212-288-0665; www.kg-ny.com; 1048 Fifth Ave, cnr E 86th St; mains $18-30; 🕒9am-6pm Mon & Wed, to 9pm Thu-Sun; 🌶👪; [S]4/5/6 to 86th St) The lines get long at this popular cafe, which evokes opulent turn-of-the-19th-century Vienna. But the well-rendered Austrian specialties make the wait worth it. Expect crepes with smoked trout, goulash soup and roasted bratwurst. There's also a long list of specialty sweets, including a divine Sacher torte (dark chocolate cake with apricot confiture).

Beyoglu Turkish **$$**

(Map p250; ☎212-650-0850; 1431 Third Ave, at 81st St; mains $16-18, sharing plates $6-8; 🕒noon-10pm Sun-Thu, to 11pm Fri & Sat; 🌶; [S]6 to 77th St, 4/5/6 to 86th St) A long-time favorite of Mediterranean-craving Upper East Siders, Beyoglu whips up meze (appetizers) platters that are ideal for sharing. Creamy rich hummus, juicy lamb kebabs, tender grape leaves and lemon-scented char-grilled octopus. It has an airy and comfy interior, though on sunny days you can head to one of the sidewalk tables in front.

Boqueria Spanish **$$**

(Map p250; ☎212-343-2227; www.boqueriany c.com; 1460 Second Ave, btwn 76th & 77th Sts; tapas $6-16, paella for two $38-46; 🕒noon-11pm Mon-Fri, 11am-11pm Sat & Sun; [S]6 to 77th St) This lively, much-loved tapas place brings a bit of downtown cool to the Upper East Side, with nicely spiced *patatas bravas* (potato chunks in tomato sauce), tender slices of *jamón ibérico* (cured Iberian ham) and rich *pulpo a gallega* (grilled octopus). Head

From left: A classic New York hot dog; Japanese cuisine on St Mark's Place; Street food vendor selling hot dogs and pretzels

chef Marc Vidal, who hails from Barcelona, also creates an exquisite seafood paella.

Tanoshi   Sushi $$$
(☏917-265-8254; www.tanoshisushinyc.com; 1372 York Ave, btwn 73rd & 74th Sts; chef's sushi selection around $80; ☉6-10:30pm Mon-Sat; Ⓢ6 to 77th St) It's not easy to snag one of the 20 stools at Tanoshi, a wildly popular sushi spot. The setting may be humble, but the flavors are simply magnificent, which might include Hokkaido scallops, Atlantic shad, seared salmon belly or mouthwatering *uni* (sea urchin). Only sushi is on offer and only *omakase* – the chef's selection of whatever is particularly outstanding that day. BYO beer, sake or whatnot. Reserve well in advance.

✖ Upper West Side & Central Park

Barney Greengrass   Deli $$
(Map p250; ☏212-724-4707; www.barneygreengrass.com; 541 Amsterdam Ave, at 86th St; mains $12-22; ☉8:30am-4pm Tue-Fri, to 5pm Sat &

Sun; Ⓢ1 to 86th St) The self-proclaimed 'King of Sturgeon' Barney Greengrass serves up the same heaping dishes of eggs and salty lox, luxuriant caviar, and melt-in-your-mouth chocolate babkas that first made it famous when it opened a century ago. Pop in to fuel up in the morning or for a quick lunch; there are rickety tables set amid the crowded produce aisles.

Jacob's Pickles   American $$
(Map p250; ☏212-470-5566; www.jacobspickles.com; 509 Amsterdam Ave, btwn 84th & 85th; mains $15-26; ☉10am-2am Mon-Thu, to 4am Fri, 9am-4am Sat, to 2am Sun; Ⓢ1 to 86th St) Jacob's elevates the humble pickle to exalted status at this inviting and warmly lit eatery on a restaurant-lined stretch of Amsterdam Ave. Aside from briny cukes and other preserves, you'll find heaping portions of upscale comfort food, such as catfish tacos, wine-braised turkey leg dinner, and mushroom mac 'n' cheese. The biscuits are top-notch.

Dovetail   Modern American $$$
(Map p250; ☏212-362-3800; www.dovetailnyc.com; 103 W 77th St, cnr Columbus Ave; tasting

menu $58-135; ⏱5:30-10pm Mon-Thu, to 11pm
Fri & Sat, 5-10pm Sun; 🍴; S A/C, B to 81st
St-Museum of Natural History, 1 to 79th St) This
Michelin-starred restaurant showcases its
Zen-like beauty in both its decor (exposed
brick, bare tables) and its delectable
seasonal menus. Think: striped bass with
sunchokes and burgundy truffle, and
venison with bacon, golden beets and
foraged greens. Each evening there are
two seven-course tasting menus: one for
omnivores ($135) and one for vegetarians
($108).

✗ Harlem &
Upper Manhattan

Red Rooster   Modern American $$
(📞212-792-9001; www.redroosterharlem.com;
310 Malcolm X Blvd, btwn 125th & 126th Sts,
Harlem; mains $18-30; ⏱11:30am-10:30pm Mon-
Thu, to 11:30pm Fri, 10am-11:30pm Sat, 10am-
10pm Sun; S 2/3 to 125th St) Transatlantic
super chef Marcus Samuelsson laces upscale comfort food with a world of flavors
at his effortlessly cool, swinging brasserie.

Here, mac 'n' cheese joins forces with
lobster, blackened catfish pairs with pickled
mango, and spectacular Swedish meatballs
salute Samuelsson's home country. The
prix-fixe lunch is a bargain at $25.

Amy Ruth's
Restaurant   American $$
(📞212-280-8779; www.amyruthsharlem.com;
113 W 116th St, btwn Malcolm X & Adam Clayton
Powell Jr Blvds, Harlem; waffles $10-18, mains
$14-25; ⏱11am-11pm Mon, 8:30am-11pm Tue-
Thu, 24hr Fri & Sat, to 11pm Sun; S B, C, 2/3 to
116th St) Perennially crowded Amy Ruth's
serves up classic soul food, from fried
catfish to mac 'n' cheese and fluffy biscuits.
But it's the waffles that really merit a
trip here – dished up 14 different ways,
including with shrimp. Our all-time favorite
is the 'Rev Al Sharpton,' waffles topped with
succulent fried chicken.

Dinosaur Bar-B-Que   Barbecue $$
(📞212-694-1777; www.dinosaurbarbque.com;
700 W 125th St, at Twelfth Ave, Harlem; mains
$12.50-25; ⏱11:30am-11pm Mon-Thu, to midnight
Fri & Sat, noon-10pm Sun; S 1 to 125th St) Jocks,
hipsters, moms and pops: everyone dives

Street art watches over outdoor tables in Williamsburg

stencil hot spots include the Brooklyn side of the Williamsburg Bridge

into this rib bar for a rockin' feed. Get messy with dry-rubbed, slow-pit-smoked ribs, slabs of juicy steak and succulent burgers, or watch the waist with the lightly seasoned grilled-chicken options. The very few vegetarian options include a fantastic version of Creole-spiced deviled eggs.

✗ Brooklyn

Champs   Vegan $
(☏718-599-2743; www.champsdiner.com; 197 Meserole St, at Humboldt St; sandwiches & salads $9-12; ◷8am-midnight; 🛜🍴; Ⓢ L to Montrose) 🍴 This airy little diner whips up delicious plates of comfort food – all made with vegan ingredients. The reasonable prices and all-day breakfasts keep things busy. Try the French toast slam (with tofu scramble and tempeh bacon), the chocolate chip and banana pancakes, mac 'n' cheese or a

'bacon cheeseburger' (a black bean burger with tempeh bacon and vegie cheese).

Pok Pok   Thai $$
(☏718-923-9322; www.pokpokpdx.com; 117 Columbia St, cnr Kane St, Columbia Street Waterfront District; sharing plates $12-20; ◷5:30-10pm Mon-Fri, from 10am Sat & Sun; Ⓢ F to Bergen St) Andy Ricker's NYC outpost is a smashing success, wowing diners with a rich and complex menu inspired by Northern Thailand street food. Fiery fish-sauce-slathered chicken wings, spicy green papaya salad with salted black crab, smoky grilled eggplant salad and sweet pork belly with ginger, turmeric and tamarind are among the many unique dishes. The setting is fun and ramshackle. Reserve ahead.

Roberta's   Pizza $$
(☏718-417-1118; www.robertaspizza.com; 261 Moore St, near Bogart St, Bushwick; pizzas $14-18; ◷11am-midnight Mon-Fri, from 10am Sat & Sun; 🍴; Ⓢ L to Morgan Ave) This hipster-saturated warehouse restaurant in Bushwick consistently produces some of the best pizza in New York. Service can be

lackadaisical and the waits long (lunch is best), but the brick-oven pies are the right combination of chewy and fresh. The classic margherita is sublimely simple, though more adventurous palates can opt for the seasonal hits like Speckenwolf (mozzarella, speck, crimini and onion).

Rabbit Hole   Modern American $$

(☎718-782-0910; www.rabbitholerestaurant. com; 352 Bedford Ave, btwn S 3rd & 4th Sts, Williamsburg; mains breakfast $9-14, dinner $15-22; ⏱9am-11pm; ☑; ⓢL to Bedford Ave; J/M/Z to Marcy Ave) A warm and inviting spot in South Williamsburg, the very charming Rabbit Hole is a fine spot to disappear into, particularly if you're craving breakfast (served till 5pm). There's casual cafe seating up front for good coffee and even better house-made pastries. Head to the back, or the relaxing rear garden for creamy eggs Benedict or fresh fruit and granola. In the evening, the quaint plank-floored, tin-ceilinged eatery transforms into a gastropub with lamb burgers, pan-seared striped bass, microbrews and old-fashioned cocktails.

Zenkichi   Japanese $$

(☎718-388-8985; www.zenkichi.com; 77 N 6th St, at Wythe Ave; small plates $9-18, tasting menu $65; ⏱6pm-midnight Mon-Sat, 5:30-11:30pm Sun; ⓢL to Bedford Ave) A temple of refined Japanese cuisine, Zenkichi presents beautifully prepared dishes in an atmospheric setting that has wowed foodies from far and wide. The recommendation here is the omakase (a seasonal eight-course tasting menu, featuring highlights like konbu-cured sashimi, crunchy shrimp tempura with trumpet mushrooms, tender grilled black cod and a silky miso soup).

Roman's   Italian $$

(☎718-622-5300; www.romansnyc.com; 243 Dekalb Ave, btwn Clermont & Vanderbilt Aves; mains $18-28; ⏱5-11pm Mon-Fri, from noon Sat & Sun; ⓢG to Clinton-Washington Aves) In a small buzzing space on restaurant-dotted Dekalb Ave, Roman's is a celebration of

seasonal locavorism, with a focused menu that changes nightly. Dishes feature imaginative combinations (sourced from small, sustainable farms) and are beautifully executed: beets with oranges and anchovies, maccheroni (macaroni-like pasta) with pork sausage and ricotta, and striped bass fillet with green olives.

Paulie Gee's   Pizza $$

(☎347-987-3747; www.pauliegee.com; 60 Greenpoint Ave, btwn West & Franklin Sts, Greenpoint; pizzas $14-18; ⏱6-11pm Mon-Fri, from 5pm Sat, 5-10pm Sun; ☑🐾; ⓢG to Greenpoint Ave) Greenpoint's best pizza place has a cozy cabin-in-the-woods vibe, with flickering candles and old-school beats playing overhead. Diners huddle over chunky wooden tables forking away at delicious, thin-crust creatively topped pizzas. For the full experience, add on craft brews, affordable wine selections, zesty salads and dessert decadence (flourless chocolate cake, Van Leeuwan ice cream).

Marlow & Sons   Modern American $$

(☎718-384-1441; www.marlowandsons. com; 81 Broadway, btwn Berry St & Wythe Ave, Williamsburg; mains lunch $14-18, dinner $25-28; ⏱8am-midnight; ⓢJ/M/Z to Marcy Ave; L to Bedford Ave) The dimly lit, wood-lined space feels like an old farmhouse cafe, and hosts a buzzing nighttime scene as diners and drinkers crowd in for oysters, tip-top cocktails and a changing daily menu of locavore specialties (smoked pork loin, crunchy crust pizzas, caramelized turnips, fluffy Spanish-style tortillas). Brunch is also a big draw, though prepare for lines.

Juliana's   Pizza $$

(Map p246; ☎718-596-6700; www.julianaspizza. com; 19 Old Fulton St, btwn Water & Front Sts, Dumbo; pizzas $17-32; ⏱11:30am-11pm; ⓢA/C to High St) Legendary pizza maestro Patsy Grimaldi has returned to Brooklyn, with delicious thin-crust perfection in both classic and creative combos (like the No 5, with smoked salmon, goat cheese and capers). It's in Dumbo and the Brooklyn waterfront.

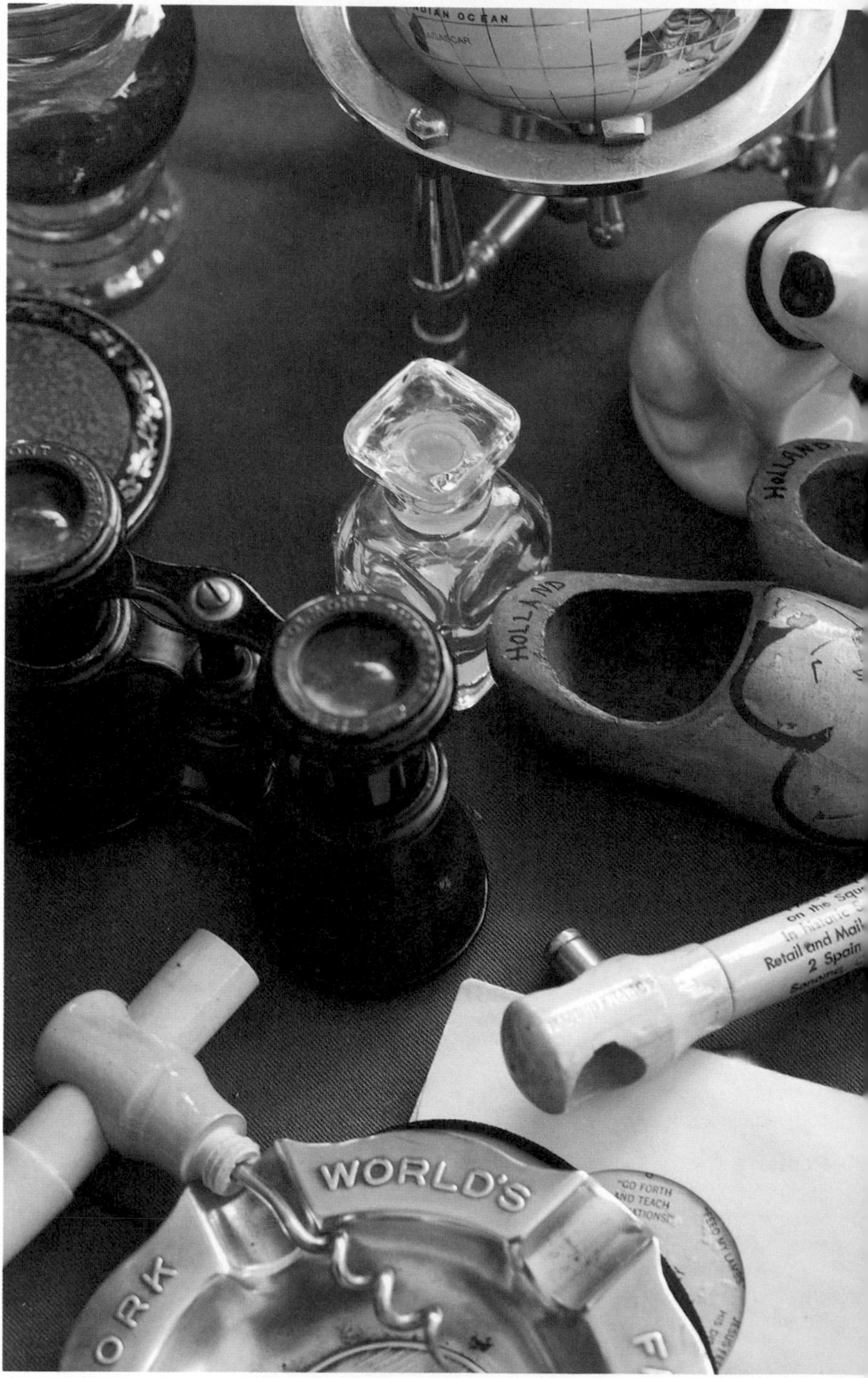

DOROTHY ALEXANDER / ALAMY STOCK PHOTO ©

TREASURE HUNT

Begin your shopping adventure

Treasure Hunt

New Yorkers live in a city of temptation. Candy-colored fashion boutiques, cutting-edge music shops, atmospheric antique stores, tea parlors – no matter what your weakness, you'll come face to face with all the objects your heart desires and plenty of curiosities you never even knew existed.

Shopping here isn't just about collecting pretty, fanciful things. It's also about experiencing the city in all its variety and connecting to New York's many subcultures: from browsing classic soul LPs at an East Village record store to jostling among fashion insiders at a Nolita sample sale, you'll find your tribe here in NYC. There are shops for old-fashioned toys, punk-rock handmade jewelry, antiquarian books, vegan clothing, gently used designer clothing, decoupage home decorations and artist monographs – indeed, if you can think of it, there's most likely a shop for it.

In This Section

Fashion Blogs

Racked (www.ny.racked.com) Informative shopping blog with its finger on the pulse.

New York Magazine (www.nymag.com) Trustworthy opinions on the Big Apple's best places to swipe your plastic.

The Glamourai (www.theglamourai. com) Glossy downtown fashion blog that's packed with cutting-edge style ideas.

Upper West Side & Central Park
The countrys most expensive boutiques
are found along Madison Ave (p158)

Midtown
Epic department stores, global chains
and the odd in-the-know treasure (p155)

West Village, Chelsea &
Meatpacking District
Boutiques and high-end shopping around Bleecker,
Washington, Hudson and W 14th Streets (p153)

Union Square, Flatiron
District & Gramercy
Vintage drinking dens, swinging cocktail bars
and a string of fun student hangouts (p154)

SoHo & Chinatown
West Broadway is a veritable outdoor
mall of encyclopedic proportions (p147)

East Village & Lower East Side
Treasure trove of vintage wares
and design goods (p150)

Financial District & Lower Manhattan
A trickle of gems, from vintage film posters and
hard-to-find vino to hipster-chic threads (p146)

Brooklyn
A healthy mix of independent
boutiques and thrift stores (p158)

Opening Hours

In general, most businesses open from 10am to around 7pm on weekdays and 11am to 8pm Saturdays. Sundays can be variable – some stores close, while others keep weekday hours. Stores tend to stay open later in the neighborhoods downtown. Small boutiques often have variable hours – many open at noon.

Sales

Clothing sales happen throughout the year, usually at the end of each season, when old stock needs to be moved out. There are also big sales during the holidays, particularly in the weeks leading up to Christmas.

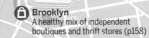

The Best...

Shop till you drop in New York City's best stores.

Fashion Boutiques

Steven Alan (p146) Heritage-inspired fashion, with branches around NYC.

Marc by Marc Jacobs (p153) A downtown and uptown favorite particularly the West Village locations.

Rag & Bone (p148) Beautifully tailored clothes for men and women.

John Varvatos (p151) Rugged but worldly wearables in a former downtown rock club.

Opening Ceremony (p147) Head-turning, cutting-edge threads and kicks for the fashion avant-garde in SoHo.

For Women

Verameat (p150) Exquisite jewelry that treads between beauty and whimsy.

Beacon's Closet (p158) Valhalla for vintage lovers at multiple locations.

MIN New York (p148) Unique perfumes in an apothecary-like setting.

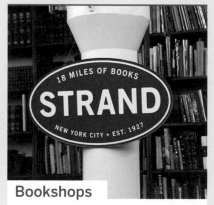

Bookshops

Strand Book Store (pictured above; p153) Hands-down NYC's best used bookstore.

McNally Jackson (p148) Great SoHo spot for book browsing and author readings.

Housing Works Book Store (p148) Used books and a cafe in an atmospheric setting in Nolita.

192 Books (p154) The perfect neighborhood book shop in Chelsea.

For Children

Dinosaur Hill (p153) In the East Village, you'll find fun and creative toys, books and music that will inspire young minds.

Books of Wonder (p155) Great gift ideas for kids, plus in-store readings at this shop near Union Square.

Music Shops

Rough Trade (p159) Vinyl is far from dead at this sprawling new music shop/concert space in Williamsburg.

Other Music (p148) Great selection of rare grooves at this downtown icon.

A-1 Records (pictured above; p151) Endless bins of records in the East Village.

For Unique Souvenirs

Obscura Antiques (pictured above; p151) A cabinet of curiosities with strange objects.

Amé Amé (p156) Beautifully made umbrellas and rain gear, plus candy!

Top Hat (p153) Lovely collectible objects from around the globe.

Bowne Stationers & Co (p146) You can score anything from vintage New York posters to city-themed stationery at this heritage printer.

For Men

By Robert James (p150) Rugged menswear by a celebrated new local designer.

Nepenthes New York (p155) Japanese collective selling covetable, in-the-know labels.

Odin (p149) Tiny downtown men's boutique for one-of-a-kind pieces.

★ Lonely Planet's Top Choices

Barneys (p115) Serious fashionistas shop (or at least browse) at Barneys, well known for its spot-on collections of in-the-know labels.

Brooklyn Flea (p151) Brooklyn's collection of flea markets offers plenty of vintage furnishings, retro clothing and bric-a-brac, plus great food stalls.

ABC Carpet & Home (p154) Spread over six floors like a museum, ABC is packed with treasures large (furniture) and small (jewelry, global gifts).

MoMA Design & Book Store (p155) The perfect one-stop shop for coffee-table tomes, art prints, edgy jewelry and 'Where-did-you-get-that?' homewares.

🔒 Financial District & Lower Manhattan

Century 21 — Fashion

(Map p246; ☎212-227-9092; www.c21stores.com; 22 Cortlandt St, btwn Church St & Broadway; ⏰7:45am-9pm Mon-Fri, 10am-9pm Sat, 11am-8pm Sun; **S**A/C, J/Z, 2/3, 4/5 to Fulton St; R to Cortlandt St) For penny-pinching fashionistas, this giant, cut-price department store is dangerously addictive. Raid the racks for designer duds at up to 65% off. Not everything is a knockout or a bargain, but persistence pays off. You'll also find accessories, shoes, cosmetics, homewares and toys.

Shinola — Accessories

(Map p246; ☎917-728-3000; www.shinola.com; 177 Franklin St, btwn Greenwich & Hudson Sts; ⏰11am-7pm Mon-Sat, noon-6pm Sun; **S**1 to Franklin St) Well known for its coveted wristwatches, Detroit-based Shinola branches out with a supercool selection of Made-in-USA life props. Bag anything from leather iPad cases, journal covers and toiletry bags to grooming products, jewelry and limited-edition bicycles with customized bags. Added bonuses include complimentary monogramming of leather goods and stationery, and an in-house espresso bar, **Smile** (Map p246; ☎917-728-3023; www.thesmilenyc.com; 177 Franklin St, btwn Greenwich & Hudson Sts; ⏰7am-7pm Mon-Fri, 8am-7pm Sat, 8am-6pm Sun; **S**1 to Franklin St), to boot.

Steven Alan — Fashion, Accessories

(Map p246; ☎212-343-0692; www.stevenalan.com; 103 Franklin St, btwn Church St & W Broadway; ⏰11:30am-7pm Mon-Wed, Fri & Sat, 11:30am-8pm Thu, noon-6pm Sun; **S**A/C/E to Canal St; 1 to Franklin St) New York designer Steven Alan mixes his hip, heritage-inspired threads for men and women with a beautiful edit of clothes from indie-chic labels like France's Arpenteur and Scandinavia's Acne and Norse Projects. Accessories include hard-to-find fragrances, bags, jewelry and a selection of shoes by cognoscenti brands such as Common Projects and Isabel Marant Étoile.

Bowne Stationers & Co — Gifts

(Map p246; ☎646-315-4478; 211 Water St, btwn Beekman & Fulton Sts; ⏰11am-7pm; **S**2/3, 4/5,

From Left: MoMA Design Store (p148); Century 21; Shinola

A/C, J/Z to Fulton St) Suitably set in cobbled South Street Seaport, this 18th-century veteran stocks vintage reproduction New York posters, city-themed notepads, pencil cases, cards, stamps and more. You can even bag New York–themed wrapping paper to wrap them in. Located next door is the printing workshop, where you can order customized business cards or hone your printing skills at one of the monthly workshops.

Citystore   Souvenirs

(Map p246; ☎212-386-0007; a856-citystore. nyc.gov; Municipal Bldg, North Plaza, 1 Centre St; ⏰10am-5pm Mon-Fri; ⓈJ/Z to Chambers St; 4/5/6 to Brooklyn Bridge-City Hall) Score all manner of New York memorabilia, from authentic taxi medallions, manhole coasters and subway-themed socks to NYPD baseball caps and wine totes featuring Manhattan and Brooklyn themes. Topping it off is a great collection of city-themed books.

Philip Williams Posters   Vintage

(Map p246; ☎212-513-0313; www.postermuseum.com; 122 Chambers St, btwn Church St & W Broadway; ⏰10am-7pm Mon-Sat; ⓈA/C, 1/2/3 to Chambers St) You'll find over half a million posters in this cavernous treasure trove, from oversized French advertisements for perfume and cognac to Soviet film posters and retro-fab promos for TWA. Prices range from $15 for small reproductions to a few thousand bucks for rare, showpiece originals. There is a second entrance at 52 Warren St.

🔒 SoHo & Chinatown

Opening Ceremony   Fashion, Shoes

(Map p246; ☎212-219-2688; www.openingceremony.us; 35 Howard St, btwn Broadway & Lafayette St; ⏰11am-8pm Mon-Sat, noon-7pm Sun; ⓈN/Q/R, J/Z, 6 to Canal St) Unisex Opening Ceremony is famed for its never-boring edit of A-list indie labels. The place showcases a changing roster of names from across the globe, both established and emerging. Complementing them is Opening Ceremony's own avant-garde creations. No matter who is hanging on the racks, you can always expect show-stopping, 'Where did you

get that?!' threads that are street-smart, bold and refreshingly unexpected.

Rag & Bone Fashion

(Map p246; ☏212-219-2204; www.rag-bone.com; 119 Mercer St, btwn Prince & Spring Sts; ☉11am-8pm Mon-Sat, noon-7pm Sat; Ⓢ N/R to Prince St) Downtown label Rag & Bone is a hit with many of New York's coolest, sharpest dressers – both men and women. Detail-oriented pieces range from clean-cut shirts and blazers, to graphic tees, monochromatic sweaters, feather-light strappy dresses, leather goods and Rag & Bone's highly prized jeans. The tailoring is generally impeccable, with accessories including shoes, hats, bags and wallets.

MiN New York Beauty

(Map p246; ☏212-206-6366; www.min.com; 117 Crosby St, btwn Jersey & Prince Sts; ☉11am-7pm Tue-Sat, noon-6pm Mon & Sun; Ⓢ B/D/F/M to Broadway-Lafayette St; N/R to Prince St) This chic, library-like apothecary curates an extraordinary, rotating collection of rare and exclusive perfumes, grooming products and scented candles. Esteemed and historic European lines aside, look out for artisanal American fragrances from the likes of Strangelove NYC and the Vagabond Prince, as well as MiN's own line of coveted hair products.

Screaming Mimi's Vintage

(Map p246; ☏212-677-6464; www.screamingmimis.com; 382 Lafayette St, btwn E 4th & Great Jones Sts; ☉noon-8pm Mon-Sat, 1-7pm Sun; Ⓢ 6 to Bleecker St; B/D/F/M to Broadway-Lafayette St) If you dig vintage threads, you may just scream too. This funtastic shop carries an excellent selection of yesteryear pieces – organized, ingeniously, by decade, from the '50s to the '90s (ask to see the small, stashed-away collection of clothing from the '20s, '30s and '40s).

Other Music Music

(Map p246; ☏212-477-8150; www.othermusic.com; 15 E 4th St, btwn Lafayette St & Broadway; ☉11am-8pm Mon-Wed, 11am-9pm Thu & Fri, noon-8pm Sat, noon-7pm Sun; Ⓢ 6 to Bleecker St; B/D/F/M to Broadway-Lafayette St) This indie-run CD store feeds its loyal fan base with a clued-in selection of, well, other types of music: offbeat lounge, psychedelic, electronica, indie rock etc, available new and used. Friendly staffers like what they do, and may be able to help translate your inner musical whims and dreams to actual CD reality. OM also stocks a small but excellent selection of new and used vinyl.

McNally Jackson Books

(Map p246; ☏212-274-1160; www.mcnallyjackson.com; 52 Prince St, btwn Lafayette & Mulberry Sts; ☉10am-10pm Mon-Sat, to 9pm Sun; Ⓢ N/R to Prince St; 6 to Spring St) Bustling indie MJ stocks an excellent selection of magazines and books covering contemporary fiction, food writing, architecture and design, art and history. The in-store cafe is a fine spot to settle in with some reading material or to catch one of the frequent readings and book signings held here.

MoMA Design Store Gifts

(Map p246; ☏646-613-1367; www.momastore.org; 81 Spring St, at Crosby St; ☉10am-8pm Mon-Sat, 11am-7pm Sun; Ⓢ N/R to Prince St; 6 to Spring St) The Museum of Modern Art's downtown retail space carries a huge collection of sleek, smart and clever objects for the home, office and wardrobe. You'll find modernist alarm clocks, sculptural vases and jewelry, surreal lamps, svelte kitchenware, plus brainy games, hand puppets, fanciful scarves, coffee-table tomes and loads of other unique gift ideas.

Housing Works Book Store Books

(Map p246; ☏212-334-3324; www.housingworks.org/usedbookcafe; 126 Crosby St, btwn E Houston & Prince Sts; ☉9am-9pm Mon-Fri, 10am-5pm Sat & Sun; Ⓢ B/D/F/M to Broadway-Lafayette St; N/R to Prince St) Relaxed, earthy and featuring a great selection of second-hand books, vinyl, CDs and DVDs you can buy for a good cause (proceeds go to the city's HIV-positive and AIDS homeless communities), this creaky hideaway is a very local place to while away a few quiet afternoon hours (there's an in-house cafe).

Evolution
Gifts
(Map p246; 212-343-1114; www.theevolution
store.com; 120 Spring St, btwn Mercer & Greene
Sts; 11am-8pm; N/R to Prince St; 6 to
Spring St) Evolution keeps things quirky with
natural-history collectibles usually seen
in museum cabinets. This is the place to
buy – or simply gawk at – framed beetles
and butterflies, bugs frozen in amber-resin
cubes, stuffed parrots, zebra hides and
shark teeth, as well as stony wonders, from
meteorites and fragments from Mars to
100-million-year-old fossils.

3x1
Fashion
(Map p246; 212-391-6969; www.3x1.us; 15
Mercer St, btwn Howard & Grand Sts; 11am-
7pm Mon-Sat, noon-6pm Sun, N/Q/R, J/Z, 6 to
Canal St) Design your most flattering pair of
jeans at this bespoke denim factory/show-
room, which offers three levels of services.
Quick, on-the-spot 'ready-to-wear service'
lets you choose the hem for ready-to-wear
denim (women's from $195, men's from
$245); 'custom service' sees you choosing
the fabric and detailing for an existing fit
($525 to $750); while the 'full bespoke
service' ($1200) designs your perfect pair
from scratch.

Odin
Fashion
(Map p246; 212-966-0026; www.odinnewyork.
com; 199 Lafayette St, btwn Kenmare & Broome
Sts; 11am-8pm Mon-Sat, noon-7pm Sun; 6
to Spring St; N/R to Prince St) Odin's flagship
men's boutique carries hip downtown
labels such as Thom Browne, Rag & Bone,
Duckie Brown and Public School NYC. Rub-
bing shoulders with them is a select edit of
imports, among them Nordic labels Acne
and Won Hundred. Other in-store tempters
include Odin candles, fragrances, jewelry
from Brooklyn creatives such as Naval Yard
and Uhuru, Oliver Peoples sunglasses, and
street-smart footwear from cult labels such
as Common Projects.

Uniqlo
Fashion
(Map p246; 877-486-4756; www.uniqlo.
com; 546 Broadway, btwn Prince & Spring Sts;
10am-9pm Mon-Sat, 11am-8pm Sun; N/R

NYC Icons
A few stores in this city have cemented
their status as NYC legends. This city
just wouldn't quite be the same without
them. For label hunters, Century 21
(p146) is a Big Apple institution, with
clothes by D&G, Prada, Marc Jacobs
and many others at low prices. Other
Music (p148) is a long-running indie
music store (CDs and some vinyl) that
thrives despite the odds. Book lovers of
the world unite at the Strand (p153), the
city's biggest and best bookseller. Run
by Hassidic Jews and employing mech-
anized whimsy, B&H Photo Video (p156)
is a mecca for digital and audio geeks.
For secondhand clothing, home furnishings and books, good-hearted Housing
Works (p154), with many locations
around town, is a perennial favorite.

Prada, Fifth Ave
RICHARD LEVINE / GETTY IMAGES ©

to Prince St; 6 to Spring St) This enormous
three-story Japanese emporium owes its
popularity to good-looking, good-quality
apparel at discount prices. You'll find Japanese denim, Mongolian cashmere, graphic
T-shirts, svelte skirts, high-tech thermals
and endless racks of colorful ready-to-wear
items – with most things falling below the
$100 mark.

Will Leather Goods
Accessories
(Map p246; 212-925-2824; www.willleather
goods.com; 29 Prince St, at Mott St; 10am-8pm
Mon-Sat, 11am-7pm Sun; N/R to Prince St; 6
to Spring St) Beautifully crafted, classically
styled leather goods fill this family-owned

Oregon import. While you'll find everything from wallets and belts to pet leashes, it's the bags that take the breath away. Made using American and Italian leathers, products include erudite satchels, briefcases, messenger bags, jet-setter duffles, clutches and cross-body bags. The store also sells vintage pieces: US Postal Service mailbag, anyone?

🔒 East Village & Lower East Side

By Robert James   Fashion
(Map p246; 📞212-253-2121; www.byrobertjames. com; 74 Orchard St; ⏱noon-8pm Mon-Sat, to 6pm Sun; Ⓢ F to Delancey St; J/M/Z to Essex St) Rugged, beautifully tailored menswear is the mantra of Robert James, who sources and manufactures right here in NYC (the design studio is just upstairs). The racks are lined with slim-fitting denim, handsome button-downs and classic-looking sports coats. Lola, James' black lab, sometimes roams the store. He also has a store in Williamsburg.

Verameat   Jewelry
(Map p246; 📞212-388-9045; www.verameat. com; 315 E 9th St, btwn First & Second Aves; ⏱noon-8pm; Ⓢ6 to Astor Pl; F to 2nd Ave) Designer Vera Balyura creates exquisite little pieces with a dark sense of humor in this delightful little shop on 9th St. Tiny, artfully wrought pendants, rings, earrings and bracelets appear almost too precious, until a closer inspection reveals zombies, godzilla robots, animal heads, dinosaurs and encircling claws – bringing a whole new level of miniaturized complexity to the realm of jewelry.

John Derian   Homewares
(Map p246; 📞212-677-3917; www.johnderian. com; 6 E 2nd St, btwn Bowery & Second Ave; ⏱11am-7pm Tue-Sun; Ⓢ F/V to Lower East Side-Second Ave) John Derian is famed for its decoupage – pieces from original botanical and animal prints stamped under glass. The result is a beautiful collection of one-of-a-kind plates, paperweights, coasters, lamps, bowls and vases.

Still House   Homewares
(Map p246; 📞212-539-0200; www.stillhousenyc. com; 117 E 7th St; ⏱noon-8pm; Ⓢ6 to Astor Pl) Step into this petite, peaceful boutique to browse sculptural glassware and pottery: handblown vases, geometric tabletop objects, ceramic bowls and cups, and other finery for the home. You'll also find minimalistic jewelry, delicately bound notebooks and small framed artworks for the wall.

Reformation   Clothing
(Map p246; 📞646-448-4925; www.thereformation.com; 156 Ludlow St, btwn Rivington & Stanton Sts; ⏱noon-8pm Mon-Sat, to 7pm Sun; Ⓢ F to Delancey St; F to 2nd Ave; J/M/Z to Essex St) 📷 This stylish boutique sells beautifully designed garments with minimal environmental impact. Aside from its green credentials, it sells unique tops, blouses, sweaters and dresses, with fair prices in comparison to other LES boutiques.

Moo Shoes   Shoes
(Map p246; 📞212-254-6512; www.mooshoes. com; 78 Orchard St, btwn Broome & Grand Sts; ⏱11:30am-7:30pm Mon-Sat, noon-6pm Sun; Ⓢ F to Delancey St; J/M/Z to Essex St) This earth- and animal-friendly boutique sells surprisingly stylish microfiber (faux leather) shoes, handbags and wallets. Look for elegant ballet flats from Love Is Mighty, rugged men's Oxfords by Novacos, and sleek Matt & Nat wallets.

Tokio 7   Fashion
(Map p246; 📞212-353-8443; www.tokio7.net; 83 E 7th St, near First Ave; ⏱noon-8pm; Ⓢ6 to Astor Pl) This revered, hip consignment shop, on a shady stretch of E 7th St, has good-condition designer labels for men and women at some fairly hefty prices. The Japanese-owned store often features lovely pieces by Issey Miyake and Yohji Yamamoto, as well as a well-curated selection of Dolce & Gabbana, Prada, Chanel and other top labels.

Obscura Antiques   Antiques

(Map p246; ☎212-505-9251; www.obscuraan-
tiques.com; 207 Ave A, btwn 12th & 13th Sts;
⏱noon-8pm Mon-Sat, to 7pm Sun; Ⓢ L to
1st Ave) This small cabinet of curiosities
pleases both lovers of the macabre and
inveterate antique hunters. Here you'll
find taxidermied animal heads, tiny rodent
skulls and skeletons, butterfly displays
in glass boxes, photos of dead people,
disturbing little (dental?) instruments,
German landmine flags (stackable so tanks
could see them), old poison bottles and
glass eyes.

Edith Machinist   Vintage

(Map p246; ☎212-979-9992; www edithma-
chinist.com; 104 Rivington St, at Ludlow St,
⏱noon-7pm Tue-Sat, to 6pm Sun & Mon; Ⓢ F
to Delancey St; J/M/Z to Essex St) To properly
strut about the Lower East Side, you've got
to dress the part. Edith Machinist can help
you get that rumpled but stylish look in a
hurry – a bit of vintage glam via knee-high
soft suede boots, 1930s silk dresses and
ballet-style flats.

John Varvatos   Fashion

(Map p246; ☎212-358-0315; www.johnvarvatos.
com; 315 Bowery, btwn 1st & 2nd Sts; ⏱noon-
8pm Mon-Sat, to 6pm Sun; Ⓢ F to 2nd Ave; 6 to
Bleecker St) Set in the hallowed halls of former punk club **CBGB** (Map p246; 315 Bowery,
btwn 1st & 2nd Sts; Ⓢ F to 2nd Ave; 6 to Bleecker
St), the John Varvatos Bowery store goes to
great lengths to tie fashion with rock and
roll, with records, '70s audio equipment
and even electric guitars for sale alongside
JV's denim, leather boots, belts and graphic
tees.

A-1 Records   Music

(Map p246; ☎212-473-2870; www.a1recordshop.
com; 439 E 6th St, btwn First Ave & Ave A; ⏱1-
9pm; Ⓢ F/V to Lower East Side-2nd Ave) One of
the last of the many record stores that once
graced the East Village, A-1 has an excellent
selection of jazz, funk and soul, and the
cramped aisles draw vinyl fans from far and
wide.

> *surprisingly stylish microfiber
> (faux leather) shoes,
> handbags and wallets*

Faux leather boots on display at Moo Shoes

SPENCER PLATT / GETTY IMAGES ©

Five Must-Buy NYC Souvenirs

Tote Bag

Boast your literary cred with a tote bag from Strand Book Store (p153), New York's biggest and best indie bookseller.

NYC Beats

New sounds (on vinyl or CD): discover underground beats from the brilliantly curated collection at Other Music (p148).

Antique Print

Reproductions of NYC at Bowne Stationers & Co (p146) make great artwork when framed – and a fine reminder of the Big Apple experience.

Manhole Cover Mat

Head to the Citystore (p147), to pick up a NYC Manhole Cover Floormat emblazoned with the poetic words 'NYC Sewer.'

Alto Vase

The undulating Alto Vase from the MoMA Design Store (p148) makes a fine conversation piece on any table.

No Relation Vintage Vintage
(Map p246; 212-228-5201; http://norelation
vintage.com; 204 First Ave, btwn 12th & 13th Sts;
noon-8pm; L to First Ave) Among the
many vintage shops of the East Village, No
Relation is a winner for its wide-ranging
collections that run the gamut from denim
and leather jackets to flannels, sneakers,
plaid shirts, candy-colored T-shirts, varsity
jackets, clutches and more. Sharpen your
elbows: hipster crowds flock here on
weekends.

Dinosaur Hill Children
(Map p246; 212-473-5850; www.dinosaurhill.
com; 306 E 9th St; 11am-7pm; 6 to Astor
Pl) A small, old-fashioned toy store that's
inspired more by imagination than Disney
movies, this shop has loads of great gift
ideas: Czech marionettes, shadow puppets,
micro building blocks, calligraphy sets, toy
pianos, art and science kits, kids' music
CDs from around the globe, and wooden
blocks in half-a-dozen different languages,
plus natural-fiber clothing for infants.

Top Hat Accessories
(Map p246; 212-677-4240; www.tophatnyc.
com; 245 Broome St, btwn Ludlow & Orchard Sts;
noon-8pm; B/D to Grand St) Sporting
curios from around the globe, this whimsical little shop is packed with intrigue: from
vintage Italian pencils and handsomely
miniaturized leather journals to beautifully
carved wooden bird whistles. If you're
looking for an endless rain album, a toy
clarinet, Japanese fabrics, a crumpled map
of the night sky or geometric Spanish cups
and saucers, you'll find all these and more
at fanciful Top Hat.

West Village, Chelsea & Meatpacking District

Strand Book Store Books
(Map p246; 212-473-1452; www.strandbooks.
com; 828 Broadway, at 12th St; 9:30am-
10:30pm Mon-Sat, from 11am Sun; L, N/Q/R,

4/5/6 to 14th St-Union Sq) Book fiends (or
even those who have casually skimmed
one or two) shouldn't miss New York's most
loved and famous bookstore. In operation
since 1927, the Strand sells new, used and
rare titles, spreading an incredible 18 miles
of books (over 2.5 million of them) among
three labyrinthine floors.

Story Gifts
(Map p252; http://thisisstory.com; 144 Tenth Ave,
btwn 18th & 19th Sts; 11am-8pm Mon-Fri, from
10am Sat & Sun; C/E to 23rd St; 1 to 18th St)
This concept shop near the High Line func-
tions like a gallery, showcasing new themes
and products every month or two. The
2000-sq-ft space covers all the bases from
crafty jewelry and eye-catching accessories
to lovely stationery, imagination-inspiring
toys for kids, thick coffee-
table books, environmentally friendly soaps
and whimsical souvenirs.

**Personnel of
New York** Fashion, Accessories
(Map p246; 212-924-0604; personnelofnew
york.com; 9 Greenwich Ave btwn Christopher &
W 10th St; 11am-8pm Mon-Sat, noon-7pm Sun;
A/C/E, B/D/F/M to W 4th St; 1 to Christopher
St-Sheridan Sq) This small, delightful indie
shop sells women's designer clothing
from unique labels from the East and West
Coasts and beyond. Look for easy-to-wear
Sunja Link dresses, soft pullover sweaters
by Ali Golden, statement-making jewelry by
Marisa Mason, comfy canvas sneakers by
Shoes Like Pottery and couture pieces by
Rodebjer.

Marc by Marc Jacobs Fashion
(Map p246; 212-924-0026; www.marcjacobs.
com; 403 Bleecker St; 11am-7pm Mon-Sat,
noon-6pm Sun; A/C/E to 14th St; L to 8th Ave)
With five small shops sprinkled around the
West Village, Marc Jacobs has established a
real presence in this well-heeled neighborhood. Large front windows allow easy
peeking – assuming there's not a sale, during which you'll only see hordes of fawning
shoppers.

A Homage to Luxury

One of the world's fashion capitals, NYC is forever setting trends for the rest of the country to follow. To check out the latest designs hitting the streets, it's worth browsing some of the city's best-loved boutiques around town – regardless of whether you intend to spend. A few favorites include Opening Ceremony, Issey Miyake, Marc Jacobs, Steven Alan, Rag & Bone, John Varvatos, By Robert James and Piperlime.

If time is limited, or you simply want to browse a plethora of labels in one go, then head to those heady conglomerations known worldwide as department stores. New York has a special blend of alluring draws – in particular don't miss Barneys (p115), Bergdorf Goodman (p155), **Macy's** (Map p252; ☏212-695-4400; www.macys.com; 151 W 34th St, at Broadway; ◷9:30am-10pm Mon & Wed-Fri, to 9:30pm Tue, 10am-10pm Sat, 11am-9pm Sun; ⓢB/D/F/M, N/Q/R to 34th St-Herald Sq) and Bloomingdale's (p155).

Opening Ceremony (p147)

Housing Works Thrift Shop Vintage
(Map p252; ☏718-838-5050; 143 W 17th St, btwn Sixth & Seventh Aves; ◷10am-7pm Mon-Fri, to 6pm Sat, noon-6pm Sun; ⓢ1 to 18th St) This shop, with its swank window displays, looks more boutique than thrift, but its selections of clothes, accessories, furniture, books and records are great value. All proceeds benefit the charity serving the city's HIV-positive and AIDS homeless communities. There are 11 other branches around town.

192 Books Books
(Map p252; ☏212-255-4022; www.192books.com; 192 Tenth Ave, btwn 21st & 22nd Sts; ◷11am-7pm; ⓢC/E to 23rd St) Located right in the gallery district is this small indie bookstore, with sections on fiction, history, travel, art and criticism. Its rotating art exhibits are a special treat, during which the owners organize special displays of books that relate thematically to the featured show or artist. Weekly book readings feature acclaimed (often NY-based) authors.

McNulty's Tea & Coffee Co, Inc Food & Drink
(Map p246; ☏212-242-5351; http://mcnultys.com; 109 Christopher St; ◷10am-9pm Mon-Sat, 1-7pm Sun; ⓢ1 to Christopher St-Sheridan Sq) Just down from a few sex shops, sweet McNulty's, with worn wooden floorboards, fragrant sacks of coffee beans and large glass jars of tea, flaunts a different era of Greenwich Village. It's been selling gourmet teas and coffees here since 1895.

🔒 Union Square, Flatiron District & Gramercy

ABC Carpet & Home Homewares
(Map p252; ☏212-473-3000; www.abchome.com; 888 Broadway, at 19th St; ◷10am-7pm Mon-Wed, Fri & Sat, to 8pm Thu, 11am-6:30pm Sun; ⓢ4/5/6, N/Q/R, L to 14th St-Union Sq) A mecca for home designers and decorators brainstorming ideas, this beautifully curated, seven-level temple to good taste heaves with all sorts of furnishings, small and large. Shop for easy-to-pack knickknacks, textiles and jewelry, as well as statement furniture, designer lighting, ceramics and antique carpets. Come Christmas season the shop is a joy to behold.

DSW Shoes
(Map p246; ☏212-674-2146; www.dsw.com; 4 Union Sq S, btwn University Pl & Broadway; ◷10am-9:30pm Mon-Sat, to 8pm Sun; ⓢ4/5/6,

N/Q/R, L to 14th St-Union Sq) If your idea of paradise involves a great selection of cut-price kicks, make a beeline for this sprawling, unisex chain. Shoes range from formal to athletic, with no shortage of popular and higher-end labels.

Idlewild Books Books

(Map p252; ☎212-414-8888; www.idlewildbooks.com; 12 W 19th St, btwn Fifth & Sixth Aves; 🕐noon-7.30pm Mon-Thu, to 6pm Fri & Sat, to 5pm Sun; [S]4/5/6, N/Q/R, L to 14th St-Union Sq) Named after JFK Airport's original moniker, this indie travel bookshop gets feet seriously itchy. Books are divided by region, and cover guidebooks as well as fiction, travelogues, history, cookbooks and other stimulating fare for delving into different corners of the world. The store also runs popular language classes in French, Italian, Spanish and German; see the website for details.

Books of Wonder Books

(Map p252; ☎212-989-3270; www.booksofwonder.com; 18 W 18th St, btwn Fifth & Sixth Aves; 🕐10am-7pm Mon-Sat, 11am-6pm Sun; 👪; [S]F/M to 14th St, L to 6th Ave) Devoted to children's and young-adult titles, this wonderful bookstore is a great place to take young ones on a rainy day, especially when a kids' author is giving a reading or a storyteller is on hand. There's an impressive range of NYC-themed picture books as well as a section dedicated to rare and vintage children's books and limited-edition children's book artwork.

🛍 Midtown

MoMA Design & Book Store Gifts, Books

(Map p252; ☎212-708-9700; www.momastore.org; 11 W 53rd St, btwn Fifth & Sixth Aves; 🕐9:30am-6:30pm Sat-Thu, to 9pm Fri; [S]E, M to 5th Ave-53rd St) The flagship store at the Museum of Modern Art is a fab spot to souvenir-shop in one fell swoop. Aside from stocking gorgeous books (from art and architecture tomes to pop-culture readers and kids' picture books), it has art prints and posters, and one-of-a-kind knick-knacks. For furniture, lighting, homewares, jewelry, bags, and MUJI merchandise, head to the MoMA Design Store across the street.

Nepenthes New York Fashion

(Map p252; ☎212-643-9540; www.nepenthesny.com; 307 W 38th St, btwn Eighth & Ninth Aves, Midtown West; 🕐noon-7pm Mon-Sat, to 5pm Sun; [S]A/C/E to 42nd St-Port Authority Bus Terminal) Occupying an old sewing shop in the Garment District, this cult Japanese collective stocks edgy menswear from the likes of Engineered Garments and Needles, known for their quirky detailing and artisanal production value (think tweed lace-up pants). Accessories include bags and satchels, gloves, eyewear and footwear.

Hell's Kitchen Flea Market Market

(Map p252; ☎212-243-5343; www.annexmarkets.com; 39th St, btwn Ninth & Tenth Aves, Midtown West; 🕐9am-5pm Sat & Sun; [S]A/C/E to 42nd St) This weekend flea lures both collectors and the common curious with its wonderful booty of vintage furnishings, accessories, clothing and unidentifiable objects from past eras.

Bergdorf Goodman Department Store

(Map p250; ☎212-753-7300; www.bergdorfgoodman.com; 754 Fifth Ave, btwn 57th & 58th Sts; 🕐10am-8pm Mon-Sat, 11am-7pm Sun; [S]N/Q/R to 5th Ave-59th St; F to 57th St) Not merely loved for its Christmas windows (the city's best), The plush Bergdorf Goodman leads the fashion race with Linda Fargo, its fashion director, being a kind of Anna Wintour. The store stocks exclusive collections of Tom Ford and Chanel shoes and an excellent women's shoe department. The men's store is located across the street.

Bloomingdale's Department Store

(Map p250; ☎212-705-2000; www.bloomingdales.com; 1000 Third Ave, at E 59th St, Midtown East; 🕐10am-8:30pm Mon & Tue, to 10pm Wed-Sat, to 9pm Sun; 📶; [S]4/5/6 to 59th St; N/Q/R to Lexington Ave-59th St) Blockbuster

Bloomie's is comprehensively stocked with clothes and shoes from myriad US and global fashion designers, including a number of up-and-coming designer collections.

Amé Amé   Accessories
(Map p252; 📞646-867-2342; www.amerain.com; 17 W 29th St, at Broadway; ⊘noon-7pm; §N/R to 28th St) Rain gear and candy? Kindly owner Teresa will explain what Amé Amé means if you're perplexed by this unusual juxtaposition. She'll also set you straight on the fallacy of buying cheap disposable umbrellas. Only well-crafted, long-lasting rain gear is sold here, from perfectly fitting Aigle boots and handsome Barbour coats to elegant scarves and hats, and whimsical, out-of-the-ordinary gifts.

B&H Photo Video   Electronics
(Map p252; 📞212-444-6615; www.bhphotovideo. com; 420 Ninth Ave, btwn 33rd & 34th Sts, Midtown West; ⊘9am-7pm Mon-Thu, to 2pm Fri, 10am-6pm Sun; §A/C/E to 34th St-Penn Station) Visiting NYC's most popular camera shop is an experience in itself – it's massive and crowded, and bustling with black-clad (and tech-savvy) Hasidic Jewish salesmen. Your chosen item is dropped into a bucket, which then moves up and across the ceiling to the purchase area (which requires a second queue).

🏠 Upper East Side

Encore   Clothing
(Map p250; 📞212-879-2850; www.encoreresale. com; 1132 Madison Ave, btwn 84th & 85th Sts; ⊘10:30am-6:30pm Mon-Sat, noon-6pm Sun; §4/5/6 to 86th St) An exclusive consignment store that has been emptying out Upper East Side closets since the 1950s. (Jacqueline Kennedy Onassis used to sell her clothes here.) Expect to find a gently worn selection of name brands such as Louboutin, Fendi and Dior. Prices are high but infinitely better than retail.

SIMON LEIGH / ALAMY STOCK PHOTO ©

🔲 Flea Markets & Vintage Adventures

As much as New Yorkers gravitate toward all that's shiny and new, it can also be infinitely fun to rifle through closets of unwanted wares. The most popular flea market is the **Brooklyn Flea (**www.brooklynflea.com; 50 Kent Ave, btwn 11th & 12th Sts, Williamsburg; ⏰10am-5pm Sun Apr-Oct; **S** L to Bedford Ave; G to Nassau Ave), housed in all sorts of spaces throughout the year. The best market in Manhattan is the Hell's Kitchen Flea Market (p155), while the East Village is the city's de facto neighborhood for secondhand and vintage stores (where the unwavering legion of hipsters seek their threads).

LEFT: PICTURE PARTNERS / ALAMY STOCK PHOTO ©, RIGHT: AUDREY CONNOLLY / GETTY IMAGES ©

Top: Smorgasburg Market in Brooklyn (p131), Left and Right: Hell's Kitchen Flea Market (p155)

Blue Tree Fashion, Homewares
(Map p250; ☎212-369-2583; www.bluetreenyc.com; 1283 Madison Ave, btwn 91st & 92nd Sts; 🕙10am-6pm Mon-Fri, 11am-6pm Sat; [S]4/5/6 to 86th St) This charming (and expensive) little boutique, owned by actress Phoebe Cates Kline (of *Fast Times at Ridgemont High*) sells a dainty array of women's clothing, cashmere scarves, Lucite objects, whimsical accessories and home design.

🛍 Upper West Side & Central Park

Magpie Crafts
(Map p250; ☎646-998-3002; http://magpienewyork.com; 488 Amsterdam Ave, btwn 83rd & 84th Sts; 🕙11am-7pm Tue-Sat, to 6pm Sun; [S]1 to 86th St) 🌿 When you're short of gift ideas, stop in this charming little outpost, where you'll find a wide range of ecofriendly objects. Elegant stationery, beeswax candles, hand-painted mugs, organic cotton scarves, recycled resin necklaces and hand-dyed felt journals are a few things that may catch your eye. Most products are fair trade, made of sustainable materials or are locally designed and made.

West Side Kids Toys
(Map p250; ☎212-496-7282; www.westsidekidsnyc.com; 498 Amsterdam Ave; 🕙10am-7pm Mon-Sat, 11am-6pm Sun; [S]1 to 86th St) A great place to pick up a gift for that little someone special, no matter their age. Stocks lots of hands-on activities and fun but educational games, as well as puzzles, mini musical instruments, science kits, magic sets, snap circuits, old-fashioned wooden trains and building kits.

🛍 Harlem & Upper Manhattan

Flamekeepers Hat Club Accessories
(☎212-531-3542; www.flamekeepershatclub.com; 273 W 121st St, at St Nicholas Ave; 🕙noon-7pm Sun-Wed, to 8pm Thu & Fri, to 9pm Sat; [S]A/C, B/D to 125th St) Sharpen your kudos at this sassy little hat shop, owned by affable Harlem local Marc Williamson. His carefully curated stock reads like a hat-lover's dream: buttery Barbisio fedoras from Italy, Selentino top hats from the Czech Republic, and woolen patchwork caps from Ireland's Hanna Hats of Donegal. Prices range from $85 to $350, with an optional customization service for true individualists.

Trunk Show Designer Consignment Vintage
(Map p250; ☎212-662-0009; www.trunkshowconsignment.com; 275-277 W 113th St, at Eighth Ave; 🕙1:30-7pm Mon-Thu, usually by appointment Fri-Sun; [S]B, C to 110th St-Cathedral Parkway, 2/3 to 110th St-Central Park North) Step into this hot little consignment store in Harlem for a unisex edit of fabulous preloved finds. With merchandise delivered every second day, you're pretty much assured of a couture catch, whether it's a John Varvatos leather coat, a Valentino frock or a pair of Lanvin python pumps. Opening times can vary, so consider calling ahead.

🛍 Brooklyn

Beacon's Closet (Greenpoint) Thrift Store
(☎718-486-0816; www.beaconscloset.com; 74 Guernsey St, btwn Nassau & Norman Aves, Greenpoint; 🕙11am-8pm; [S]L to Bedford Ave) Twenty-something groovers find this massive 5500-sq-ft warehouse of vintage clothing part gold mine, part grit. Lots of coats, polyester tops and '90s-era T-shirts are handily displayed by color, but the sheer mass can take time to conquer. You'll also find shoes of all sorts, flannels, hats, handbags, chunky jewelry and brightly hued sunglasses.

Artists & Fleas Flea Market
(www.artistsandfleas.com; 70 N 7th Ave, btwn Wythe & Kent Aves, Williamsburg; 🕙10am-7pm Sat & Sun; [S]L to Bedford Ave) At this popular

artists', designers' and vintage flea market in Williamsburg, in operation for over a decade, you'll find an excellent selection of crafty goodness. Over 100 vendors sell their wares, which include vintage clothing, records, paintings, photographs, hats, handmade jewelry, one-of-a-kind T-shirts, canvas bags and more. There's also a smaller location (open daily) inside the Chelsea Market.

Buffalo Exchange   Clothing

(🖉718-384-6901; www.buffaloexchange.com; 504 Driggs Ave, at 9th St, Williamsburg; ⊙11am-8pm Mon-Sat, noon-7pm Sun; S L to Bedford Ave) This new and used clothing shop, featuring clothes (designer and not), shoes, jewelry and accessories, is a go-to spot for Brooklynites on a budget. It's a generally well-curated collection, though you'll still want to bank on spending some quality time here.

Spoonbill & Sugartown   Books

(🖉718 387 7322; www.spoonbillbooks.com; 218 Bedford Ave, at 5th St, Williamsburg; ⊙10am-10pm; S L to Bedford Ave) Williamsburg's favorite bookshop has an intriguing range of art and coffee-table books, cultural journals, used and rare titles, and locally made works not found elsewhere.

A&G Merch   Homewares

(🖉718-388-1779; http://aandgmerch.com; 111 N 6th St, btwn Berry & Wythe Sts, Williamsburg; ⊙11am-7pm; S L to Bedford Ave) A&G Merch is a fun shop to explore, with its mix of whimsy and elegance. Check out antique plates adorned with animal heads, rustic wicker baskets, cast-iron whale bookends, silver tree-branch-like candleholders, brassy industrial table lamps and more goods to give your nest that artfully rustic look so prominent in Brooklyn these days.

Rough Trade   Music

(🖉718-388-4111; www.roughtradenyc.com; 64 N 9th St, btwn Kent & Wythe Aves, Williamsburg; ⊙11am-11pm Mon-Sat, to 9pm Sun; S L to Bedford Ave) This sprawling, 10,000-sq-ft record store – a London import – stocks thousands of titles on vinyl and CD. It also has in-store DJs, listening stations, art exhibitions, and coffee and tea from Greenpoint purveyor Five Leaves.

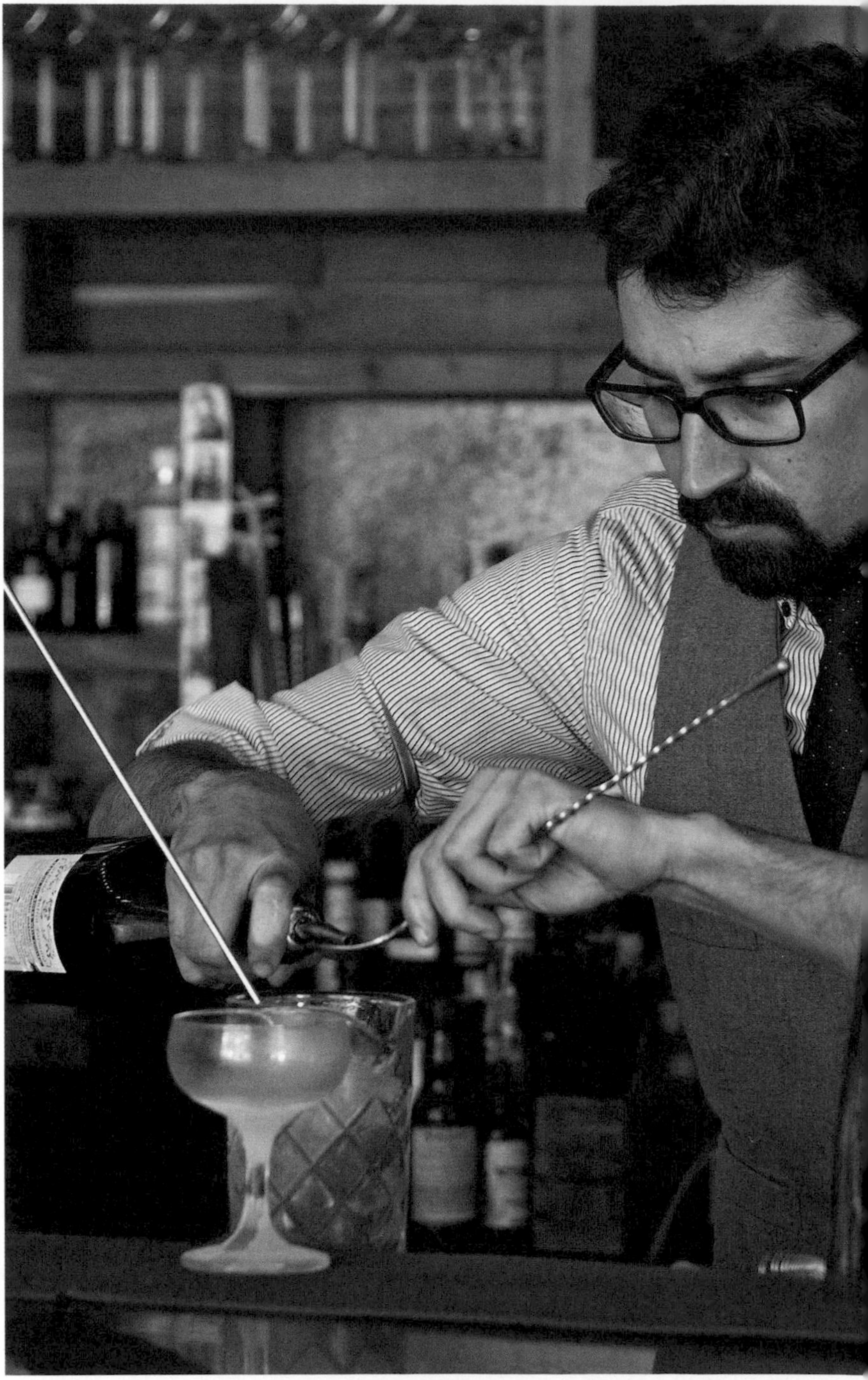

BAR OPEN

Afternoon beers, midnight cocktails and beyond

Bar Open

Considering that 'Manhattan' is thought to be a derivation of the Munsee word manahactanienk ('place of general inebriation'), it shouldn't be surprising that New York truly lives up to its nickname: 'the city that never sleeps.' You'll find all species of thirst-quenching venues here, from award-winning cocktail lounges and historic dive bars to an ever-growing number of specialty tap rooms. Then there's the city's legendary club scene, spanning everything from celebrity staples to gritty, indie hangouts.

Here in the land where the term 'cocktail' was born, mixed drinks are still stirred with the utmost gravitas. The city's craft beer culture is equally dynamic, with an ever-expanding booty of breweries, bars and shops showcasing local artisanal brews. No matter what your poison, NYC has you covered.

In This Section

Opening Hours

Opening times vary. While some dive bars open as early as 8am, most drinking establishments get rolling around 5pm. Numerous bars stay open until 4am, while others close at around 1am early in the week and at 2am from Thursday to Saturday. Clubs generally operate from 10pm to 4am or 5pm.

Harlem & Upper Manhattan
A burgeoning mix of speakeasy-style bars,
hipster hangouts and old-school dives with
soul-stirring jazz and blues (p179)

Midtown
Rooftop bars with skyline views, historic cocktail salons
and rough-n-ready dive bars (p175)

**West Village, Chelsea &
Meatpacking District**
Jet-setters flock here for wine bars,
backdoor lounges and gay hangouts (p171)

Union Square, Flatiron District & Gramercy
Vintage drinking dens, swinging cocktail bars
and a string of fun student hangouts (p172)

East Village & Lower East Side
Lower East Side is cool and edgy. East Village
is brimming with dive-bar options (p169)

**Financial District &
Lower Manhattan**
Specialist beer and brandy bars, and
revered cocktail hot spots. Crowds
pack Stone St in summer (p166)

Brooklyn
Brooklyn offers everything on the nightlife
spectrum with Williamsburg as its heart (p179)

Costs/Tipping

A draft beer costs $6 and up in most
places; a glass of wine starts around $9,
and cocktails run $12 and up.

If you grab a beer at the bar, bartenders
will expect at least a $1 tip *per drink;* tip
$2 to $3 for fancier cocktails.

Blogs/Websites

New York Magazine (www.nymag.com/night
life) Myriad nightlife options by the people
who know best.

Thrillist (www.thrillist.com) An on-the-ball
round up of what's hot or coming soon on the
NYC bar scene.

Urbandaddy (www.urbandaddy.com) Up-to-
the-minute info.

Time Out (www.timeout.com/newyork/night
life) Reviews and on-the-ball listings of where
to drink and dance.

The Best...

Drinking and Nightlife spots to sip the night away

Cocktails

Dead Rabbit (p166) Well-researched cocktails, punches and pop-inns – lightly hopped ales spiked with flavors – in a FiDi den.

Employees Only (p171) Award-winning barkeeps and arresting libations in the timeless West Village.

Lantern's Keep (p175) Classic, elegant drinks in a historic Midtown hotel.

Genuine Liquorette (p167) A Cali-style bodega in Little Italy, where innovative drinks meet playful irreverence.

Beer

Spuyten Duyvil (p180) A much-loved Williamsburg spot serving unique craft beer.

Keg No 229 (p166) A who's who of boutique American brews.

West End Hall (p178) A grand beer hall that showcases craft brews from Belgium, Germany, the US and beyond.

Classic Date Bars

Pegu Club (p167) Made-from-scratch concoctions in a Burma-inspired SoHo hideaway.

Ten Bells (p169) Candlelit beauty with great drinks and tapas in the Lower East Side.

Buvette (p171) A buzzing, candlelit wine bar on a tree-lined West Village street.

Wine Selection

La Compagnie des Vins Surnaturels (p168) A love letter to Gallic wines.

Barcibo Enoteca (p178) Go-to spot for vinophiles before or after a show at the nearby Lincoln Center.

Immigrant (p170) Wonderful wines and service in a skinny East Village setting.

Spirits

Rum House (p175) Unique, coveted rums, and a pianist to boot, in Midtown.

Mayahuel (p171) A sophisticated East Village temple to mescal and tequila.

Dead Rabbit (p166) NYC's finest collection of rare Irish whiskeys in the Financial District.

Dance Clubs & House DJs

Cielo (p172) A thumping, modern classic in the Meatpacking District.

Le Bain (p172) Well-dressed crowds still pack this favorite near the High Line.

Berlin (p171) Yesteryear's free-spirited dance days live on at this concealed East Village bolthole.

Bossa Nova Civic Club (p181) A hip little Bushwick haunt for those craving off-the-radar thrills

Dive Bars

Spring Lounge (p168) Soaks, ties and cool kids unite at this veteran Nolita rebel.

Jimmy's Corner (p177) Boxing legends grace the walls at this lowdown bar off Times Square.

★ Lonely Planet's Top Choices

Campbell Apartment (p177) Sip Kentucky Gingers in the lavish Grand Central office of a 1920s bigwig.

Little Branch (p172) Speakeasy-chic is all the craze, but no one does it quite like this West Village hideout.

Maison Premiere (p179) Absinthe, juleps and oysters shine bright at this Big Easy tribute in Williamsburg.

🍷 Financial District & Lower Manhattan

Dead Rabbit Cocktail Bar

(Map p246; ☎646-422-7906; www.deadrabbitnyc.com; 30 Water St; 🕐taproom 11am-4am; parlor 5pm-2am Mon-Wed, to 3am Thu-Sat; [S]R to Whitehall St; 1 to South Ferry) Named in honor of a dreaded Irish-American gang, this rabbit is regularly voted one of the world's best bars. During the day, hit the sawdust-sprinkled taproom for specialty beers, historic punches and pop-inns (lightly hopped ale spiked with different flavors). Come evening, scurry upstairs to the cozy Parlor for over 70 meticulously researched cocktails. Tip: head in before 5.30pm to avoid a long wait for a Parlor seat.

Keg No 229 Beer Hall

(Map p246; ☎212-566-2337; www.kegno229.com; 229 Front St, btwn Beekman St & Peck Slip; 🕐11:30am-midnight Sun-Wed, to 2am Thu-Sat; [S]A/C, J/Z, 2/3, 4/5 to Fulton St; R to Cortlandt St) If you know that a Flying Dog Raging Bitch is a craft beer – not a nickname for your ex – then this curated beer bar is for you. From Elysian Space Dust to Abita Purple Haze, its battalion of drafts, bottles and cans are a who's who of boutique American brews. Across the street, Bin No 220 is its wine-loving sibling.

Ward III Cocktail Bar

(Map p246; ☎212-240-9194; www.ward3tribeca.com; 111 Reade St, btwn Church St & W Broadway; 🕐4pm-4am Mon-Fri, 5pm-4am Sat, to 2am Sun; [S]A/C, 1/2/3 to Chambers St) Dark and bustling, Ward III channels old-school jauntiness with its elegant libations, vintage vibe (including old Singer sewing tables behind the bar) and gentlemanly house rules (No 2: 'Don't be creepy'). Reminisce over a Moroccan martini, or sample the bar's coveted collection of whiskeys. If you need to line the stomach, top-notch bar grub is served till close.

"rooftop bars with skyline views, historic cocktail salons and rough-n-ready dive bars"

Midtown and SoHo light up at night

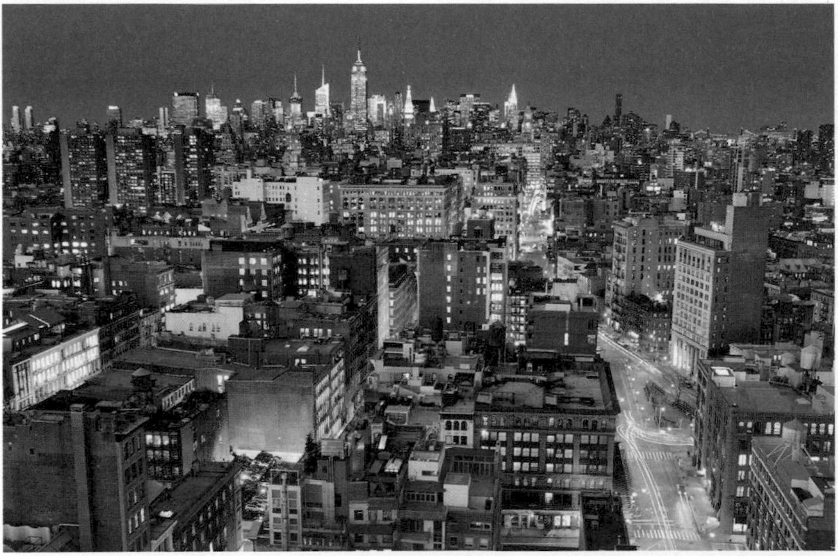

RYAN D. BUDHU / GETTY IMAGES ©

Weather Up   Cocktail Bar
(Map p246; ☎212-766-3202; www.weatherupnyc.com; 159 Duane St, btwn Hudson St & W Broadway; ⏱5pm-late Mon-Sat; Ⓢ1/2/3 to Chambers St) Softly lit subway tiles, amiable barkeeps and seductive cocktails make for a bewitching trio at Weather Up. Sweet talk the staff over a Whizz Bang (scotch whisky, dry vermouth, house-made grenadine, orange bitters and absinthe). Failing that, comfort yourself with some satisfying snacks.

Pier A Harbor House   Bar
(Map p246; ☎212-785-0153; www.piera.com; 22 Battery Pl; ⏱11am-4am; 🛜; Ⓢ4/5 to Bowling Green; R to Whitehall St; 1 to South Ferry) Looking dashing after a major restoration, Pier A is now a superspacious, casual eating and drinking house right on New York Harbor. If the weather's on your side, try for a seat on the waterside deck. Here, picnic benches, sun umbrellas and an eyeful of New York skyline make for a brilliant spot to sip craft beers or one of the house cocktails on tap.

🍷 SoHo & Chinatown

Pegu Club   Cocktail Bar
(Map p246; ☎212-473-7348; www.peguclub.com; 77 W Houston St, btwn W Broadway & Wooster St; ⏱5pm-2am Sun Thu, to 4am Fri & Sat; ⓈB/D/F/M to Broadway-Lafayette St; C/E to Spring St) Dark, elegant Pegu Club (named after a legendary gentleman's club in colonial-era Rangoon) is an obligatory stop for cocktail connoisseurs. Sink into a velvet lounge and savor seamless libations such as the silky smooth Earl Grey MarTEAni (tea-infused gin, lemon juice and raw egg white). Grazing options are suitably Asianesque, among them sloppy duck (braised duck with tropical fruit BBQ sauce on toasted mini-brioche buns).

Genuine Liquorette   Cocktail Bar
(Map p246; http://genuineliquorette.com; 191 Grand St, at Mulberry St; ⏱6pm-midnight Tue & Wed, to 2am Thu-Sat; ⓈJ/Z, N/Q/R, 6 to Canal St; B/D to Grand St) What's not to love about a jamming basement bar with Cha-Chunkers

 Cocktail Crazed

From Jillian Vose at Dead Rabbit to Eben Freeman at Genuine Liquorette, the city's top barkeeps are virtual celebrities, their deft precision creating some of the world's most sophisticated and innovative libations. Often, it's a case of history in a glass: New York's obsession with rediscovered recipes and Prohibition style continues to drive many a cocktail list. Once-obscure bartenders such as Harry Johnson and Jerry Thomas are now born-again legends, their vintage concoctions revived by a new generation of braces-clad mixologists. Historic ingredients such as crème de violette, Old Tom gin and Batavia arrack are back in vogue. In the Financial District, cocktail bar Dead Rabbit (p166) has gone one step further, reintroducing the 17th-century practice of pop-inns, drinks that fuse ale, liqueurs, spices and botanicals.

Then there are the city's revered single-spirit establishments, among them tequila- and mescal-focused Mayahuel (p171) in the East Village, whiskey-versed Ward III (p166) in Tribeca, and the self-explanatory Rum House (p175) in Midtown.

MICHAEL MARQUAND / GETTY IMAGES ©

(canned cocktails) and a Farah Fawcett–themed restroom? Hell, you're even free to grab the bottles and mixers and make your own drinks (bottles are weighed before and after you're done). At the helm is prolific mixologist Eben Freeman, who regularly

 Microbreweries

Beer brewing was once a thriving indus-try in the city – by the 1870s, Brooklyn boasted 48 breweries. Most of these were based in Williamsburg, Bushwick and Greenpoint, neighborhoods packed with German immigrants with extensive brewing know-how. By the eve of Prohi-bition in 1919, the borough was one of the country's leading beer peddlers, as famous for kids carrying growlers (beer jugs) as for its bridges. By the end of Prohibition in 1933, most breweries had shut up shop. And while the industry rose from the ashes in WWII, local flavor gave in to big-gun Midwestern brands.

Fast-forward to today, and Brooklyn is once more a catchword for a decent brewski, as a handful of craft brew-eries put integrity back on tap. While Brooklyn may no longer be the major beer exporter of yesteryear, hipster breweries such as Brooklyn Brewery (www.brooklynbrewery.com), Sixpoint (www.sixpoint.com) and KelSo (www.kelsobeer.com) have put it back on the map. Queens has seen the launch of an even greater number of micro- and nano-breweries. Standouts include Rockaway Brewing Company (www.rockawaybrewco.com), SingleCut Beersmiths (www.singlecutbeer.com) and Big Alice Brewery (www.bigalice-brewing.com). Urban explorers can also venture out to Gun Hill Brewing Co (www.gunhillbrewing.com) in the Bronx, or to Flagship Brewery (www.theflag-shipbrewery.com) in Staten Island.

invites New York's finest barkeeps to create cocktails using less-celebrated hooch.

Apothéke
Cocktail Bar

(Map p246; 212-406-0400; www.apotheke nyc.com; 9 Doyers St; 6:30pm-2am Mon-Sat, 8pm-2am Sun; J/Z to Chambers St; 4/5/6 to Brooklyn Bridge-City Hall) It takes a little effort to track down this former opium-den-turned-apothecary bar on Doyers St. Inside, skilled barkeeps work like careful chemists, using local, seasonal produce from greenmarkets to produce intense, flavorful 'prescriptions.' Toast to your health with the likes of MVO Negative, a smoky concoction of Lapsang tea–infused gin, Antica Formula, Campari and Peychauds Bitters.

La Compagnie des Vins Surnaturels
Wine Bar

(Map p246; 212-343-3660; www.compagnie nyc.com; 249 Centre St, btwn Broome & Grand Sts; 5pm-1am Mon-Wed, to 2am Thu-Sat; 6 to Spring St; N/R to Prince St) A snug mélange of Gallic-themed wallpaper, svelte arm-chairs and tea lights, La Compagnie des Vins Surnaturels is an offshoot of a Paris bar by the same name. Head sommelier Caleb Ganzer steers an impressive, French-heavy wine list, with some 600 drops and no shortage of arresting drops by the glass. A short, sophisticated menu of bites includes house-made charcuterie and (if you're lucky) buffalo chicken rillettes.

Spring Lounge
Bar

(Map p246; 212-965-1774; www.thespring lounge.com; 48 Spring St, at Mulberry St; 8am-4am Mon-Sat, from noon Sun; 6 to Spring St; N/R to Prince St) This neon-red rebel has never let anything get in the way of a good time. In Prohibition days it peddled buckets of beer. In the '60s its basement was a gambling den. These days, it's best known for its kooky stuffed sharks, early-start regulars and come-one, come-all late-night revelry.

Spring Lounge

🍷 East Village & Lower East Side

Ten Bells   Bar

(Map p246; 🕿 212-228-4450; www.tenbellsnyc.
com; 247 Broome St, btwn Ludlow & Orchard Sts;
🕙 5pm-2am Mon-Fri, from 3pm Sat & Sun; **S** F to
Delancey St; J/M/Z to Essex St) This charming-
ly tucked-away tapas bar has a grotto-like
design, with flickering candles, dark tin
ceilings, brick walls and a U-shaped bar
that's an ideal setting for a conversation
with a new friend.

The chalkboard menu hangs on both
walls and features excellent wines by the
glass, which go nicely with *boquerones*
(marinated anchovies), *txipirones en su tin-
ta* (squid in ink sauce) and regional cheeses. Come for happy hour when oysters are
$1 each, and a carafe of wine costs $15. The
unsigned entrance is easy to miss. It's right
next to the shop Top Hat.

Barrio Chino   Cocktail Bar

(Map p246; 🕿 212-228-6710; www.barriochino
nyc.com; 253 Broome St, btwn Ludlow & Orchard

Sts; 🕙 11:30am-4:30pm & 5:30pm-1am; **S** F,
J/M/Z to Delancey-Essex Sts) An eatery that
spills easily into a party scene, with an airy
Havana-meets-Beijing vibe and a focus on
fine sipping tequilas. Or stick with fresh
blood-orange or black-plum margaritas,
guacamole and chicken tacos.

Ten Degrees Bar   Wine Bar

(Map p246; 🕿 212-358-8600; www.10dogrooo
bar.com; 121 St Marks Pl, btwn First Ave & Ave
A; 🕙 noon-4am; **S** F to Second Ave; L to First
Ave; L to Third Ave) This small, candlelit St
Marks charmer – with leather couches,
friendly bartenders and an excellent wine
and cocktails list – is a great spot to start
out the night. Come from noon to 8pm for
two-for-one drink specials (otherwise, it's
$11 to $15 for cocktails), or get half-price
bottles of wine on Monday night. Go for the
couches up front or grab a tiny table in the
back nook.

Wayland   Bar

(Map p246; 🕿 212-777-7022; www.thewaylandnyc.
com; 700 E 9th St, cnr Ave C; 🕙 5pm-4am; **S** L
to 1st Ave) Whitewashed walls, weathered

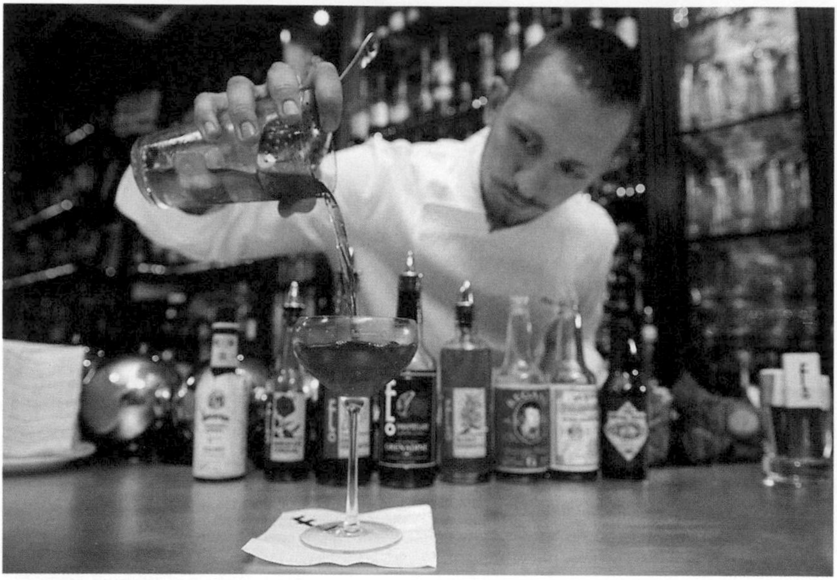

BRYAN SMITH/ZUMAPRESS /ALAMY STOCK PHOTO ©

Bartender serving a Manhattan at Employees Only (p171)

> *fizzing up crazy, addictive libations such as the Ginger Smash and the Mata Hari*

floorboards and salvaged lamps give this urban outpost a Mississippi flair, which goes well with the live music (bluegrass, jazz, folk) played on Monday to Wednesday nights. The drinks, though, are the real draw – try the 'I Hear Banjos,' made of Apple Pie Moonshine, rye whiskey and applewood smoke, which tastes like a campfire (but slightly less burning).

Angel's Share Bar

(Map p246; ☎212-777-5415; 2nd fl, 8 Stuyvesant St, near Third Ave & E 9th St; 🕒6pm-1:30am Sun-Thu, to 2:30am Fri & Sat; [S]6 to Astor Pl) Show up early and snag a seat at this hidden gem, behind a Japanese restaurant on the same floor. It's quiet and elegant with creative cocktails, but you can't stay if you don't have a table or a seat at the bar, and they tend to go fast.

Rue B Bar

(Map p246; www.ruebnyc188.com; 188 Ave B, btwn 11th & 12th Sts; 🕒noon-4am; [S]L to 1st Ave) There's live jazz (and the odd rockabilly group) every night from about 8:30pm at this tiny, amber-lit drinking den on a bar-dappled stretch of Avenue B. It draws a young, celebratory crowd, and the space is quite small, so mind the tight corners, lest the trombonist ends up in your lap.

Bar Goto Bar

(Map p246; ☎212-475-4411; http://bargoto.com; 245 Eldridge St, btwn E Houston & Stanton Sts; 🕒5pm-midnight Tue-Thu & Sun, to 2am Fri & Sat; [S]F to 2nd Ave) Maverick mixologist Kenta Goto has cocktail connoisseurs spellbound at his eponymous hot spot. Expect meticulous, elegant drinks that revel in Koto's Japanese heritage (the sake-spiked Sakura Martini is utterly smashing), paired with authentic Japanese comfort bites such as *okonomiyaki* (savory pancakes).

Immigrant Bar

(Map p246; ☎646-308-1724; 341 E 9th St, btwn First & Second Aves; 🕒5pm-1am Sun-Wed, to

2am Thu-Sat; [S]L to 1st Ave; 4/6 to Astor Pl)
Wholly unpretentious, these twin boxcar-sized bars could easily become your neighborhood local if you decide to stick around town. The staff are knowledgeable and kind, mingling with faithful regulars while dishing out tangy olives and topping up glasses with imported snifters.

Enter the right side for the wine bar, with an excellent assortment of wines by the glass. The left entrance takes you into the tap room, where the focus is on unique microbrews. Both have a similar design – chandeliers, exposed brick, vintage charm.

Berlin   Club
(Map p246; 25 Ave A, btwn 1st & 2nd Aves; 10pm-4am; [S]F to 2nd Ave) Like a secret bunker hidden beneath the ever-gentrifying streets of the East Village, Berlin is a throwback to the neighborhood's more riotous days of wildness and dancing. Once you find the unmarked entrance, head downstairs to the grotto-like space with vaulted brick ceilings, a long bar and tiny dance floor, with funk and rare grooves spilling all around.

Death + Co   Lounge
(Map p246; 212-388-0882; www.deathand company.com; 433 E 6th St, btwn First Ave & Ave A; 6pm-1am Sun-Thu, to 2am Fri & Sat; [S]F to 2nd Ave; L to 1st Ave; 6 Astor Pl) Relax amid dim lighting and thick wooden slatting and let the bartenders – with their PhDs in mixology – work their magic as they shake, rattle and roll some of the most perfectly concocted cocktails (from $15) in town.

Mayahuel   Cocktail Bar
(Map p246; 212-253-5888; www.mayahuelny. com; 304 E 6th St, at Second Ave; 6pm-2am; [S]L to 3rd Ave; L to 1st Ave; 6 Astor Pl) About as far from your typical Spring Break tequila bar as you can get, Mayahuel is more like the cellar of a monastery. Devotees of the fermented agave can seriously indulge themselves experimenting with dozens of varieties (all cocktails $15); in between drinks, snack on quesadillas and tamales.

♥ West Village, Chelsea & Meatpacking District

Employees Only   Bar
(Map p246; 212-242-3021; www.employees onlynyc.com; 510 Hudson St, near Christopher St; 6pm-4am; [S]1 to Christopher St-Sheridan Sq) Duck behind the neon 'Psychic' sign to find this hidden hangout. The bar gets busier as the night wears on. Bartenders are ace mixologists, fizzing up crazy, addictive libations such as the Ginger Smash and the Mata Hari. Great for late-night drinking and eating, courtesy of the on-site restaurant that serves till 3:30am.

Buvette   Wine Bar
(Map p246; 212-255-3590; www.ilovebuvette. com; 42 Grove St, btwn Bedford & Bleecker Sts; 9am-2am; [S]1 to Christopher St-Sheridan Sq; A/C/E, B/D/F/M to W 4th St) The rustic-chic decor here (think delicate tin tiles and a swooshing marble counter) make it the perfect place for a glass of wine – no matter the time of day. For the full experience at this self-proclaimed *gastrotèque*, grab a seat at one of the surrounding tables and nibble on small plates while enjoying the Old World wines (mostly from France and Italy).

Bell Book & Candle   Bar
(Map p246; 212-414-2355; www.bbandcnyc. com; 141 W 10th St, btwn Waverley Pl & Greenwich Ave; 5:30pm-2am Sun-Wed, to 4am Thu-Sat; [S]A/B/C, B/D/F/M to W 4th St, 1 to Christopher St-Sheridan Sq) Step down into this candlelit gastropub for strong, inventive libations (try the *canela* margarita, with cinnamon-infused tequila) and hearty pub grub. A twenty-something crowd gathers around the small, packed bar (for $1 oysters and happy hour drink specials early in the night), though there's a lot more seating hidden in the back, with big booths ideal for larger groups.

Marie's Crisis   Bar
(Map p246; 212-243-9323; 59 Grove St, btwn Seventh Ave & Bleecker St; 4pm-4am; [S]1 to Christopher St-Sheridan Sq) Ageing Broadway

queens, wide-eyed out-of-town gay boys, giggly tourists and various other fans of musical theater assemble around the piano here and take turns belting out campy show tunes, often joined by the entire crowd – and the occasional celebrity (Jimmy Fallon joined in singing 'Summer Nights' from *Grease* in 2015).

Happiest Hour   Cocktail Bar

(Map p246; ☎212-243-2827; www.happiest hournyc.com; 121 W 10th St, btwn Greenwich St & Avenue of the Americas/Sixth Ave; ⏰5pm-late Mon-Fri, from 2pm Sat & Sun; Ⓢ A/C/E, B/D/F/M to W 4th St; 1 to Christopher St-Sheridan Sq) A supercool, tiki-licious cocktail bar splashed with palm prints, '60s pop and playful mixed drinks. Below it sits serious sibling, Slowly Shirley, a subterranean temple to beautifully crafted, thoroughly researched libations.

Little Branch   Cocktail Bar

(Map p246; ☎212-929-4360; 20 Seventh Ave, at Leroy St; ⏰7pm-3am; Ⓢ 1 to Houston St) If it weren't for the doorman, you'd never guess that a charming drinking den lurked beyond the plain metal door positioned at this triangular intersection. When you get the go-ahead to enter, you'll find a basement bar that feels like a throwback to Prohibition times. Old-time jazz tunes waft overhead as locals clink glasses and sip inventive, artfully prepared cocktails.

Cielo   Club

(Map p246; ☎212-645-5700; www.cieloclub. com; 18 Little W 12th St; cover charge $15-25; ⏰10pm-5am Mon & Wed-Sat; Ⓢ A/C/E, L to 8th Ave-14th St) This long-running club boasts a largely attitude-free crowd and an excellent sound system. Join dance lovers on Deep Space Monday when DJ François K spins dub and underground beats. Other nights feature various DJs from Europe who mix entrancing, seductive sounds that pull everyone to their feet.

Le Bain   Club

(Map p246; ☎212-645-7600; www.standardcul-ture.com/lebain.com; 848 Washington St, btwn 13th & Little W 12th Sts; ⏰4pm-midnight Mon, to 4am Tue-Thu, 2pm-4am Fri-Sun; Ⓢ L to 8th Ave; 1/2/3, A/C/E to 14th St) The sweeping rooftop venue at the tragically hip Standard Hotel, Le Bain sees a garish parade of party promoters who do their thang on any day of the week. Brace yourself for skyline views, a dance floor with a giant Jacuzzi built right into it and an eclectic crowd getting wasted on pricey snifters.

When hunger strikes, you can hit up the rooftop crepe stand, which is open all night.

Frying Pan   Bar

(Map p252; ☎212-989-6363; www.fryingpan. com; Pier 66, at W 26th St; ⏰noon-midnight May-Oct; Ⓢ C/E to 23rd St) Salvaged from the bottom of the sea (or at least the Chesapeake Bay), the lightship *Frying Pan* and the two-tiered dockside bar where it's parked are fine go-to spots for a sundowner. On warm days, the rustic open-air space brings in the crowds, who come to laze on deck chairs and drink ice-cold beers ($7 for a microbrew; $25 for a pitcher).

You can also come for burgers, cooked up on the sizzling grill, or just sit back and admire the fine views across the water to, uh, New Jersey.

Bathtub Gin   Cocktail Bar

(Map p252; ☎646-559-1671; www.bathtubgin nyc.com; 132 Ninth Ave, btwn 18th & 19th Sts; ⏰6pm-1:30am Sun-Tue, to 3:30am Wed-Sat; Ⓢ A/C/E to 14th St; L to 8th Ave; A/C/E to 23rd St) Amid New York City's obsession with speakeasy-styled hangouts, Bathtub Gin manages to poke its head above the crowd with its supersecret front door hidden on the wall of an unassuming cafe (the Stone Street Coffee Company). Once inside, chilled-out seating, soft background beats and kindly staff make it a great place to sling back bespoke cocktails with friends.

🍷 Union Square, Flatiron District & Gramercy

Old Town Bar & Restaurant   Bar

(Map p252; ☎212-529-6732; www.oldtownbar. com; 45 E 18th St, btwn Broadway & Park Ave S;

🍷 The Club Scene

New Yorkers are always looking for the next big thing, so the city's club scene changes faster than a New York minute. Promoters drag revelers around the city for weekly events held at all of the finest addresses, and when there's nothing on, it's time to hit the dancefloor stalwarts.

When clubbing, it never hurts to plan ahead; having your name on a guest list can relieve unnecessary frustration and disappointment. If you're an uninitiated partier, dress the part. If you're fed the 'private party' line, try to bluff – chances are high that you've been bounced. Also, don't forget a wad of cash as many nightspots (even the swankiest ones) often refuse credit cards, and in-house ATMs scam a fortune in fees.

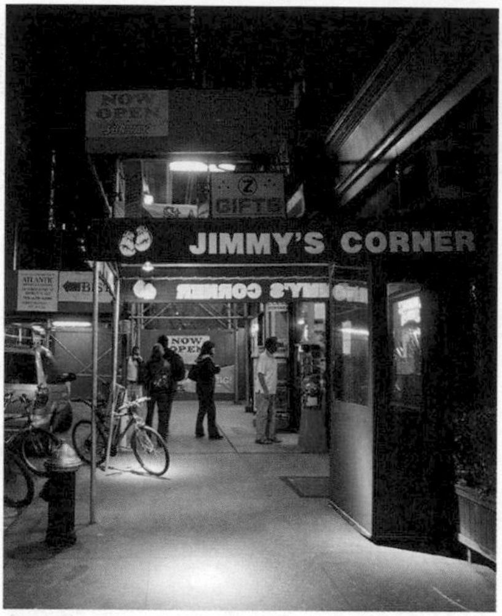

SERGI REBOREDO / ALAMY STOCK PHOTO ©

From left: Jimmy's Corner (p177); Cocktails at Ginny's Super Club (p179); Rum House

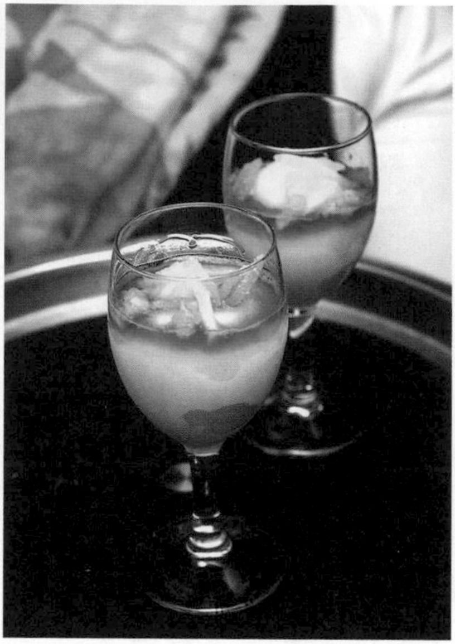

ANDREW H. WALKER / GETTY IMAGES ©

⏰11:30am-1am Mon-Fri, noon-2am Sat, 1pm-midnight Sun; [S]4/5/6, N/Q/R, L to 14th St-Union Sq) It still looks like 1892 in here, with the original tile floors and tin ceilings – the Old Town is an 'old world' drinking-man's classic (and woman's: Madonna lit up at the bar here, when lighting up was still legal, in her 'Bad Girl' video). There are cocktails around, but most come for beers and a burger (from $12.50).

Raines Law Room Cocktail Bar

(Map p252; www.raineslawroom.com; 48 W 17th St, btwn Fifth & Sixth Aves; ⏰5pm-2am Mon-Wed, to 3am Thu-Sat, 7pm-1am Sun; [S]F/M to 14th St, L to 6th Ave, 1 to 18th St) A sea of velvet drapes and overstuffed leather lounge chairs, the perfect amount of exposed brick, and expertly crafted cocktails using meticulously aged spirits – these guys are about as serious as a mortgage payment when it comes to amplified atmosphere. Reservations (recommended) are only possible Sunday to Tuesday. Whatever the night, style up for taste of a far more sumptuous era.

Pete's Tavern Bar

(Map p252; ☎212-473-7676; www.petestavern.com; 129 E 18th St, at Irving Pl; ⏰11am-2am; [S]4/5/6, N/Q/R, L to 14th St-Union Sq) Adorned with its original 19th-century mirrors, pressed-tin ceiling and rosewood bar, this dark, atmospheric watering hole has all the earmarks of a New York classic. You can get a respectable prime-rib burger here and choose from 17 draft beers. The bar draws in everyone from post-theater couples and Irish expats to no-nonsense NYU students and the odd celebrity (see photos by the restrooms).

Flatiron Lounge Cocktail Bar

(Map p252; ☎212-727-7741; www.flatironlounge.com; 37 W 19th St, btwn Fifth & Sixth Aves; ⏰4pm-2am Mon-Wed, to 3am Thu, to 4am Fri, 5pm-4am Sat, 5pm-2am Sun; 📶; [S]F/M, N/R, 6 to 23rd St) Head through a dramatic archway and into a dark, swinging, deco-inspired fantasy of lipstick-red booths, racy jazz tunes and sassy grown-ups downing seasonal drinks. The Beijing Mule (jasmine vodka, lime juice, ginger syrup and pomegranate molasses) is scrumptious,

while the genial Flight of the Day (a trio of mini-sized cocktails) is head-spinning enlightenment. Happy hour cocktails go for $10 a pop (4pm to 6pm weekdays).

🍷 Midtown

SixtyFive   Cocktail Bar
(Map p252; 📞212-632-5000; www.rainbowroom. com, 30 Rockefeller Plaza, entrance on W 49th St; ⏰5pm-midnight Mon-Fri; Ⓢ B/D/F/M to 47th-50th Sts-Rockefeller Center) Not to be missed, sophisticated SixtyFive sits on level 65 of the GE Building at Rockefeller Center. Dress well (no sportswear or guests under 21) and arrive by 5pm for a seat with a multi-million-dollar view. Even if you don't score a table on the balcony or by the window, head outside to soak up that sweeping New York panorama.

At the other end of the corridor is the revamped Rainbow Room, a legendary, elite nightclub turned swanky nosh spot serving Sunday brunch as well as dinner on select evenings (see the website).

Rum House   Cocktail Bar
(Map p252; 📞646-490-6924; www.therumhouse nyc.com; 228 W 47th St, btwn Broadway & Eighth Ave, Midtown West; ⏰1pm-4am; Ⓢ N/Q/R to 49th St) This sultry, revamped slice of old New York is revered for its cognoscenti rums and whiskeys. Savor them straight up or mixed in impeccable cocktails like a Dark & Stormy (rum, ginger beer and lime). Adding to the magic is nightly live music, spanning solo piano tunes to jaunty jazz trios and sentimental torch divas.

Lantern's Keep   Cocktail Bar
(Map p252; 📞212-453-4287; www.thelanterns keep.com; Iroquois Hotel, 49 W 44th St, btwn Fifth & Sixth Aves, ⏰5-11:30pm Mon-Fri, 7pm-12:30am Sat; Ⓢ B/D/F/M to 42nd St-Bryant Park) Can you keep a secret? If so, cross the lobby of the Iroquois Hotel and slip into this dark, intimate cocktail salon. Its specialty is classic drinks, shaken and stirred by passionate, personable mixologists. If you're feeling spicy, request a Gordon's Breakfast, a fiery melange of gin, Worcestershire sauce, hot sauce, muddled lime and cucumber, salt and pepper. Reservations are recommended.

New York City in a Glass

60ml (2fl oz) Rye whiskey

30ml (1fl oz) Sweet vermouth

maraschino cherry

orange peel

2 dashes of Angostura bitters

ice cubes

Manhattan Cocktail

How to Make a Manhattan

Place ice in a cocktail shaker.
Add the whiskey, vermouth and bitters.
Rub the orange peel around the rim of the cocktail glass.
Strain the drink into the glass.
Add a maraschino cherry and enjoy!

Story Behind the Cocktail

Complex, elegant and timeless, the Manhattan is quite simply one of the world's greatest cocktails. According to legend, it was created on 26th St and Madison Ave, at the long-gone Manhattan Club. The occasion was a party in 1874, allegedly thrown by Jennie Churchill (mother of Winston). One of the barmen decided to create a drink to mark the occasion, naming it in honor of the bar.

★ NYC's Top Five Bars

Pegu Club (p167)

Pouring Ribbons (Map p246; ☎917-656-6788; www.pouringribbons.com; 2nd fl, 225 Avenue B; ⏰6pm-2am; [S]L to 1st Ave)

Little Branch (p172)

Lantern's Keep (p175)

Flatiron Room (Map p252; ☎212-725-3860; www.theflatironroom.com; 37 W 26th St, btwn Sixth Ave & Broadway; ⏰4pm-2am Mon-Fri, 5pm-2am Sat, 5pm-midnight Sun; [S]N/R to 28th St, F/M to 23rd St)

Campbell Apartment Cocktail Bar
(Map p252; ☎212-953-0409; www.hospitalityholdings.com; Grand Central Terminal, 15 Vanderbilt Ave, at 43rd St; 🕐noon-1am Mon-Thu, to 2am Fri & Sat, to midnight Sun; [S]S, 4/5/6, 7 to Grand Central-42nd St) Party like it's 1928! This sublime, deliciously buttoned-up gem in Grand Central was once the office of a '20s railroad magnate fond of Euro eccentricities: think Florentine-style carpets, decorative wooden ceiling beams and a soaring leaded glass window. Suitably tucked away from the hordes, it is reached from the lift beside the Oyster Bar or the stairs to the West Balcony.

Jimmy's Corner Bar
(Map p252; ☎212-221-9510; 140 W 44th St, btwn Sixth & Seventh Aves, Midtown West; 🕐11am-4am Mon-Fri, from 12:30pm Sat, from 3pm Sun; [S]N/Q/R, 1/2/3, 7 to 42nd St-Times Sq; B/D/F/M to 42nd St-Bryant Park) This welcoming, completely unpretentious dive off Times Square is run by an old boxing trainer – as if you wouldn't guess by all the framed photos of boxing greats (and lesser-known fighters, too). The jukebox covers Stax to Miles Davis, kept low enough for postwork gangs to chat away.

Waylon Bar
(Map p252; ☎212-265-0010; www.thewaylon.com; 736 Tenth Ave, at 50th St, Midtown West; 🕐2pm-4am Mon-Fri, from noon Sat & Sun; [S]C/E to 50th St) Slip on your spurs, partner, there's a honky-tonk in Hell's! Celebrate Dixie at this saloon-style watering hole, where the jukebox keeps good folk dancing to Tim McGraw's broken heart, where the barkeeps pour American whiskeys and tequila, and where the bar bites include Texan-style Frito pie and country-fried steak sandwiches. For live country-and-western sounds, head in on Thursdays between 8pm and 11pm.

Industry Gay
(Map p252; ☎646-476-2747; www.industry-bar.com; 355 W 52nd St, btwn Eighth & Ninth Aves, Midtown West; 🕐4pm-4am; [S]C/E, 1 to 50th St) What was once a parking garage is now one of the hottest gay bars in Hell's Kitchen – a slick 4000-sq-ft watering hole with handsome lounge areas, a pool table and a stage for top-notch drag divas. Head in between 4pm and 9pm for the two-for-one drinks special or squeeze in later to party with the eye-candy party hordes. Cash only.

🍷 Upper East Side

The Daisy Bar
(Map p250; ☎646-964-5756; 1641 Second Ave, at 85th St; 🕐4pm-1am Sun-Wed, to 2am Thu-Sat; [S]4/5/6 to 86th St) Billing itself as an 'agave gastropub,' the Daisy serves up mescal cocktails and creative Latin-inspired drinks (Michelada) and dishes (rice with duck) alongside bistro fare like duck-fat fries and grilled octopus. Unlike most other UES bars, there are no TVs or bros here – it's a laid-back, low-lit spot, with good grooves, skilled bartenders and a friendly crowd.

The Penrose Bar
(Map p250; ☎212-203-2751; www.penrosebar.com; 1590 Second Ave, btwn 82nd & 83rd Sts; 🕐noon-4am Mon-Fri, 10am-4am Sat & Sun; [S]4/5/6 to 86th St) The Penrose brings a dose of style to the Upper East Side, with craft beers, exposed brick walls, vintage mirrors, floral wallpaper, reclaimed wood details and friendly bartenders setting the stage for a fine evening outing among friends.

Drunken Munkey Lounge
(Map p250; ☎646-998-4600; www.drunkenmunkeynyc.com; 338 E 92nd St, btwn First & Second Aves; 🕐11am-2am Mon-Thu, to 3am Fri-Sun; [S]6 to 96th St) This playful lounge channels colonial-era Bombay with vintage wallpaper, cricket-ball door handles and jauntily attired waitstaff. The monkey chandeliers may be pure whimsy, but the craft cocktails and tasty curries (small, meant for sharing) are serious business. Gin, not surprisingly, is the drink of choice. Try the Bramble (Bombay gin, blackberry liqueur and fresh lemon juice and blackberries).

From left: White wine; Radegast Hall & Biergarten (p180); Spuyten Duyvil (p180)

🍷 Upper West Side & Central Park

Barcibo Enoteca   Wine Bar

(Map p250; ☎212-595-2805; www.barciboenote-ca.com; 2020 Broadway, cnr 69th St; ⏰4:30-11:30pm Tue-Fri, from 3:30pm Sat-Mon; 🚇1/2/3 to 72nd St) Just north of Lincoln Center, this casual chic marble-table spot is ideal for sipping, with a long list of vintages from all over Italy, including 40 different varieties sold by the glass. There is a short menu of small plates and light meals. The staff is knowledgeable; ask for recommendations.

Manhattan Cricket Club   Cocktail Lounge

(Map p250; ☎646-823-9252; www.mccnewyork.com; 226 W 79th St, btwn Amsterdam Ave & Broadway; ⏰6pm-2am; 🚇1 to 79th St) Above Burke & Wills Australian bistro, this elegant drinking lounge is modeled on the classy Anglo-Aussie cricket clubs of the early 1900s. Sepia-toned photos of batsmen adorn the gold brocaded walls, while mahogany bookshelves and Chesterfield sofas create a fine setting for quaffing well-made,

but pricey, cocktails. It's a guaranteed date pleaser.

West End Hall   Beer Garden

(Map p250; ☎212-662-7200; www.westendhall.com; 2756 Broadway, btwn 105th & 106th Sts; ⏰4pm-1am Mon-Fri, from 11am Sat & Sun; 🚇1 to 103rd St) Beer drinkers of the UWS have much to celebrate with the arrival of this grand beer hall that showcases craft brews from around Belgium, Germany, the US and beyond. There are around 20 draft beers on rotation along with another 30 bottle choices, most of which go nicely with the meaty menu of sausages, schnitzel, pork sliders and an excellent truffle burger.

Dead Poet   Bar

(Map p250; ☎212-595-5670; www.thedeadpoet.com; 450 Amsterdam Ave, btwn 81st & 82nd Sts; ⏰noon-4am; 🚇1 to 79th St) This skinny, mahogany-paneled pub has been a neighborhood favorite for over a decade, with a mix of locals and students nursing pints of Guinness. There are cocktails named after dead poets, including a Walt Whitman Long Island iced tea ($11) and a Pablo Neruda spiced rum sangria ($9). Funny, because

we always pegged Neruda as a pisco sour kind of guy.

🍷 Harlem & Upper Manhattan

Paris Blues   Bar

(📞212-222-9878; www.parisbluesharlem.com; 2021 Adam Clayton Powell Jr Blvd, at 121st St, Harlem; 🕐noon-3am; 🚇A/C, B to 116th St, 2/3 to 125th St) This down-home dive is named after the 1961 Sidney Poitier and Paul Newman flick about two expats living and loving in Paris. It's a little worn in places and the booze selection is limited, but it makes up for it with buckets of charm, generous pours and nightly jazz gigs from around 9pm.

Ginny's Supper Club   Cocktail Bar

(📞212-421-3821, brunch reservations 212-792-9001; www.ginnyssupperclub.com; 310 Malcolm X Blvd, btwn 125th & 126th Sts, Harlem; 🕐6pm-11pm Thu, to 3am Fri & Sat, 10:30am-2pm Sun; 🚇2/3 to 125th St) Looking straight out of *Boardwalk Empire,* this roaring basement supper club is rarely short of styled-up

punters sipping cocktails, nibbling on soul and global bites (from the Red Rooster kitchen upstairs) and grooving to live jazz from 7:30pm Thursday to Saturday and DJ-spun beats from 11pm Friday and Saturday. For a spirited start to your Sunday, don't miss the weekly Sunday gospel brunch (reservations recommended).

🍺 Brooklyn

Maison Premiere   Cocktail Bar

(📞347-335-0446; www.maisonpremiere.com; 298 Bedford Ave, btwn S 1st & Grand Sts, Williamsburg; 🕐4pm-2am Mon-Fri, from 11am Sat & Sun; 🚇L to Bedford Ave) We kept expecting to see Dorothy Parker stagger into this old-timey place, which features an elegant bar full of syrups and essences, suspendered bartenders and a jazzy soundtrack to further channel the French Quarter New Orleans vibe. The cocktails are serious business: the epic list includes more than a dozen absinthe drinks, various juleps and an array of specialty cocktails.

Wily Tom Collins

One New York classic was born in the 1870s – the summer-centric Tom Collins. A mix of dry gin, sugar, lemon juice and club soda, the long drink's name stems from an elaborate hoax in which hundreds of locals were informed that a certain Tom Collins had been sullying their good names. While many set out to track him down, clued-in bartenders relished the joke by making the drink and naming it for the fictitious troublemaker. When the aggrieved stormed into the bars looking for a Tom Collins, they were served the drink to cool their tempers.

IVAN MATEEV / SHUTTERSTOCK ©

A raw bar doles out delicious oysters, while there's more serious dining (and an outdoor patio) behind the bar.

Hotel Delmano   Cocktail Bar
(☎718-387-1945; www.hoteldelmano.com; 82 Berry St, at N 9th St, Williamsburg; ⏰5pm-2am Mon-Fri, from 2pm Sat & Sun; Ⓢ L to Bedford Ave) This low-lit cocktail bar aims for a speakeasy vibe, with old smoky mirrors, unpolished floorboards and vintage chandeliers. Nestle into one of the nooks in back or have a seat at the curving marble-topped bar and watch moustached barkeeps whip up a changing array of inventive cocktails (rye, gin and mescal are favored spirits).

It also offers charcuterie, cheese boards and a raw bar (oysters, littleneck clams, shrimp cocktail). Enter on N 9th St.

Spuyten Duyvil   Bar
(☎718-963-4140; www.spuytenduyvilnyc. com; 359 Metropolitan Ave, btwn Havemayer & Roebling, Williamsburg; ⏰5pm-late Mon-Fri, from noon Sat & Sun; Ⓢ L to Lorimer St; G to Metropolitan Ave) This low-key Williamsburg bar looks like it was pieced together from a rummage sale. The ceilings are painted red, there are vintage maps on the walls and the furniture consists of tattered armchairs. But the beer selection is staggering, the locals from various eras are chatty and there's a decent-sized patio with leafy trees that is open in good weather.

There's also a fine jukebox.

Skinny Dennis   Bar
(www.skinnydennisbar.com; 152 Metropolitan Ave, btwn Wythe Ave & Berry St, Williamsburg; ⏰noon-4am; Ⓢ L to Bedford Ave) No need to fly to Austin. You can get your honky-tonk right here in Billyburg at this roadhouse saloon on bustling Metropolitan Ave. Aside from Kinky Friedman posters, a reverential painting of Willie Nelson, peanut shells on the floor and a Patsy Cline–heavy jukebox in the corner, you'll find country crooners playing nightly to a garrulous beer-swilling crowd.

Radegast Hall &
Biergarten   Beer Hall
(☎718-963-3973; www.radegasthall.com; 113 N 3rd St, at Berry St, Williamsburg; ⏰noon-2am Mon-Fri, from 11am Sat & Sun; Ⓢ L to Bedford Ave) This Austro-Hungarian beer hall in Williamsburg offers up a huge selection of Bavarian brews as well as a kitchen full of munchable meats. You can hover in the dark, woody bar area or sit in the adjacent hall, which has a retractable roof and communal tables to feast at – perfect for pretzels, sausages and burgers.

OTB   Bar
(www.otbbk.com; 141 Broadway, btwn Bedford & Driggs Aves, Williamsburg; ⏰5pm-2am Mon-Fri, from 2pm Sat & Sun; Ⓢ J/M to Marcy Ave) OTB, which stands for 'off-track betting,' pays homage to those gamble-worthy thoroughbreds with horse-themed decor (betting-

form menus, black-and-white photos of shapely ponies and horse wallpaper in the bathrooms) – though low-lit chandeliers, flickering candles and dark-wood furniture somehow create a classy rather than kitschy vibe.

61 Local   Bar
(718-875-1150; www.61local.com; 61 Bergen St, btwn Smith St & Boerum Pl, Cobble Hill; 7am-midnight Mon-Fri, from 9am Sat & Sun; ; F, G to Bergen) A roomy brick-and-wood hall in Cobble Hill manages to be both chic and warm, with large communal tables, a mellow vibe and a good selection of craft beers (including KelSo, Ommegang and Allagash). There's a simple menu of charcuterie, cheese boards and other snacks, including pulled pork tacos, quiche and Mediterranean platters (hummus, labne, olives).

Royal Palms   Bar
(www.royalpalmsshuffle.com; 514 Union St, btwn 3rd Ave & Nevins St, Gowanus; 6pm-midnight Mon-Thu, to 2am Fri, noon-2am Sat, noon-10pm Sun; R to Union St) If you're hankering for a bit of sport, but don't want to drift too far from the bar stool, the Royal Palms should figure high on your itinerary. Inside this 17,000-sq-ft space, you'll find 10 full shuffleboard courts, plus board games (massive Jenga, oversize Connect Four), draft brews, cocktails and filling snacks provided by a food truck (with a different rotation each week).

The ambience veers toward subtropical Floridian, though it's hipsters rather than old-timers finessing those discs across the shiny courts. It's strictly age 21 and up.

Pine Box Rock Shop   Bar
(718-366-6311; www.pineboxrockshop.com; 12 Grattan St, btwn Morgan Ave & Bogart St, Bushwick; 4pm-4am Mon-Fri, from 2pm Sat & Sun; L to Morgan Ave) The cavernous Pine

Box is a former Bushwick casket factory that has 16 drafts to choose from, as well as spicy, pint-sized Bloody Marys. Run by a friendly musician couple, the walls are filled with local artwork, and a performance space in the back hosts regular gigs.

Rookery   Bar
(www.therookerybar.com; 425 Troutman St, btwn St Nicholas & Wyckoff Aves, Bushwick; noon-4am; L to Jefferson St) Every week Rookery brings a new crop of farm-to-table restaurants and creative drinking dens. A mainstay of the Bushwick scene is the industrialesque Rookery, with outdoor seating on mural-lined Troutman Ave. Come for cocktails, craft brews, reconfigured pub fare (curried goat shepherds pie, oxtail sloppy joe), obscure electro-pop and a relaxed vibe.

Der Schwarze Köelner   Pub
(347-841-4495; http://dsk-brooklyn.com; 710 Fulton St, cnr Hanson Pl, Fort Greene; 3pm-1am Mon-Fri, from 2pm Sat & Sun; C to Lafayette Ave; G to Fulton St) This casual beer garden with checkered floors, lots of windows and a lively, mixed crowd is located just a few blocks away from the Brooklyn Academy of Music. There are 18 beers on tap, all of which go swimmingly with a hot *brezel* (soft German pretzel).

Bossa Nova Civic Club   Club
(www.bossanovacivicclub.com; 1271 Myrtle Ave, btwn Evergreen & Central Aves, Bushwick; 7pm-4am; M to Central Ave) Yet another reason why you never need to leave Brooklyn, this smallish hole-in-the-wall club is a great place to get your groove on, with DJs spinning a wide mix of sounds in a somewhat tropical-themed interior. Great sound system, fairly priced drinks (at least as far as clubs are concerned) and snacks on hand when hunger strikes (empanadas, slow-cooked pork, arepas).

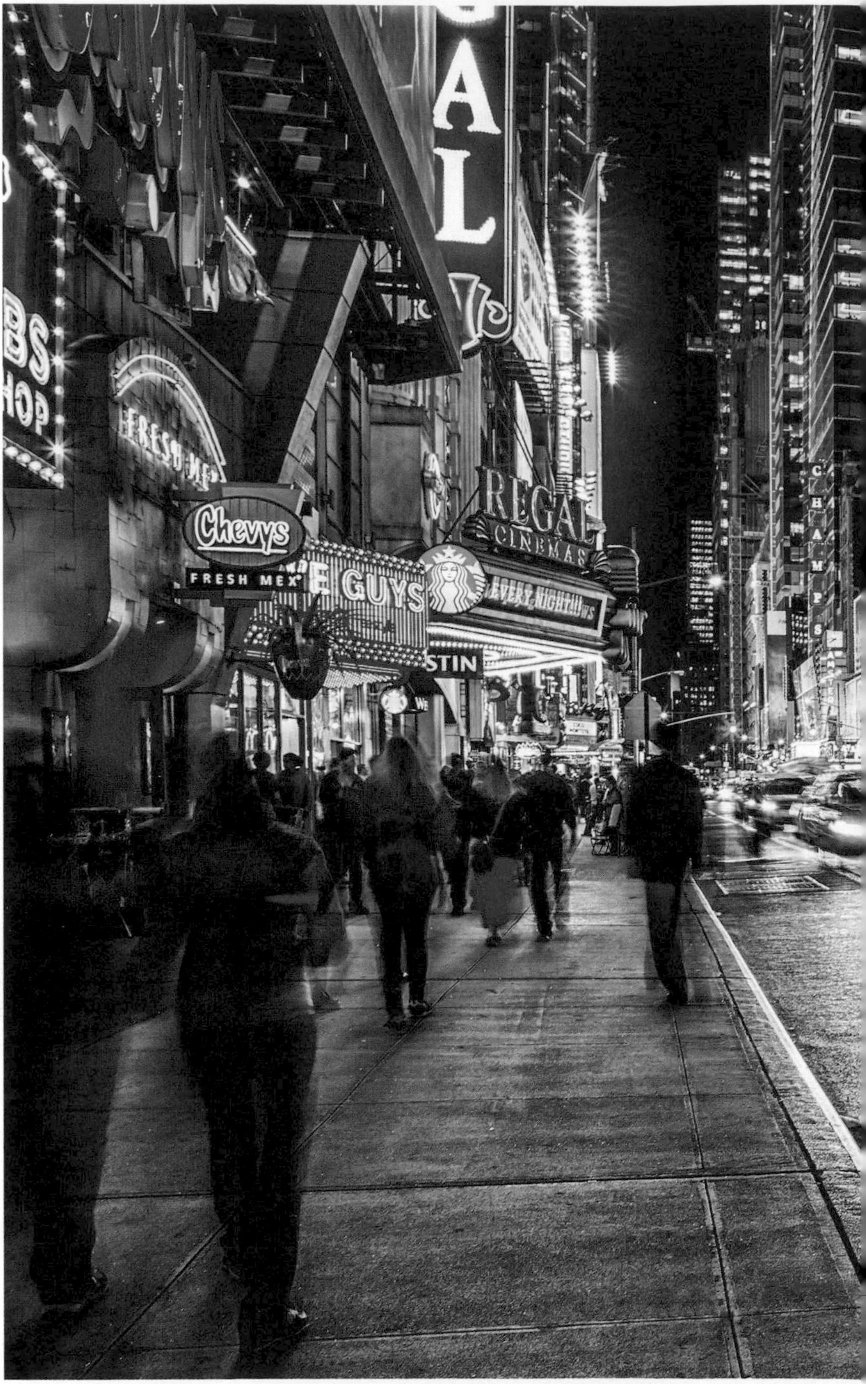

MBBIRDY / GETTY IMAGES ©

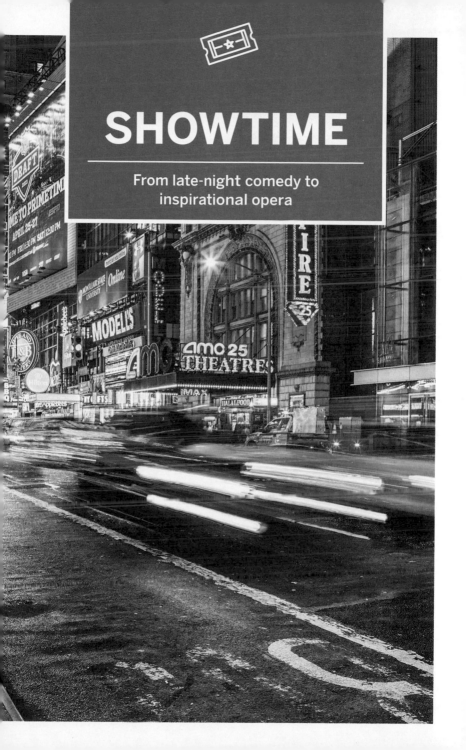

SHOWTIME

From late-night comedy to
inspirational opera

Showtime

Dramatically lit stages, basement jazz joints, high-ceilinged dance halls, and opera houses set for melodramatic tales – for more than a century, New York City has been America's capital of cultural production. And while gentrification has pushed many artists out to the city's fringes and beyond, New York nonetheless remains a nerve center for music, theater and dance.

When it comes to entertainment, the city is perhaps best known for its Broadway musicals. These are presented in any one of 40 official Broadway theaters – lavish early 20th-century jewels that surround Times Square – and are a major component of cultural life in New York. Beyond Broadway, you'll find experimental downtown playhouses, the hallowed concert halls of the Met, and live music joints scattered in all corners of the city. The biggest challenge is deciding where to begin.

In This Section

Tickets

To purchase tickets for shows, you can either head directly to the venue's box office, or use a ticket agency such as Telecharge (www.telecharge.com) or Ticketmaster (www.ticketmaster.com).

For cut-price same-day Broadway tickets, visit a TKTS Booth (www.tdf.org). And for non-Broadway entertainment (comedy, cabaret, performance art, music, dance and downtown theater), check out SmartTix (www.smarttix.com).

Times Square (p62)

The Best...

Broadway Shows

Book of Mormon (p190) Award-winning show by the creators of *South Park*.

Chicago (p191) One of the most scintillating shows on Broadway.

Kinky Boots (p190) Book well ahead to score seats for this over-the-top musical.

An American in Paris (p191) Exuberant choreography and a romantic Parisian setting.

Live Music

Jazz at Lincoln Center (p192) Innovative fare under the guidance of jazz luminary Wynton Marsalis.

Village Vanguard (p187) Legendary West Village jazz club.

Smalls (p188) Tiny West Village basement joint that evokes the feel of decades past.

Barbès (p194) Obscure but celebratory global rhythms in Park Slope.

Birdland (p192) Sleek Midtown space that hosts big-band sounds, Afro-Cuban jazz and more.

Minton's (p193) Swanky crowds, bewitching brass and a Sunday jazz brunch in Harlem.

☆ Financial District & Lower Manhattan

Flea Theater — Theater
(Map p246; ☎ tickets 212-352-3101; www.theflea. org; 41 White St, btwn Church St & Broadway; Ⓢ 1 to Franklin St; A/C/E, N/Q/R, J/Z, 6 to Canal St) One of NYC's top off-off-Broadway companies, Flea is famous for performing innovative, timely new works in its two performance spaces. Luminaries, including Sigourney Weaver and John Lithgow, have trodden the boards here, and the year-round program also includes music and dance performances.

☆ SoHo & Chinatown

Joe's Pub — Live Music
(Map p246; ☎ 212-539-8500, tickets 212-967-7555; www.joespub.com; Public Theater, 425 Lafayette St, btwn Astor Pl & 4th St; Ⓢ 6 to Astor Pl; R/W to 8th St-NYU) Part bar, part cabaret and performance venue, intimate Joe's serves up both emerging acts and top-shelf

performers. Performers have included caustic comic Sandra Bernhard and British songstress Adele. In fact, it was right here that Adele gave her very first American performance back in 2008.

Film Forum — Cinema
(Map p246; ☎ 212-727-8110; www.filmforum.com; 209 W Houston St, btwn Varick St & Sixth Ave; Ⓢ 1 to Houston St) This three-screen cinema screens an astounding array of independent films, revivals and career retrospectives from greats such as Sidney Lumet. Theaters are small, as are the screens, so get there early for a good viewing spot. Showings are often combined with director talks or other film-themed discussions.

☆ East Village & Lower East Side

La MaMa ETC — Theater
(Map p246; ☎ 646-430-5374; www.lamama. org; 74A E 4th St; admission $25; Ⓢ F to Second Ave) A long-standing home for onstage experimentation (the ETC stands for

From left: Rockwood Music Hall; Village Vanguard; Blue Note

Experimental Theater Club), La MaMa is now a three-theater complex with a cafe, an art gallery and a separate studio building that features cutting-edge dramas, sketch comedy and readings of all kinds. Ten $10 tickets are available for each show. Book early to score a deal!

New York Theatre Workshop Theater

(Map p246; ☎212-460-5475; www.nytw.org; 79 E 4th St, btwn Second & Third Aves; [S]F to 2nd Ave) Recently celebrating its 25th year, this innovative production house is a treasure to those seeking cutting-edge plays with purpose. It was the originator of two big Broadway hits, *Rent* and *Urinetown*, and offers a constant supply of high-quality drama.

Rockwood Music Hall Live Music

(Map p246; ☎212-477-4155; www.rockwoodmusichall.com; 196 Allen St, btwn Houston & Stanton Sts; 🕒6pm-2am Mon-Fri, from 3pm Sat & Sun; [S]F/V to Lower East Side-Second Ave) Opened by indie rocker Ken Rockwood, this bread-box-sized concert space has three stages that see a rapid-fire flow of bands and singer-songwriters. If cash and time are limited, head to stage 1, which has free shows, with a maximum of one hour per band (die-hards can see five or more performances a night). Music kicks off at 3pm on weekends and 6pm on weeknights.

☆ West Village, Chelsea & Meatpacking District

Village Vanguard Jazz

(Map p246; ☎212-255-4037; www.villagevanguard.com; 178 Seventh Ave, at 11th St; cover around $33; 🕒7:30pm-12:30am; [S]1/2/3 to 14th St) Possibly the city's most prestigious jazz club, the Vanguard has hosted literally every major star of the past 50 years. It started as a home to spoken-word performances and occasionally returns to its roots, but most of the time it's just big, bold jazz all night long.

Blue Note Jazz

(Map p246; ☎212-475-8592; www.bluenote.net; 131 W 3rd St, btwn Sixth Ave & MacDougal St; [S]A/C/E, B/D/F/M to W 4th St-Washington Sq)

PIO3 / SHUTTERSTOCK ©

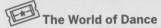

The World of Dance

For nearly 100 years, New York City has been at the center of American dance. It is here that the American Ballet Theatre (ABT; www.abt.org) – led by the fabled George Balanchine – was founded in 1949. The company promoted the idea of cultivating American talent, hiring native-born dancers and putting on works by choreographers such as Jerome Robbins, Twyla Tharp and Alvin Ailey. The company continues to perform in New York and around the world.

But NYC is perhaps best known for nurturing a generation of modern-dance choreographers – figures such as Martha Graham, who challenged traditional notions of dance with boxy, industrial movements on bare, almost abstract sets. The boundaries were pushed ever further by Merce Cunningham, who disassociated dance from music. Today, companies such as Streb (www.streb.org) are pushing dance to its limits. Lincoln Center (p76) and Brooklyn Academy of Music (p193) host regular performances, while up-and-coming acts feature at spaces including Chelsea's Kitchen (p189), Joyce Theater and New York Live Arts (www.newyorklivearts.org), as well as Midtown's Baryshnikov Arts Center (www.bacnyc.org).

This is by far the most famous (and expensive) of the city's jazz clubs. Most shows are $30 at the bar or $45 at a table, but can rise for the biggest jazz stars. There are also a few cheaper $20 shows, as well as jazz brunch on Sundays at 11:30am. Go on an off night, and be quiet – all attention is on the stage!

Smalls Jazz

(Map p246; ☎212-252-5091; www.smallslive.com; 183 W 10th St; cover from 7:30pm-12:30am $20, after 12:30am $10; 🕐7:30pm-4am Mon-Thu, from 4pm Fri-Sun; [S]1 to Christopher St-Sheridan Sq) Living up to its name, this cramped but appealing basement jazz den offers a grab-bag collection of jazz acts who take the stage nightly. Cover for the evening is $20, with a come-and-go policy if you need to duck out for a bite.

Joyce Theater Dance

(Map p252; ☎212-691-9740; www.joyce.org; 175 Eighth Ave; [S]C/E to 23rd St; A/C/E to Eighth Ave-14th St; 1 to 18th St) A favorite among dance junkies thanks to its excellent sight lines and offbeat offerings, this is an intimate venue, seating 472 in a renovated cinema. Its focus is on modern companies such as Pilobolus, Stephen Petronio Company and Parsons Dance as well as global stars, such as Dance Brazil, Ballet Hispanico and MalPaso Dance Company.

Sleep No More Theater

(Map p252; www.sleepnomorenyc.com; McKittrick Hotel, 530 W 27th St; tickets from $91; 🕐7pm-midnight Mon-Sat; [S]C/E to 23rd St) One of the most immersive theater experiences ever conceived, *Sleep No More* is a loosely based retelling of *Macbeth* set inside a series of Chelsea warehouses that have been redesigned to look like an abandoned hotel.

It's a choose-your-own adventure kind of experience where audience members are free to wander the elaborate rooms (ballroom, graveyard, taxidermy shop, lunatic asylum) and interact with the actors, who perform a variety of scenes that border on the bizarre to the risqué. Be prepared: you must check in everything when you arrive (jackets, handbag, cell phone), and you will wear a mask, à la *Eyes Wide Shut*.

Comedy Cellar lies beneath sidewalk cafes

Upright Citizens Brigade Theatre Comedy

(Map p252; ☎212-366-9176; www.ucbtheatre.com; 307 W 26th St, btwn Eighth & Ninth Aves; admission free-$10; 🕒7pm-midnight; [S]C/E to 23rd St) Pros of comedy sketches and outrageous improvisations reign at this popular 74-seat venue, which gets drop-ins from casting directors. Getting in is cheap, and so is the beer and wine. You may recognize pranksters on stage from late-night comedy shows. It's free on Sundays after 9:30pm and on Mondays after 11pm, featuring up-and-coming comics. You'll find quality shows happening nightly, from about 7:30pm, though the Sunday-night Asssscat Improv session is always a riot.

Kitchen Theater, Dance

(Map p252; ☎212-255-5793; www.thekitchen.org; 512 W 19th St, btwn Tenth & Eleventh Aves; [S]A/C/E to 14th St; L to 8th Ave) A loftlike experimental space in west Chelsea that also produces edgy theater, readings and music performances, Kitchen is where you'll find new, progressive pieces and works-in-progress from local movers and shakers.

Le Poisson Rouge Live Music

(Map p246; ☎212-505-3474; www.lepoissonrouge.com; 158 Bleecker St; [S]A/C/E, B/D/F/M to W 4th St-Washington Sq) This high-concept art space hosts a highly eclectic lineup of live music, with the likes of Deerhunter, Marc Ribot and Cibo Matto performing in past years. There's a lot of experimentation and cross-genre pollination between classical, folk music, opera and more.

Comedy Cellar Comedy

(Map p246; ☎212-254-3480; www.comedycellar.com; 117 MacDougal St, btwn W 3rd & Minetta Lane; cover $12-24; [S]A/C/E, B/D/F/M to W 4th St-Washington Sq) This long-established comedy club in Greenwich Village features mainstream material and a good list of regulars (Colin Quinn, *Saturday Night Live's* Darrell Hammond, Wanda Sykes), plus an occasional high-profile drop-in like Dave Chappelle. Its success continues: Comedy Cellar now boasts another location around the corner on W 3rd St.

Duplex Cabaret
(Map p246; ☎212-255-5438; www.theduplex.com; 61 Christopher St; cover $5-15; 🕓4pm-4am; [S]1 to Christopher St-Sheridan Sq) Cabaret, karaoke and campy dance moves are par for the course at the legendary Duplex. Pictures of Joan Rivers line the walls, and the performers like to mimic her sassy form of self-deprecation, while getting in a few jokes about audience members as well. It's a fun and unpretentious place, and certainly not for the bashful.

At the downstairs piano bar (from 9pm onwards), you can sing a tune, or simply watch some extremely talented regulars (including Broadway performers) and staff belt out the hits. There's a two-drink minimum.

IFC Center Cinema
(Map p246; ☎212-924-7771; www.ifccenter.com; 323 Sixth Ave, at 3rd St; tickets $14; [S]A/C/E, B/D/F/M to W 4th St-Washington Sq) This art-house cinema in NYU-land has a solidly curated lineup of new indies, cult classics and foreign films. Catch shorts, documentaries, '80s revivals, director-focused series, weekend classics and frequent special series, such as cult favorites (*The Shining*, *Taxi Driver*, *Aliens*) at midnight.

☆ Midtown

Book of Mormon Show
(Eugene O'Neill Theatre; Map p252; ☎tickets 212-239-6200; www.bookofmormonbroadway.com; 230 W 49th St, btwn Broadway & Eighth Ave, Midtown West; [S]N/Q/R to 49th St; 1 to 50th St; C/E to 50th St) Subversive, obscene and ridiculously hilarious, this cutting musical satire is the work of *South Park* creators Trey Parker and Matt Stone and *Avenue Q* composer Robert Lopez. Winner of nine Tony Awards, it tells the story of two naive Mormons on a mission to 'save' a Ugandan village.

Kinky Boots Show
(Hirschfeld Theatre; Map p252; ☎tickets 212-239-6200; www.kinkybootsthemusical.com; 302 W 45th St, btwn Eighth & Ninth Aves, Midtown West; [S]A/C/E to 42nd St-Port Authority Bus Terminal) Adapted from a 2005 British indie

Kinky Boots

AF ARCHIVE / ALAMY STOCK PHOTO ©

film, Harvey Fierstein and Cyndi Lauper's smash hit tells the story of a doomed English shoe factory unexpectedly saved by Lola, a business-savvy drag queen. Its solid characters and energy have not been lost on critics, the musical winning six Tony Awards, including Best Musical in 2013.

Hamilton Show
(Richard Rodgers Theatre; Map p252; tickets 877-250-2929; www.hamiltonbroadway.com; 226 W 46th St, btwn Seventh & Eighth Aves, Midtown West; S N/Q/R to 49th St) Lin-Manuel Miranda's acclaimed new musical is Broadway's hottest ticket, using contemporary hip-hop beats to recount the story of America's founding father, Alexander Hamilton. Inspired by Ron Chernow's biography *Alexander Hamilton*, the musical has won a swath of awards, including Outstanding Musical at the Drama Desk Awards and Best Musical at the New York Drama Critics' Circle Awards.

An American in Paris Show
(Palace Theatre; Map p252; 212-730-8200, tickets 877-250-2929; www.anamericaninparis broadway.com; 1564 Broadway, at 47th St, Midtown West; S N/Q/R to 49th St) Adapted from the 1951 film starring Gene Kelly, this elegant, critically acclaimed stage musical tells the story of an American ex-GI in post-WWII Paris, following his artistic dreams and falling head over heels for an alluring dancer. Packed with toe-tapping Gershwin tunes (including rarer numbers), it's directed by renowned English choreographer Christopher Wheeldon.

Chicago Show
(Ambassador Theater; Map p252; tickets 212-239-6200; www.chicagothemusical.com; 219 W 49th St, btwn Broadway & Eighth Ave, Midtown West; S N/Q/R to 49th St; 1, C/E to 50th St) A little easier to score tickets to than some of the newer Broadway musicals, this beloved Bob Fosse/Kander & Ebb classic tells the story of showgirl Velma Kelly, wannabe Roxie Hart, lawyer Billy Flynn and the fabulously sordid goings-on of the Chicago underworld. Revived by director

Performing Arts

The classics are alive and well at Lincoln Center (p77). Here, the Metropolitan Opera (p192) delivers a wide array of celebrated operas, from Verdi's *Aida* to Mozart's *Don Giovanni*. The New York Philharmonic (p193), the symphony that was once directed by Leonard Bernstein, one of the 20th century's great maestros, is also based here. Carnegie Hall (p192), the Merkin Concert Hall (www.kaufman-center.org/mch) and the **Frick Collection** (Map p250; 212-288-0700; www.frick.org; 1 E 70th St, at Fifth Ave; admission $40; S 6 to 68th St-Hunter College) also offer wonderful – and more intimate – spaces to enjoy great classical music.

For more avant-garde fare, try the Center for Contemporary Opera (www.centerforcontemporaryopera.org) and the Brooklyn Academy of Music (p193) – the latter is one of the city's vital opera and classical-music hubs. Another excellent venue, featuring highly experimental work, is St Ann's Warehouse (p195) in Brooklyn. If you like your performance outré, keep an eye on its calendar.

New York Philharmonic (p193)
HIROYUKI ITO / GETTY IMAGES ©

Walter Bobbie, its sassy, infectious energy more than makes up for the theater's tight-squeeze seating.

Jazz at Lincoln Center Jazz
(Map p250; tickets to Dizzy's Club Coca-Cola 212-258-9595, tickets to Rose Theater & Appel

 Musical Metropolis

This is the city where jazz players such as Ornette Coleman, Miles Davis and John Coltrane pushed the limits of improvisation in the '50s. It's where various Latin sounds – from cha-cha-cha to rumba to mambo – came together to form the hybrid we now call salsa, where folks singers such as Bob Dylan and Joan Baez crooned protest songs in coffeehouses, and where bands such as the New York Dolls and the Ramones tore up the stage in Manhattan's gritty downtown. It was the ground zero of disco. And it was the crucible where hip-hop was grew – then exploded.

The city remains a magnet for musicians to this day. The local indie rock scene is especially vibrant: groups including the Yeah Yeah Yeahs, LCD Soundsystem and Animal Collective all emerged out of NYC. Williamsburg is at the heart of the action, packed with clubs and bars, as well as indie record labels and internet radio stations.

Room 212-721-6500; www.jazz.org; Time Warner Center, Broadway, at 60th St, Midtown West; **S** A/C, B/D, 1 to 59th St-Columbus Circle) Perched high atop the Time Warner Center, Jazz at Lincoln Center consists of three state-of-the-art venues: the midsized Rose Theater; the panoramic, glass-backed Appel Room; and the intimate Dizzy's Club Coca-Cola. It's the last of these that you're most likely to visit given its nightly shows.

The talent is often exceptional, as are the dazzling Central Park views.

Carnegie Hall　　　　　　　Live Music
(Map p252; **☎** 212-247-7800; www.carnegiehall. org; W 57th St, at Seventh Ave, Midtown West; ☺tours 11:30am, 12:30pm, 2pm & 3pm Mon-Fri, 11:30am & 12:30pm Sat, 12:30pm Sun Oct-Jun; **S** N/Q/R to 57th St-7th Ave) This legendary music hall may not be the world's biggest, nor grandest, but it's definitely one of the most acoustically blessed venues around. Opera, jazz and folk greats feature in the Isaac Stern Auditorium, with edgier jazz, pop, classical and world music in the hugely popular Zankel Hall. The intimate Weill Recital Hall hosts chamber-music concerts, debut performances and panel discussions.

Jazz Standard　　　　　　　　　Jazz
(Map p252; **☎** 212-576-2232; www.jazzstandard. com; 116 E 27th St, btwn Lexington & Park Aves; **S** 6 to 28th St) One of the city's other great jazz clubs is the Jazz Standard. The service is impeccable. The food is great. There's no minimum and it's programmed by Seth Abramson, a guy who really knows his stuff.

Birdland　　　　　　　Jazz, Cabaret
(Map p252; **☎** 212-581-3080; www.birdlandjazz. com; 315 W 44th St, btwn Eighth & Ninth Aves, Midtown West; cover $20-50; ☺5pm-1am; 📶; **S** A/C/E to 42nd St-Port Authority Bus Terminal) This bird's got a slick look, not to mention the legend – its name dates from bebop legend Charlie Parker (aka 'Bird'), who headlined at the previous location on 52nd St, along with Miles, Monk and just about everyone else (you can see their photos on the walls). Covers run from $20 to $50 and the lineup is always stellar.

☆ Upper West Side & Central Park

Metropolitan Opera House　　Opera
(Map p250; **☎** tickets 212-362-6000, tours 212-769-7028; www.metopera.org; Lincoln Center, 64th St, at Columbus Ave; **S** 1 to 66th St-Lincoln Center) The Metropolitan Opera hosts well-

known theatre classics as well as brilliant contemporary works. The season runs from September to April.

New York City Ballet   Dance
(Map p250; [2]212-496-0600; www.nycballet.com; David H Koch Theater, Lincoln Center, Columbus Ave, at 62nd St; [S]1 to 66th St-Lincoln Center) Russian-born choreographer George Balanchine first directed the city's ballet company in the 1940s. The company is the largest ballet organization in the country and has 90 dancers. Lincoln Center's David H Koch Theater hosts performances, which run for 23 weeks a year.

New York Philharmonic   Classical Music
(Map p250; [2]212-875-5656; www.nyphil.org; Avery Fisher Hall, Lincoln Center, cnr Columbus Ave & 65th St; [S]1 to 66 St-Lincoln Center) The Philharmonic holds its season every year at Avery Fisher Hall. It is the oldest professional orchestra in the country and plays a mix of classic and contemporary concerts, plus shows for children.

Beacon Theatre   Live Music
(Map p250; [2]212-465-6500; www.beacontheatre.com; 2124 Broadway, btwn 74th & 75th Sts; [S]1/2/3 to 72nd St) This historic 1929 theater is a perfect medium-size venue with 2600 seats (not a terrible one in the house) and a constant flow of popular acts from Nick Cave to Bryan Adams. A recent restoration has left the gilded interiors – a mix of Greek, Roman, Renaissance and rococo design elements – totally sparkling.

Symphony Space   Live Music
(Map p250; [2]212-864-5400; www.symphonyspace.org; 2537 Broadway, btwn 94th & 95th Sts; [S]1/2/3 to 96th St) Symphony Space is a multidisciplinary gem supported by the local community. It often hosts three-day series that are dedicated to one musician, and has an affinity for world music, theater, film, dance and literature (with appearances by acclaimed writers).

Film Society of Lincoln Center   Cinema
(Map p250; [2]212-875-5610; www.filmlinc.com; [S]1 to 66th St-Lincoln Center) The Film Society is one of New York's cinematic gems, providing an invaluable platform for a wide gamut of documentary, feature, independent, foreign and avant-garde art pictures. Films screen in one of two facilities at Lincoln Center: the **Elinor Bunin Munroe Film Center** (Map p250; [2]212-875-5232), a more intimate, experimental venue, or the **Walter Reade Theater** (Map p250; [2]212-875-5601), with wonderfully wide, screening-room-style seats.

☆ Harlem & Upper Manhattan

Minton's   Jazz
([2]212-243-2222; www.mintonsharlem.com; 206 W 118th St, btwn St Nicholas Ave & Adam Clayton Powell Jr Blvd; ☺6-11pm Wed-Sat, noon-3pm & 6-11pm Sun; [S]B/C, 2/3 to 116th St) Birthplace of bebop, this Harlem jazz-and-dinner club is a musical holy grail. Everyone from Dizzy Gillespie to Louis Armstrong has jammed here, and dinner (mains $20 to $46) or Sunday brunch (prix fixe $32) in its dining room is an experience to behold.

☆ Brooklyn

Brooklyn Academy of Music   Performing Arts
(BAM; [2]718-636-4100; www.bam.org; 30 Lafayette Ave, at Ashland Pl, Fort Greene; ☎; [S]D, N/R to Pacific St; B, Q, 2/3, 4/5 to Atlantic Ave) At this performing-arts complex, the Howard Gilman Opera House and Harvey Lichtenstein Theater host their share of ballet, modern and world dance performances. Among other groups, they've presented the Alvin Ailey American Dance Theater, the Mark Morris Dance Group and the Pina Bausch Dance Theater.

Buy tickets early for the Next Wave Festival (September to December), featuring

From left: Bell House; Les Fêtes Vénitiennes perform at Brooklyn Academy of Music (p193); Brooklyn Bowl

cutting-edge theater and dance from around the globe. Also onsite are the **BAM Rose Cinemas** (tickets $12-18), which screen first-run, indie and foreign films. Around the corner is the **BAM Fisher Building** (www. bam.org/fisher; 321 Ashland Pl, Fort Greene; S D, N/R to Pacific St; B, Q, 2/3, 4/5 to Atlantic Ave) with its more intimate 250-seat theater.

Brooklyn Bowl
Live Music

(718-963-3369; www.brooklynbowl.com; 61 Wythe Ave, btwn 11th & 12th Sts, Williamsburg; 6pm-2am Mon-Fri, from 11am Sat & Sun; S L to Bedford Ave; G to Nassau Ave) This 23,000-sq-ft venue inside the former Hecla Iron Works Company combines bowling (p205), microbrews, food and groovy live music. In addition to the live bands that regularly tear up the stage, there are NFL game days, karaoke and DJ nights.

Music Hall of Williamsburg
Live Music

(www.musichallofwilliamsburg.com; 66 N 6th St, btwn Wythe & Kent Aves, Williamsburg; show $15-40; S L to Bedford Ave) This popular Williamsburg music venue is *the* place to see indie bands in Brooklyn. (For many

groups traveling through New York, this is their one and only spot.) It is intimate and the programming is solid.

Bell House
Live Music

(718-643-6510; www.thebellhouseny.com; 149 7th St, Gowanus; 5pm-4am; ; S F, G, R to 4th Ave-9th St) A big, old venue in the mostly barren neighborhood of Gowanus, the Bell House features live performances, indie rockers, DJ nights, comedy shows and burlesque parties. The converted warehouse has a spacious concert area, plus a bar in the front room with candles, leather armchairs and 10 or so beers on tap.

Barbès
Live Music

(347-422-0248; www.barbesbrooklyn.com; 376 9th St, at Sixth Ave, Park Slope; suggested donation for live music $10; 5pm-2am Mon-Thu, 2pm-4am Fri & Sat, to 2am Sun; S F to 7th Ave) This bar and performance space is owned by a French musician and longtime Brooklyn resident, Olivier Conan, who sometimes takes the stage with his Latin-themed band Las Rubias del Norte. The line-up here is impressive and eclectic (the bar is named after the North African neighborhood in

Paris), featuring Afro-Peruvian grooves and French chanson among other sounds.

Jalopy   Live Music
(📞718-395-3214; www.jalopy.biz; 315 Columbia St, at Woodhull St, Red Hook; 🚇F, G to Carroll St) This Carroll Gardens/Red Hook banjo shop has a fun DIY space with cold beer for its bluegrass, country and ukulele shows.

LoftOpera   Opera
(www.loftopera.com; tickets from $30) True to its name, this Brooklyn-based outfit performs operas at lofts in Gowanus and elsewhere in Brooklyn. Even if you're not an opera fan, it's an extraordinary experience.

Nitehawk Cinema   Cinema
(www.nitehawkcinema.com; 136 Metropolitan Ave, btwn Berry & Wythe, Williamsburg; 🚇L to Bedford Ave) This triplex has a fine lineup of first-run and indie films, a good sound system and comfy seats, but Nitehawk's big draw is that you are able to dine and drink while watching a movie. Munch on hummus plates, sweet potato risotto balls or short rib empanadas, matched by a Blue Point toasted lager or perhaps a Negroni.

Many shows sell out (especially on weekends). Purchase tickets in advance online to avoid disappointment.

St Ann's Warehouse   Theater
(Map p246; 📞718-254-8779; www.stannswarehouse.org; 45 Water St, Dumbo; 🚇A/C to High St) This avant-garde performance company hosts innovative theater and dance happenings that attract the Brooklyn literati. The line-up has featured rock opera, genre-defying music by new composers, and strange and wondrous puppet theater. In 2015, St Ann's moved to a new location in the historic Tobacco Warehouse facing Brooklyn Bridge Park.

ACTIVE NEW YORK

Baseball, jogging in Central Park and more

Active New York

Although hailing cabs in New York City can feel like a blood sport, and waiting on subway platforms in summer heat is steamier than a sauna, New Yorkers still love to stay active in their spare time. And considering how limited the green spaces are in the city, it's surprising for some visitors just how active the locals can be. Non-rainy days see New Yorkers taking to the paths of Central Park, cycling along Hudson River Park and joining in pick-up basketball games on outdoor courts across town.

For those who prefer their sport sitting down, there's a packed calendar of athletic artistry, with over half a dozen pro teams playing within the metropolitan area. Football, basketball, baseball, hockey, tennis – there's lots of excitement right on your doorstep.

In This Section

What to Watch/Sports Seasons

Baseball season runs from April to October. Basketball follows on its heels, running from October to May or June. It overlaps a bit with football season (August to January) and pro hockey (September to April). Meanwhile, the US Open is America's biggest tennis event, happening in late August and September.

The Brooklyn Nets play the Toronto Raptors

The Best...

NYC Activities Spots

Central Park (p36) The city's wondrous playground has rolling hills, forested paths, open green spaces and a beautiful lake.

Chelsea Piers Complex (p201) Every activity imaginable – from kickboxing to ice hockey – under one gigantic roof.

Brooklyn Bridge Park (p106) This brand new green space is Brooklyn's pride and joy.

Prospect Park (p102) Escape the crowds at Brooklyn's gorgeous park, with trails, hills, a canal, lake and meadows.

NYC Sports Teams

New York Yankees (p200) One of the country's most successful baseball teams.

New York Giants (p200) Football powerhouse that, despite the name, plays their home games in New Jersey.

New York Knicks (p200) See the Knicks sink a few three-pointers at Madison Square Garden.

Brooklyn Nets (p200) The hot new NBA team in town and symbol of Brooklyn's resurgence.

New York Mets (p200) NYC's other baseball team play their games at Citi Field in Queens.

⚡ Baseball

New York is one of the last remaining corners of the USA where baseball reigns supreme over football and basketball. Tickets start at around $15 – a great deal for seeing the home teams playing in their recently opened stadiums. The two Major League Baseball teams play 162 games during the regular season from April to October, when the playoffs begin. Head to Yankee Stadium to cheer on the **New York Yankees** (☎718-293-4300, tours 646-977-8687; www.yankees.com; E 161st St, at River Ave; tours $20; Ⓢ B/D, 4 to 161st St-Yankee Stadium), also known as the Bronx Bombers, the USA's greatest baseball dynasty, with over two dozen World Series championship titles since 1900. Or queue up at Citi Field station to catch the **New York Mets** (☎718-507-8499; www.mets.com; 123-01 Roosevelt Ave, Flushing; tickets $19-130; Ⓢ 7 to Mets-Willets Point), New York's 'new' baseball team (in

> ❝ cheer on the New York Yankees, also known as the Bronx Bombers ❞

the National League since 1962), who won the pennant in 2015.

⚡ Basketball

Two National Basketball Association (NBA) teams now play in New York City. The blue-and-orange **New York Knicks** (Map p252; www.nyknicks.com; Madison Sq Garden, Seventh Ave btwn 31st & 33rd Sts, Midtown West; tickets from $75.50; Ⓢ A/C/E, 1/2/3 to 34th St-Penn Station) are loved by New Yorkers, occasional scandal aside, while the **Brooklyn Nets** (www.nba.com/nets; tickets from $15; 🚌351 from Port Authority), formerly the New Jersey Nets, is Brooklyn's new pro team (the first since the Dodgers left town) and has gained a strong local following.

⚡ Football

Most of New York tunes into its National Football League (NFL) teams: the **New York Giants** (☎201-935-8222; www.giants.com; Meadowlands Stadium, Meadowlands Sports Complex, East Rutherford, NJ; 🚌351 from

Yankee Stadium

Port Authority, 🚇NJ Transit from PennStation to Meadowlands), one of the NFL's oldest teams, with four Super Bowl victories, most recently in 2011, and the **New York Jets** (☎800-469-5387; www.newyorkjets.com; Meadowlands Stadium, Meadowlands Sports Complex, East Rutherford, NJ; 🚌351 from Port Authority, 🚇NJ Transit from Penn Station to Meadowlands), whose games are always packed and new fans get swept away by the contagious 'J-E-T-S' chants.

Both teams play at the new Metlife Stadium at the Meadowlands Sports Complex in New Jersey (from Manhattan take NJ Transit via Seacaucus Junction).

🏒 Hockey

The National Hockey League (NHL) has three franchises in the greater New York area; each team plays three or four games weekly during the season from September to April.

The **New York Rangers** (Map p252; ☎212-465-6000, tickets 800-745-3000; www.nyrangers.com; Madison Square Garden, Seventh Ave, btwn 31st & 33rd Sts, Midtown West; tickets from $55; 🚇A/C/E, 1/2/3 to 34th St-Penn Station) are Manhattan's favorite hockey squad.

New York City hasn't given much love to the **New York Islanders** (☎Barclays Center 917-618-6700, tickets 844-334-7537; www.newyorkislanders.com; Nassau Veterans Memorial Coliseum, 1255 Hempstead Turnpike, Long Island; tickets from $19; 🚃LIRR to Hempstead station, then bus N70, N71 or N72) since the remarkable four-consecutive-year Stanley Cup streak in the '80s. Their stock is on the rise, however, since their move to Brooklyn's Barclay Center in 2015.

🏃 Health & Fitness

Chelsea Piers
Complex   Health & Fitness
(Map p252; ☎212-336-6666; www.chelseapiers.com; Hudson River, at end of W 23rd St; 🚇C/E to 23rd St) This massive waterfront sports center caters to the athlete in everyone.

 Running the Big Apple

Central Park's loop roads are best during traffic-free hours, though you'll be in the company of many cyclists and in-line skaters. The 1.6-mile path surrounding the Jacqueline Kennedy Onassis Reservoir (where Jackie O used to run) is for runners and walkers only; access it between 86th and 96th Sts. The loop around the whole park is 6 miles.

Running along the Hudson River is a popular path, best from about 30th St to Battery Park in Lower Manhattan. The Upper East Side has a path that runs along FDR Dr and the East River (from 63rd St to 115th St). Brooklyn's Prospect Park has plenty of paths (and a 3-mile loop), while 1.3-mile-long Brooklyn Bridge Park has incredible views of Manhattan (reach it via Brooklyn Bridge to up the mileage). The New York Road Runners Club (www.nyrr.org) organizes weekend runs citywide, including the New York City Marathon.

You can set out to hit a bucket of golf balls at the four-level driving range, ice skate on the complex's indoor rink or rack up a few strikes in a jazzy bowling alley. There's Hoop City for basketball, a sailing school for kids, batting cages, a huge gym facility with an indoor pool (day passes for nonmembers are $50), indoor rock-climbing walls – the works.

From left: Citibike rental station; Rock climbing at Brooklyn Boulders; New York Trapeze School

Central Park Tennis Center Tennis

(Map p250; 📞212-316-0800; www.centralpark tenniscenter.com; Central Park, btwn 94th & 96th Sts, enter at 96th St & Central Park West; ⏰6:30am-dusk Apr-Oct or Nov; 🚇B, C to 96th St) This daylight-hours-only facility has 26 clay courts for public use and four hard courts for lessons. You can buy single-play tickets ($15) here, and can reserve a court if you pick up a $15 permit at the **Arsenal** (Map p250; 📞212-360-8131; www.nycgovparks. org; Central Park, at 5th Ave & E 64th St; ⏰9am-5pm Mon-Fri; 🚇N/R/Q to 5th Ave-59th St). The least busy times are roughly from noon to 4pm on weekdays.

Bike and Roll
Bike Rentals Bicycle Rental

(Map p246; 📞212-260-0400; www.bikenewyork city.com; State & Water Sts; rentals per day from $44, tours from $50; ⏰varies, check website; 🚇4/5 to Bowling Green; 1 to South Ferry) Just northwest of Staten Island Ferry terminal, this is one of several Bike and Roll Bike Rental outlets in the city. The outfit also leads bike tours, including across the

Brooklyn Bridge and along the Hudson River.

Russian & Turkish Baths Bathhouse

(Map p246; 📞212-674-9250; www.russianturk-ishbaths.com; 268 E 10th St, btwn First Ave & Ave A; per visit $40; ⏰noon-10pm Mon-Tue & Thu-Fri, from 10am Wed, from 9am Sat, from 8am Sun; 🚇L to First Ave; 6 to Astor Pl) Since 1892, this has been the spa for anyone who wants to get naked (or stay in their swimsuit) and romp in steam baths, an ice-cold plunge pool, a sauna or on the sundeck. The baths are open to both men and women most hours (wearing shorts is required at these times), though at some times it's men or women only.

Check the website for more detailed opening hours.

Great Jones Spa Spa

(Map p246; 📞212-505-3185; www.greatjones spa.com; 29 Great Jones St, btwn Lafayette St & Bowery; ⏰9am-10pm; 🚇6 to Bleecker St; B/D/F/M to Broadway-Lafayette St) Don't skimp on the services at this downtown feng shui master, whose offerings include

Moroccan rose sea salt scrubs and stem-cell facials. If you spend over $100 per person (not hard: hour-long massages start at $145, hour-long facials start at $135), you get three-hour access to the water lounge and its thermal hot tub, river rock sauna, chakra-light steam room and cold plunge pool. Swimwear is essential.

New York
Trapeze School   Adventure Sports

(Map p246; ☏212-242-8769; www.newyork. trapezeschool.com; Pier 40, at West Side Hwy; per class $50-60; ⓢ1 to Houston St) Fulfill your circus dreams, like Carrie did on *Sex and the City,* flying trapeze to trapeze in this open-air tent by the river. It's open from May to September, on top of Pier 40. The school also has an indoor facility inside the Circus Warehouse in Long Island City, Queens, that's open from October to April. Call or check the website for daily class times. There's a one-time $22 registration fee.

Jivamukti   Yoga

(Map p246; ☏212-353-0214; www.jivamukti yoga.com; 841 Broadway, btwn 13th & 14 Sts;

classes $15-22; ⓧclasses 7am-9pm Mon-Thu, 7am-8pm Fri, 8am-8pm Sat & Sun; ⓢ4/5/6, N/Q/R, L to 14th St-Union Sq) *The* yoga spot in Manhattan, Jivamukti – in a 12,000-sq-ft locale on Union Sq – is a posh place for vinyasa, hatha and Ashtanga classes. The center's 'open classes' are suitable for both rookies and experienced practitioners, and there's an organic, vegan cafe on-site too. Gratuitous celebrity tidbit: Uma's little bro Dechen Thurman teaches classes here.

Brooklyn Boulders   Rock Climbing

(www.brooklynboulders.com; 575 Degraw St, at Third Ave, Boerum Hill; day pass $28, shoe rental $6; ⓧ8am-midnight; ⓢR to Union St) It's Brooklyn's biggest indoor climbing arena for scaling aficionados and folks looking to reach new heights. Ceilings top out at 30ft inside this 18,000-sq-ft facility, and its caves and freestanding 17ft boulder and climbing walls offer numerous routes for beginners to experts. There are overhangs of 15, 30 and 45 degrees. Climbing classes are available.

Street Sports

With all that concrete around, New York has embraced a number of sports and events played directly on the streets themselves. Those with hoop dreams will find pick-up basketball games all over the city, the most famous courts being the West 4th Street Basketball Courts, known as 'the Cage.' Or try Holcombe Rucker Park up in Harlem – that's where many NBA big shots cut their teeth. You'll also find pick-up games in Tompkins Square Park and Riverside Park. Hudson River Park has courts at Canal St and on W 11th Ave at 23rd St.

Lesser-known handball and stickball are also popular in NYC; you'll find one-wall courts in outdoor parks all over the city. For stickball, link up with the Bronx-based Emperors Stickball League (www.stickball.com) to check out its Sunday games during the warmer months.

Street basketball, Greenwich Village
CITIZEN OF THE PLANET / ALAMY STOCK PHOTO ©

🏃 Aquatic Activities

Downtown Boathouse   Kayaking
(Map p246; www.downtownboathouse.org; Pier 26, near N Moore St; ⊙9am-4:30pm Sat & Sun mid-May–mid-Oct, 5-6:30pm Mon-Fri Jul & Aug; S1 to Houston St) New York's most active public boathouse offers free walk-up 20-minute kayaking sessions (including equipment) in a protected embayment on the Hudson River on weekends and some weekday evenings. For more activities –

kayaking trips, stand-up paddle boarding and classes – check out www.hudsonriverpark.org for the four other kayaking locations on the Hudson River. There's also a summer-only kayaking location on Governors Island (p109).

Schooner Adirondack   Boating
(Map p252; ☑212-913-9991; www.sail-nyc.com; Chelsea Piers, Pier 62 at W 22th St; tours $48-78; SC, E to 23rd St) The two-masted 'Dack hits the New York Harbor with four two-hour sails daily from May to October. The 1920s-style, 80ft Manhattan yacht sails daily at 3:30pm and 6pm, with other tours throughout the week. Call or check the website for the latest times.

🏃 Family Activities

Belvedere Castle   Birdwatching
(Map p250; ☑212-772-0288; Central Park, at 79th St; ⊙10am-5pm ; 👪; S1/2/3, B, C to 72nd St) FREE For a DIY birding expedition with kids, borrow a 'Discovery Kit' at Belvedere Castle in Central Park. It comes with binoculars, a bird book, colored pencils and paper – a perfect way to get the kids excited about birds. Picture ID required.

Loeb Boathouse   Kayaking, Cycling
(Map p250; ☑212-517-2233; www.thecentralparkboathouse.com; Central Park, btwn 74th & 75th Sts; boating per hr $15, bike rental per hr $9-15; ⊙10am-6pm Apr-Nov; 👪; SB, C to 72nd St, 6 to 77th St) Central Park's boathouse has a fleet of 100 rowboats as well as a Venetian-style gondola that seats up to six if you'd rather someone else do the paddling. Bicycles are also available, weather permitting. Rentals require ID and a credit card, and helmets are included.

Wollman Skating Rink   Skating
(Map p250; ☑212-439-6900; www.wollmanskatingrink.com; Central Park, btwn 62nd & 63rd Sts; adult Mon-Thu/Fri-Sun $11/18, child $6, skate rentals $8, lock rental $5, spectator fee $5; ⊙10am-2:30pm Mon & Tue, to 10pm Wed-Sat, to 9pm Sun Nov-Mar; 👪; SF to 57 St, N/Q/R to

5th Ave-59th St) Larger than the Rockefeller Center skating rink, and allowing all-day skating, this rink is at the southeastern edge of Central Park and offers nice views. Cash only.

Rink at Rockefeller Center Skating
(Map p252; 212-332-7654; therinkatrock-center.com; Rockefeller Center, Fifth Ave, btwn 49th & 50th Sts; adult $25-32, child $15, skate rental $12; 8:30am-midnight mid-Oct–Apr; ; B/D/F/M to 47th-50th Sts-Rockefeller Center) From mid-October to April, Rockefeller Plaza is home to New York's most famous ice-skating rink. Incomparably magical, it's also undeniably small and crowded. Opt for the first skating period (8:30am) to avoid a long wait. Come summer, the rink becomes a cafe.

Lakeside Skating, Boating
(718-462-0010; www.lakesideprospectpark. com; Prospect Park, near Ocean & Parkside Aves; ice-skating $6-9, skate rental $6; 10am-6:30pm Mon-Thu, to 9pm Fri, 11am-9pm Sat, 11am-6:30pm Sun Nov-Mar; ; B, Q to Prospect Park) Two brand-new rinks (one open and one covered) in Prospect Park opened in late 2013 as part of Lakeside Center, a $74-million project which reconfigured 26 acres of parkland in a beautiful, ecofriendly showcase. In the summer, kids can splash about in wading pools and sprinklers; the other rink features old-school roller skating.

In the summer, pedal boats and kayaks are available for leisurely rides on the lake.

Brooklyn Bowl Bowling
(718-963-3369; www.brooklynbowl.com; 61 Wythe Ave, btwn 11th & 12th Sts, Williamsburg; lane rental per hr $50, shoe rental $5; 6pm-2am Mon-Fri, from 11am Sat & Sun; L to Bedford; G to Nassau Ave) This incredible alley is housed in the 23,000-sq-ft former Hecla Iron Works Company, which provided ornamentation for several NYC landmarks

at the turn of the 20th century. There are 16 lanes surrounded by cushy sofas and exposed-brick walls. In addition to bowling, Brooklyn Bowl hosts concerts throughout the week, and there's always good food on hand.

🏃 Tours

New York City Audubon Walking Tour
(Map p252; 212-691-7483; www.nycaudubon. org; 71 W 23rd St, Suite 1523, at Sixth Ave; tours & classes free-$170; F/M to 23rd St) Throughout the year, the New York City Audubon Society runs bird-watching field trips (including seal- and waterbird-spotting on New York Harbor and eagle-watching in the Hudson Valley), lectures and beginner birding classes.

Municipal Art Society Walking Tour
(Map p250; 212-935-3960; www.mas.org; tours adult/child from $20/15; F to 57th St) The Municipal Art Society offers various scheduled tours focusing on architecture and history. Among them is a 75-minute tour of Grand Central Terminal, departing daily at 12:30pm from the station's Main Concourse.

Circle Line Boat Tours Boat Tour
(Map p252; 212-563-3200; www.circleline42. com; Pier 83, 42nd St, at Twelfth Ave, Midtown West; cruises adult/child from $29/20; westbound M42 or M50, A/C/E to 42nd-Port Authority) The classic Circle Line guides you through all the big sights from the safe distance of a boat. Options include a 2½-hour full-island cruise, a shorter (90-minute) 'semi-circle' journey and a two-hour evening cruise. From May to October, the outfit also operates adrenaline-fueled cruises aboard the high-speed *Beast*. See the website for schedules.

ALIJA / GETTY IMAGES ©

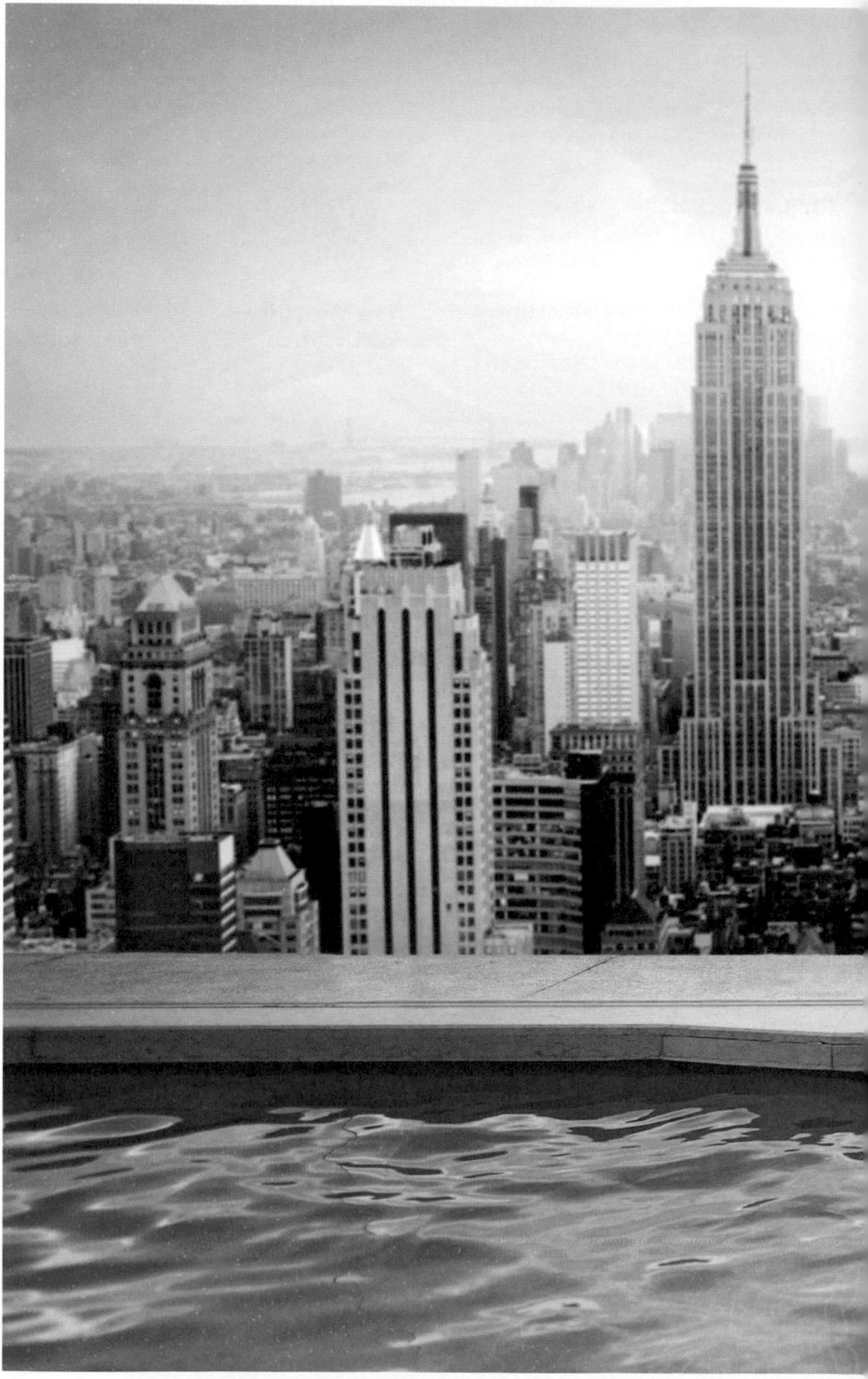

REST YOUR HEAD

Top tips for the best accommodations

Rest Your Head

Like the student with the hand up at the front of class, NYC just seems to know how to do everything well, and its lodging scene is no exception. Creative minds have descended upon the 'city that never sleeps' to create memorable spaces for those who might just want to grab a bit of shut-eye during their stay.

In This Section

Prices/Tipping

A 'budget hotel' in NYC generally costs up to $150 for a standard double room including breakfast. For a modest mid-range option, plan on spending $150 to $350. Luxury options run $350 and higher.

Tip the maid $3 to $5 per night, tip porters $1 to $2 per bag. Staff providing service (hailing cabs, room service, concierge help) should be tipped accordingly.

PHILIPPE MARION / GETTY IMAGES ©

Reservations

Reservations are essential – walk-ins are practically impossible and rack rates are almost always unfavorable relative to online deals. Reserve your room as early as possible and make sure you understand your hotel's cancellation policy. Expect check-in to always be in the middle of the afternoon and check-out in the late morning. Early check-ins are rare, though high-end establishments can often accommodate with advance notice.

Useful Websites

newyorkhotels.com (www.newyork hotels.com) The self-proclaimed official website for hotels in NYC.

NYC (www.nycgo.com/hotels) Loads of listings from the NYC Official Guide.

Lonely Planet (lonelyplanet.com/usa/ new-york-city/hotels) Accommodation reviews and online booking service.

Renting Rooms & Apartments Online

More and more travelers are bypassing hotels and staying in private apartments listed online through companies such as Airbnb. The wealth of options is staggering, with more than 25,000 listings per night scattered in every corner of New York City. If you want a more local, neighborhood-oriented experience, then this can be a great way to go.

There are a few things, however, to keep in mind. First off: many listings are actually illegal. Laws in NYC dictate that apartments can be rented out for less than 30 days only if the occupants are present. Effects on the immediate community are another issue, with some neighbors complaining about noise, security risks and the unexpected transformation of their residence into a hotel of sorts. There are also the larger impacts on the housing market: some landlords are cashing in, knowing they can earn more from holiday rentals than with long-term tenants. Taking thousands of possible rentals off the market is only driving rental prices for NYC residents ever higher.

🛏 Booking Accommodations

In New York City, the average room rate is well over $300. But don't let that scare you, as there are great deals to be had – almost all of which can be found through savvy on-line snooping. To get the best deals, launch a two-pronged approach: if you don't have your heart set on a particular property, then check out the generic booking websites. If you do know where you want to stay – it might sound simple – but it's best to start at your desired hotel's website. These days it's not uncommon to find deals and package rates directly on the site of your accommodation of choice.

🛏 Room Rates

New York City doesn't have a 'high season' in the common way that beach destinations do. Sure, there are busier times of the year when it comes to tourist traffic, but, with over 50 million visitors per annum, the Big Apple never needs to worry when it comes to filling up beds. As such, room rates fluctuate based on availability; in fact, most hotels have a booking algorithm in place that spits out a price quote relative to the number of rooms already booked on the same night, so the busier the evening the higher the price goes.

If you're looking to find the best room rates, then flexibility is key: weekdays are often cheaper, and you'll generally find that accommodations in winter months have smaller price tags. If you are visiting over a weekend, try for a business hotel in the Financial District, which tends to empty out when the workweek ends.

🛏 Accommodations Types

B&Bs & Family-Style Guesthouses

Offer mix-and-match furnishings and some serious savings (if you don't mind some Victorian styles or eating breakfast with strangers).

Boutique Hotels

Usually have tiny rooms decked out with fantastic amenities and at least one celebrity-filled basement bar, rooftop bar or hip, flashy eatery on-site.

Classic Hotels

Typified by old-fashioned, small-scale European grandeur; these usually cost the same as boutiques and aren't always any larger.

Hostels

Functional dorms (bunk beds and bare walls) that are nonetheless communal and friendly. Many have a backyard garden, kitchen and a pretty lounge that make up for the soulless rooms.

Where to Stay

Upper West Side
& Central Park

Upper East Side

Midtown

West Village, Chelsea &
Meatpacking District

Union Square, Flatiron
District & Gramercy

SoHo &
Chinatown

East Village &
Lower East Side

Financial District &
Lower Manhattan

Brooklyn

Neighborhood	Atmosphere
Financial District & Lower Manhattan	Convenient to Tribeca's nightlife and ferries. Business hotel cheap weekend rates. The area can feel impersonal, corporate and even a bit desolate after business hours.
SoHo & Chinatown	Shop to your heart's content right on your doorstep. Crowds swarm the streets of SoHo almost any time of day.
East Village & Lower East Side	The area feels the most quintessentially 'New York' to visitors and Manhattanites. Not a great deal to choose from when it comes to hotel sleeps.
West Village, Chelsea & Meatpacking District	Close-to-everything feel in a thriving part of town that has an almost-European feel. Prices soar for traditional hotels, but remain reasonable for B&Bs. Rooms can be on the small side.
Union Square, Flatiron District & Gramercy	Good subway access to all over the city. Steps away from the Village and Midtown. Prices are high and there's not much neighborhood flavor.
Midtown	Postcard NYC: skyscrapers, museums, shopping and Broadway shows. One of the most expensive areas in the city; expect small rooms.
Upper East Side	A stone's throw from top-notch museums and the rolling hills of Central Park. Sleeping options are scarce and wallet-busting prices are not uncommon; also not particularly central.
Upper West Side & Central Park	Close to Central Park and the Museum of Natural History. More familial feel if you're looking for a livelier scene.
Brooklyn	Cheaper; great for exploring NYC's most creative area. Long commute to Midtown and north.

Flatiron Building

In Focus

ERIN CADIGAN / SHUTTERSTOCK ©

New York City Today

With almost 60 million smitten visitors pouring into the city each year, New York remains a mighty force to be reckoned with. Statement architecture is reinvigorating the skyline, while ambitious greenhouse targets attest to a city determined to build a cleaner, greener future. Yet, like any metropolis, the world's 'can-do' capital is not without its challenges, from rising crime rates to social harmony in the Age of Terror.

Above: Looking at the Manhattan skyline from Liberty State Park
/ WIBOWO RUSLI/GETTY IMAGES ©

De Blasio Blues

According to a *Wall Street Journal*–NBC4 New York–Marist poll taken in late 2015, mayor Bill de Blasio's approval rating slid from 44% in the spring to just 38% in the fall, suggesting the love affair between de Blasio and NYC could be on the rocks. The swing was especially significant among black voters, among whom his approval rating tumbled from 59% to 50% in the same period. White voters are even less impressed according to a poll by the *New York Times* and Siena College, which declared their support for the mayor to be just 28% in late 2015. Some detractors argue that the city's two-year rise in gun crime (the first increase in almost two decades) reflects de Blasio's 'soft' stance on law enforcement. The Democrat is a prolific critic of the 'stop and frisk' policy supported by former mayor

housing
(% of population)

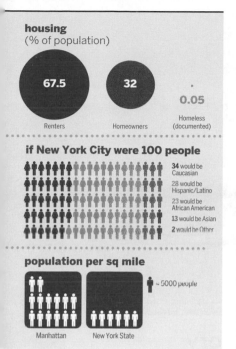

67.5 — Renters

32 — Homeowners

0.05 — Homeless (documented)

if New York City were 100 people

34 would be Caucasian

28 would be Hispanic/Latino

23 would be African American

13 would be Asian

2 would be Other

population per sq mile

Manhattan

New York State

~5000 people

Michael Bloomberg, which allows police officers to randomly stop, question and search citizens.

Clean & Green

Never one to take things lying down, NYC is fighting climate change with fervor. The city's current goal is to slash citywide greenhouse gas emissions 80% below 2005 levels by 2050. The goal complements de Blasio's 'One City, Built to Last,' a scheme in which 3000 city-owned buildings will be upgraded with more efficient power, cooling and heating systems by 2025. Private buildings will be given target reductions, which, if not met voluntarily, will be followed by mandated reductions. Given around three-quarters of NYC's greenhouse gases are produced by buildings, the program will go a long way to meeting the 2050 targets. De Blasio's commitments build on the original New York City Carbon Challenge launched by his predecessor, Michael Bloomberg. Kick-started in 2007, the program encouraged universities, businesses and other private bodies to slash greenhouse gas emissions by 30% in 10 years.

Thin is In

New York's Midtown skyline is undergoing an upgrade thanks to a new wave of pencil-thin, super-tall towers. Mostly residential, these architecture supermodels include the recently completed 432 Park Ave, a 1396ft-tall, elongated cube tower designed by Uruguayan architect Rafael Viñoly. Currently NYC's tallest building to roof level, it will be superseded by the 1522ft Central Park Tower (aka Nordstrom Tower) in 2019. The latter's total height will reach 1550ft, making it the world's tallest residential building by both roof and total architectural height. The building – located at 225 W 57th St – is the work of Chicago-based firm Adrian Smith + Gordon Gill Architecture (AS+GG), the team behind the record-breaking, mile-high Joddah Tower currently under construction in Saudi Arabia. Just up the street from Central Park Tower, the 1438ft-tall 111 W 57th St condominium will take slender to a whole new level with a width-to-height ratio of 1:24, which will make it the city's skinniest show pony. The most spectacular newcomer, however, will arguably be 53W53 at 53 W 53rd, a mixed-use tower designed by French architect Jean Nouvel with a head-turning, skeletal form.

History

This is the tale of a city that never sleeps, of a kingdom where tycoons and world leaders converge, of a place that's seen the highest highs and the most devastating lows. Yet through it all, it continues to reach for the sky (both figuratively and literally). And to think it all started with $24 and a pile of beads...

From left: Ellis Island (p43); 'Tribute in Light' for the anniversary of September 11

c AD 1500	1625–26	1646
About 15,000 Native Americans live in 80 sites around the island. The groups include the feuding Iroquois and Algonquins.	The Dutch West India Company imports slaves from Africa to work in the fur trade and construction.	The Dutch found the village of Breuckelen on the eastern shore of Long Island, naming it after Breukelen in the Netherlands.

ANDRIA PATINO / GETTY IMAGES ©

Buying Manhattan

The Dutch West India Company sent 110 settlers to begin a trading post here in 1624. They settled in Lower Manhattan and called their colony New Amsterdam, touching off bloody battles with the unshakable Lenape, a people who had roots on the island dating back 11,000 years. It all came to a head in 1626, when the colony's first governor, Peter Minuit, became the city's first but certainly not the last – unscrupulous real estate agent by purchasing Manhattan's 14,000 acres from the Lenape for 60 guilders ($24) and some glass beads.

By the time peg-legged Peter Stuyvesant arrived to govern the colony in 1647, the Lenape population had dwindled to about 700. In 1664 the English arrived in battleships. Stuyvesant avoided bloodshed by surrendering without a shot. King Charles II renamed the colony after his brother the Duke of York. New York became a prosperous British port and the population rose to 11,000 by the mid-1700s; however, colonists started to become resentful of British taxation.

1784	**1811**	**1853**
Alexander Hamilton founds America's first bank, the Bank of New York, with holdings of $500,000.	Manhattan's grid plan is developed by Mayor DeWitt Clinton, reshaping the city and laying plans for the future.	The State Legislature authorizes the allotment of public lands for what will later become Central Park.

Lower East Side Tenement Museum

LONELY PLANET / GETTY IMAGES ©

Revolution & War

By the 18th century the economy was so robust that the locals were improvising ways to avoid sharing the wealth with London, and New York became the stage for the fatal confrontation with King George III. Revolutionary battle began in August 1776, when General George Washington's army lost about a quarter of its men in just a few days. The general retreated, and fire engulfed much of the colony. But soon the British left and Washington's army reclaimed their city. In 1789 the retired general found himself addressing crowds at Federal Hall, gathered to witness his presidential inauguration. Alexander Hamilton, as Washington's secretary of the treasury, began rebuilding New York and working to establish the New York Stock Exchange.

Population Bust, Infrastructure Boom

There were setbacks at the start of the 19th century: the bloody Draft Riots of 1863, cholera epidemics, tensions among 'old' and 'new' immigrants, and poverty and crime in Five Points, the city's first slum. But the city prospered and found resources for mighty public works. Begun in 1855, Central Park was a vision of green reform and a boon to real-estate speculation. It also offered work relief when the Panic of 1857 shattered the nation's finance system. Another vision was realized by German-born engineer John Roebling who designed the Brooklyn Bridge, spanning the East River and connecting lower Manhattan and Brooklyn.

The Burgeoning Metropolis

By the turn of the 20th century, elevated trains carried a million people a day in and out of the city. Rapid transit opened up areas of the Bronx and Upper Manhattan. Tenements were overflowing with immigrants arriving from southern Italy and Eastern Europe, who increased the metropolis to about three million. Newly wealthy folks – boosted by an

1863	**1882**	**1883**
Civil War draft riots erupt, lasting for three days; order is restored by the Federal Army.	Thomas Edison switches on the city's first electric lights at the JP Morgan bank at 23 Wall St.	The Brooklyn Bridge, built at a cost of $15.5 million (and 27 lives), opens on May 24.

economy jump-started by financier JP Morgan – built splendid mansions on Fifth Ave. Reporter and photographer Jacob Riis illuminated the widening gap between the classes, leading the city to pass much-needed housing reforms.

Factory Tragedy, Women's Rights

Wretched factory conditions – low pay, long hours, abusive employers – in the early 20th century were highlighted by a tragic event in 1911. The infamous Triangle Shirtwaist Company fire saw rapidly spreading flames catch onto the factory's piles of fabrics, killing 146 of the 500 female workers who were trapped behind locked doors. The event led to sweeping labor reforms after 20,000 female garment workers marched to City Hall. Nurse and midwife Margaret Sanger opened the first birth-control clinic in Brooklyn and suffragists held rallies to obtain the vote for women.

Move to the Beats

The 1960s ushered in an era of legendary creativity and anti-establishment expression, with many of its creators centered right downtown in Greenwich Village. One movement was Abstract Expressionism, a large-scale outbreak of American painters – Mark Rothko, Jackson Pollock, Lee Krasner, Helen Frankenthaler and Willem de Kooning among them – who offended and intrigued with incomprehensible squiggles and blotches and exuberant energy. Then there were the writers, such as Beat poets Allen Ginsberg and Jack Kerouac and novelist-playwright Jane Bowles. They gathered in Village coffeehouses to exchange ideas and find inspiration, which was often discovered in the form of folk music from burgeoning big names, such as Bob Dylan.

The Jazz Age

The 1920s saw the dawning of the Jazz Age, when Prohibition outlawed the sale of alcohol, encouraging bootlegging and speakeasies, as well as organized crime. Congenial mayor James Walker was elected in 1925, Babe Ruth reigned at Yankee Stadium and the Great Migration from the South led to the Harlem Renaissance, when the neighborhood became a center of African American culture and society. Harlem's nightlife attracted the flappers and gin-soaked revelers that marked the complete failure of Prohibition.

Hard Times

The stock market crashed in 1929 and the city dealt with the Great Depression through grit, endurance, rent parties, militancy and public works projects. Texas-born, Yiddish-speaking Mayor Fiorello La Guardia worked to bring relief in the form of New Deal-funded projects. World War II brought troops to the city, ready to party in Times Square before

1913
Though not yet complete, Grand Central Terminal opens for business on February 2.

1939
The World's Fair opens in Queens. With the future as its theme, the exposition invites visitors to take a look at 'the world of tomorrow.'

1969
Police officers raid the gay-friendly Stonewall Inn, sparking days of rioting and the birth of the modern gay-rights movement.

shipping off to Europe. Converted to war industries, factories hummed, staffed by women and African Americans who had rarely before had access to good, unionized jobs. With few evident controls on business, Midtown bulked up with skyscrapers after the war.

Enter Robert Moses

Working with Mayor La Guardia to usher the city into the modern age was Robert Moses, an urban planner who would influence the physical shape of the city more than anyone else in the 20th century. He was the mastermind behind the Triborough Bridge (now the Robert F Kennedy Bridge), Jones Beach State Park, the Verrazano–Narrows Bridge, the West Side Hwy and the Long Island parkway system – not to mention endless highways, tunnels and bridges, which shifted this mass-transit area into one largely dependent on the automobile.

'Drop Dead'

By the early 1970s deficits had created a fiscal crisis. President Ford refused to lend federal aid – summed up by the *Daily News* headline 'Ford to City, Drop Dead!' Massive layoffs decimated the working class; untended bridges, roads and parks reeked of hard times. The traumatic '70s – which reached a low point in 1977 with a citywide blackout and the existence of serial killer Son of Sam – drove down rents, helping to nourish an alternative culture that transformed the former industrial precincts of SoHo and Tribeca into energized nightlife districts.

Out of the Ashes

While the stock market boomed for much of the 1980s, neighborhoods struggled with the spread of crack cocaine; the city reeled from the impact of addiction, crime and AIDS. Squatters in the East Village fought back when police tried to clear a big homeless encampment, leading to the Tompkins Square Park riots of 1988. In South Bronx, a wave of arson reduced blocks of apartments to cinders. But amid the smoke, an influential hip-hop culture was born there and in Brooklyn.

Still convalescing from the real-estate crash of the late 1980s, the city faced crumbling infrastructure, jobs leaking south and Fortune 500 companies leaving for suburbia. Then the dot-com market roared in, turning the New York Stock Exchange into a speculator's fun park and the city launched a frenzy of building and partying unparalleled since the 1920s.

With pro-business, law-and-order Rudy Giuliani as mayor, the dingy and destitute were swept from Manhattan's yuppified streets to the outer boroughs, leaving room for Generation X to live the high life. Giuliani grabbed headlines with his campaign to stamp out crime, even kicking the sex shops off notoriously seedy 42nd St.

1977	**1988**	**2001**
A summer blackout leaves New Yorkers in the dark for 24 sweltering hours, which leads to rioting around the city.	Squatters riot when cops attempt to remove them from their de facto home in the East Village's Tompkins Square Park.	On September 11, terrorist hijackers fly two planes into the Twin Towers, destroying the World Trade Center and killing nearly 3000 people.

The Naughts in New York

The decade after September 11 was a period of rebuilding – both physically and emotionally. In 2002 Mayor Michael Bloomberg began the unenviable task of picking up the pieces of a shattered city. Much to Bloomberg's pleasure, New York did see a great deal of renovation and reconstruction, especially after the city hit its stride with spiking tourist numbers in 2005. By the latter part of Bloomberg's second term as mayor, the entire city seemed to be under construction, with luxury high-rise condos sprouting up in every neighborhood.

Soon the economy buckled under its own weight in what has largely become known as the Global Financial Crisis. The city was paralyzed as the cornerstones of the business world were forced to close shop. Although hit less badly than many pockets of the country, NYC still saw a significant dip in real-estate prices and many cranes turned to frozen monuments of a broken economy.

In 2011 the city commemorated the 10th anniversary of the September 11 attacks with the opening of a remembrance center and a half-built Freedom Tower – a new corporate behemoth – that loomed overhead.

September 11

On September 11, 2001, terrorists flew two hijacked planes into the World Trade Center's Twin Towers, turning the whole complex to dust and rubble and killing nearly 3000 people. Downtown Manhattan took months to recover from the ghastly fumes wafting from the ruins as forlorn missing-person posters grew ragged on brick walls. While the city mourned its dead and recovery crews coughed their way through the debris, residents braved constant terrorist alerts and an anthrax scare. Shock and grief drew people together, uniting the oft-fractious citizenry in a determined effort not to succumb to despair.

Storms & Political Change

New York's resilience would be tested again in 2012 by superstorm Hurricane Sandy. On October 29, cyclonic winds and drenching rain pounded the city, causing severe flooding and property damage in all five boroughs, including to the NYC subway system, Hugh L Carey Tunnel and World Trade Center site. A major power blackout plunged much of Lower Manhattan into surreal darkness, while trading at the New York Stock Exchange was suspended for two days in its first weather-related closure since 1888. In the neighborhood of Breezy Point, Queens, a devastating storm surge hindered the efforts of firefighters confronted with a blaze that reduced over 125 homes to ashes. The fire went down as one of the worst in NYC's history, while the storm itself claimed 44 lives in the city alone.

The winds of political change swept through the city in November 2013, when Bill de Blasio became the city's first Democrat mayor since 1989. The 52-year-old self-proclaimed 'progressive' also became the first white mayor of NYC with an African American spouse.

2008–09	2012	2016
The stock market crashes due to mismanagement by major American financial institutions.	Superstorm Sandy hits NYC in October, cutting power and causing major flooding and property damage.	Architect Santiago Calatrava's landmark World Trade Center Transportation Hub officially opens in Lower Manhattan.

/GETTY IMAGES ©

Art & Architecture

Peel back the concrete urban landscape, and you discover one of the world's great artistic centers. The city has been a showcase for talents great and small, who've added their mark to the city's canvas – both on its gallery walls and onto its gritty streets in the form of architectural icons that soar above the crowded sidewalks.

Above: Graffiti covering rooftops in Chinatown (p86) MAREMAGNUM / GETTY IMAGES ©

An Artistic Heavyweight

That New York claims some of the world's mightiest art museums attests to its enviable artistic pedigree. From Pollock and Rothko to Warhol and Rauschenberg, the city has nourished many of America's greatest artists and artistic movements.

The Birth of an Arts Hub

In almost all facets of the arts, New York really got its sea legs in the early 20th century, when the city attracted and retained a critical mass of thinkers, artists, writers and poets. It was at this time that the homegrown art scene began to take shape. In 1905, photographer (and husband of Georgia O'Keeffe) Alfred Stieglitz opened Gallery 291, a Fifth Ave space that provided a vital platform for American artists and helped establish photography as a credible art form.

In the 1940s, an influx of cultural figures fleeing the carnage of WWII saturated the city with fresh ideas – and New York became an important cultural hub. Peggy Guggenheim established the Art of this Century gallery on 57th St, a space that helped launch the careers of painters such as Jackson Pollock, Willem de Kooning and Robert Motherwell. These Manhattan-based artists came to form the core of the Abstract Expressionist movement – also known as the New York School – creating an explosive and rugged form of painting that changed the course of modern art as we know it.

An American Avant-Garde

The Abstract Expressionists helped establish New York as a global arts center. Another generation of artists then carried the ball. In the 1950s and '60s, Robert Rauschenberg, Jasper Johns and Lee Bontecou turned paintings into off-the-wall sculptural constructions that included everything from welded steel to taxidermy goats. By the mid-1960s, pop art – a movement that utilized the imagery and production techniques of popular culture – had taken hold, with Andy Warhol at the helm.

Graffiti & Street Art

Contemporary graffiti as we know it was cultivated in New York City. In the 1970s, the graffiti-covered subway train became a potent symbol of the city and work by figures such as Dondi, Blade and Lady Pink became known around the world. In addition, fine artists such as Jean-Michel Basquiat, Kenny Scharf and Keith Haring began incorporating elements of graffiti into their work.

The movement received new life in the late 1990s when a new generation of artists – many with art-school pedigrees – began using materials such as cut paper and sculptural elements (all illicitly). Well-known NYC artists working in this vein include John Fekner, Stephen 'Espo' Powers, Swoon and the twin-brother duo Skewville.

These days, spray-can and stencil hot spots include the Brooklyn side of the Williamsburg Bridge and the corner of Troutman St and St Nicholas Ave in Bushwick, also in Brooklyn. In Astoria, Queens, explore the Technicolor artworks around Welling Ct and 30th Ave.

By the '60s and '70s, when New York's economy was in the dumps and much of SoHo lay in a state of decay, the city became a hotbed of conceptual and performance art. Gordon Matta-Clark sliced up abandoned buildings with chainsaws and the artists of Fluxus staged happenings on downtown streets. Carolee Schneemann organized performances that utilized the human body; at one famous 1964 event, she had a crew of nude dancers roll around in an unappetizing mix of paint, sausages and dead fish in the theater of a Greenwich Village church.

Art Today

New York remains the world's gallery capital, with more than 800 spaces showcasing all kinds of art all over the city. The blue-chip dealers can be found clustered in Chelsea and the Upper East Side. Galleries that showcase emerging and mid-career artists dot the Lower East Side, while prohibitive rents have pushed the city's more emerging and experimental scenes further out, with current hot spots including Harlem and the Brooklyn neighborhoods of Bushwick, Greenpoint, Clinton Hill and Bedford-Stuyvesant (Bed-Stuy).

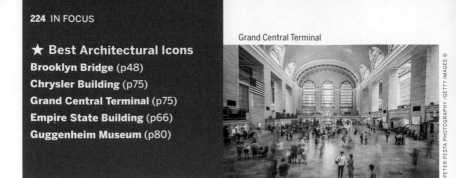

Grand Central Terminal

PETER PESTA PHOTOGRAPHY/GETTY IMAGES ©

Architecture

New York's architectural history is a layer cake of ideas and styles – one that is literally written on the city's streets. Humble colonial farmhouses and graceful Federal-style buildings can be found alongside ornate beaux-arts palaces from the early 20th century. There are the unadorned forms of the International Style, and, in recent years, there has been the addition of the torqued forms of deconstructivist architects. For the architecture buff, it's a bricks-and-mortar bonanza.

Beaux-Arts Blockbusters

At the turn of the 20th century, New York entered a gilded age. Architects, many of whom trained in France, came back with European design ideas. Gleaming white limestone began to replace all the brownstone, first stories were elevated to allow for dramatic staircase entrances, and buildings were adorned with sculptured keystones and Corinthian columns.

McKim, Mead & White's Villard Houses, from 1884 (now the Palace Hotel), show the movement's early roots. Loosely based on Rome's Palazzo della Cancelleria, they channeled the symmetry and elegance of the Italian Renaissance. Other classics include the central branch of the New York Public Library (1911) designed by Carrère and Hastings, the 1902 extension of the Metropolitan Museum of Art by Richard Morris Hunt, and Warren and Wetmore's stunning Grand Central Terminal (1913), which is capped by a statue of Mercury, the god of commerce.

Reaching Skyward

By the time New York settled into the 20th century, elevators and steel-frame engineering had allowed the city to grow up – literally. This period saw a building boom of skyscrapers, starting with Cass Gilbert's neo-Gothic 57-story Woolworth Building (1913). To this day it remains one of the 50 tallest buildings in the United States.

Others soon followed. In 1930, the Chrysler Building, the 77-story art-deco masterpiece designed by William Van Alen, became the world's tallest structure. The following year, the record was broken by the Empire State Building, a clean-lined moderne monolith crafted from Indiana limestone. Its spire was meant to be used as a mooring mast for dirigibles (airships) – an idea that made for good publicity, but which proved to be impractical and unfeasible.

The influx of displaced European architects and other thinkers who had resettled in New York by the end of WWII fostered a lively dialogue between American and European architects. This was a period when urban planner Robert Moses furiously rebuilt vast swaths of New York – to the detriment of many neighborhoods – and designers and artists became obsessed with the clean, unadorned lines of the International Style.

One of the earliest projects in this vein were the UN buildings (1948–52), the combined effort of a committee of architects, including the Swiss-born Le Corbusier, Brazil's Oscar Niemeyer and America's Wallace K Harrison. The Secretariat employed New York's first glass curtain wall – which looms over the ski-slope curve of the General Assembly. Other significant modernist structures from this period include Gordon Bunshaft's Lever House (1950–52), a floating, glassy structure on Park Ave and 54th St, and Ludwig Mies van der Rohe's austere, 38-story Seagram Building (1956–58), located just two blocks to the south.

The New Guard

By the late 20th century, numerous architects began to rebel against the hard-edged, unornamented nature of modernist design. Among them was Philip Johnson. His pink granite AT&T Building (now Sony Tower; 1984) – topped by a scrolled, neo-Georgian pediment – has become a postmodern icon of the Midtown skyline.

What never became an icon was Daniel Libeskind's twisting, angular design for the One World Trade Center (2013) tower, replaced by a boxier architecture-by-committee glass obelisk. On the same site, budget blowouts led to tweaks of Santiago Calatrava's luminous design for the World Trade Center Transportation Hub (2016). According to critics, what should have looked like a dove in flight now resembles a winged dinosaur.

Starchitects on the Line

Frank Gehry's IAC Building (2007) – a billowing, white-glass structure often compared to a wedding cake – is one of a growing number of starchitect creations appearing around railway-turned-urban-park, the High Line. The most prolific of these is Renzo Piano's new Whitney Museum (2015). Dramatically asymmetrical and clad in blue-gray steel, the building has received significant praise for melding seamlessly with the elevated park. Turning heads eight blocks to the north is 100 Eleventh Ave (2010), a 23-story luxury condominium by French architect Jean Nouvel. Its exuberant arrangement of angled windows is nothing short of mesmerizing, both cutting-edge in its construction and sensitive to the area's heritage. That the facade's patterning evokes West Chelsea's industrial masonry is not coincidental.

The area's next darling is set to be Zaha Hadid's apartment complex at 520 W 28th St. Rising 11 stories, the luxury structure will be the Iraqi-British architect's first residential project in the city, its voluptuous, sci-fi curves to be complemented by a 2500-sq-ft sculpture deck showcasing art presented by Friends of the High Line

Sir Norman Foster has also bequeathed his cutting-edge style upon the city. The British architect's Hearst Tower (2006) – a glass skyscraper zigzagging its way out of a 1920s sandstone structure – remains a Midtown trailblazer. The building is one of numerous daring 21st-century additions to the city's architectural portfolio, among them Brooklyn's sci-fi arena Barclays Center (2012), Thom Mayne's folded-and-slashed 41 Cooper Square (2009) in the East Village, and Frank Gehry's rippling, 76-story apartment tower New York by Gehry (2011) in the Financial District.

LGBTIQ New York City

New York City is out and damn proud. It was here that the Stonewall Riots took place, that the modern gay-rights movement bloomed and that America's first Pride march hit the streets. Yet even before the days of 'Gay Lib,' the city had a knack for all things queer and fabulous, from Bowery sex saloons and Village Sapphic poetry to drag balls in Harlem. It hasn't always been smooth sailing, but it's been one hell of a ride.

Above: NYC Pride March (p11) along Fifth Ave LEV RADIN / SHUTTERSTOCK ©

Divas, Drag & Harlem

While Times Square had developed a reputation for attracting gay men – many of them working in the district's theaters, restaurants and speakeasy bars – the hottest gay scene in the 1920s was found further north, in Harlem.

Harlem's drag balls were a hit with both gay and straight New Yorkers in the Roaring Twenties. The biggest of the lot was the Hamilton Lodge Ball, held annually at the swank Rockland Palace on 155th St. Commonly dubbed the Faggot's Ball, it was a chance for both gay men and women to (legally) cross-dress and steal a same-sex dance, and for fashionable 'normals' to indulge in a little voyeuristic titillation. The evening's star attraction was the beauty pageant, which saw the drag-clad competitors compete for the title of 'Queen of the Ball.' Langston Hughes proclaimed it the 'spectacles of color' and the gay writer was one of many members of New York's literati to attend the ball. It was also attended by everyone from prostitutes to high-society families, including the Astors and the Vanderbilts. Even the papers covered the extravaganza, its outrageous frocks the talk of the town.

The Stonewall Revolution

The relative transgression of the early 20th century was replaced with a new conservatism in the following decades, as the Great Depression, WWII and the Cold War took their toll. Conservatism was helped along by Senator Joseph 'Joe' McCarthy, who declared that homosexuals in the State Department threatened America's security and children. Tougher policing aimed to eradicate queer visibility in the public sphere, forcing the scene further underground in the 1940s and '50s. Although crackdowns on gay venues had always occurred, they became increasingly common.

Gay Pride Beyond Manhattan

Sure, the annual Gay Pride march and flood of parties in Manhattan is a wild and wonderful thing. But New York City's outer boroughs have queer folks, too – and their lives and cultures can often feel worlds away from the Manhattan scene. Going to one of these smaller, nontouristy celebrations can be a joyously unique experience. Queens Pride (www.queenspride.org), held the first Sunday in June, takes place in the multiculti neighborhood of Jackson Heights and has a strong pan-Latin flavor. Brooklyn Pride (www.brooklynpride.org) kicks off the second Sunday in June and features a street fair and nighttime parade in Park Slope, with parties radiating throughout the borough at nightfall.

Yet on June 28, 1969, when eight police officers raided the Stonewall Inn – a gay-friendly watering hole in Greenwich Village – patrons did the unthinkable: they revolted. Fed up with both the harassment and corrupt officers receiving payoffs from the bars' owners (who were mostly organized crime figures), they began bombarding the officers with coins, bottles, bricks and chants of 'gay power' and 'we shall overcome.' The cops were also met by a line of high-kicking drag queens and their now legendary chant, 'We are the Stonewall girls, we wear our hair in curls, we wear no underwear, we show our pubic hair, we wear our dungarees, above our nelly knees...'

Their collective anger and solidarity was a turning point, igniting intense and passionate debate about discrimination and forming the catalyst for the modern gay-rights movement, not just in New York, but across the US and in countries from the Netherlands to Australia.

In the Shadow of AIDS

LGBT activism intensified as HIV and AIDS hit world headlines in the early 1980s. Faced with ignorance, fear and the moral indignation of those who saw AIDS as a 'gay cancer,' activists such as writer Larry Kramer set about tackling what was quickly becoming an epidemic. Out of his efforts was born ACT UP (AIDS Coalition to Unleash Power) in 1987, an advocacy group set up to fight the perceived homophobia and indifference of the then President Ronald Reagan, as well as to end the price gouging of AIDS drugs by pharmaceutical companies.

The epidemic itself had a significant impact on New York's artistic community. Among its most high-profile victims were artist Keith Haring, photographer Robert Mapplethorpe and fashion designer Halston. Yet out of this loss grew a tide of powerful AIDS-related plays and musicals that would not only win broad international acclaim, but would become part

Industry bar in Hell's Kitchen

GAY TOURISM / ALAMY STOCK PHOTO ©

★ **Best LGBT Nightspots**

Duplex (p190)

Marie's Crisis (p171)

Industry (p177)

of America's mainstream cultural canon. Among these are Tony Kushner's political epic *Angels in America* and Jonathan Larson's rock musical *Rent*. Both works would win Tony Awards and the Pulitzer Prize.

Marriage & the New Millennium

The LGBT fight for complete equality took two massive steps forward in recent years. In 2011, a federal law banning LGBT military personnel from serving openly – the so-called 'Don't Ask, Don't Tell' policy – was repealed after years of intense lobbying. An even bigger victory arrived when in 2015 the US Supreme Court ruled that same-sex marriage is a legal right across the country, striking down the remaining marriage bans in 13 US states.

Blizzard in Central Park (p36)

Survival Guide

Directory A–Z

Customs Regulations

US Customs allows each person over the age of 21 to bring 1L of liquor and 200 cigarettes into the US duty free. Agricultural items including meat, fruits, vegetables, plants and soil are prohibited. US citizens are allowed to import, duty free, up to $800 worth of gifts from abroad, while non-US citizens are allowed to import $100 worth. For updates, check www.cbp.gov.

Discount Cards

The following discount cards offer a variety of passes and perks to some of the city's must-sees. Check the websites for more details.

Downtown CulturePass (www.downtownculturepass.org)
Explorer Pass (www.smartdestinations.com)
New York CityPASS (www.citypass.com/new-york)
The New York Pass (www.newyorkpass.com)

Electricity

120V/60Hz

120V/60Hz

Insurance

Before traveling, contact your health-insurance provider to find out what types of medical care it will cover outside your hometown (or home country). Overseas visitors should acquire travel insurance that covers medical situations in the US, as nonemergency care for uninsured patients can be very expensive. For nonemergency appointments at hospitals, you'll need proof of insurance or cash. Even with insurance, you'll most likely have to pay up front for non-emergency care and then consult with your insurance company afterwards to get your money reimbursed.

Internet Access

It's rare to find accommodations in New York City that don't offer wi-fi, though it isn't always free. Public parks with free wi-fi include the High Line, Bryant Park, Battery Park, Tompkins Square Park and Union Square Park. Other public areas with free wi-fi include **Columbia University** (www.columbia.edu; Broadway, at 116th St, Morningside Heights; **S**1 to 116th St-Columbia University) and **South Street Seaport** (Map p246; www.southstreetseaport.com; **S**A/C, J/Z, 2/3, 4/5 to Fulton St). Internet kiosks can be found at Staples and FedEx Office stores around the city, and you can also try Apple stores.

LGBTIQ Travelers

From hand-locked married couples on the streets of Hell's Kitchen to a rainbow-hued Empire State Building at Pride, there's no doubt that New York City is one of the world's great gay cities. Indeed, few places come close to matching the breadth and depth of queer offerings here, from clubs to festivals.

Money

ATMs are widely available and credit cards are widely accepted. Farmers markets, food trucks and some restaurants and bars are cash-only.

ATMs

ATMs are on practically every corner. You can either use your card at banks – usually in a 24-hour-access lobby, filled with up to a dozen monitors at major branches – or you can opt for the lone wolves, which sit in delis, restaurants, bars and grocery stores, charging fierce service fees that average $3 but can go as high as $5.

Changing Money

Banks and moneychangers, found all over New York City (including at the three major airports), will give you US currency based on the current exchange rate.

Credit Cards

Major credit cards are accepted at most hotels, restaurants and shops throughout New York City.

Opening Hours

Standard business hours are as follows:

Banks 9am to 6pm Monday to Friday, some also 9am to noon Saturday

Bars 5pm to 4am

Businesses 9am to 5pm Monday to Friday

Clubs 10pm to 4am

Restaurants Breakfast 6am to 11am, lunch 11am to around 3pm, and dinner 5pm to 11pm. Weekend brunch 11am to 4pm.

Shops 10am to 7pm weekdays, 11am to 8pm Saturday, and Sunday can be variable – some stores stay closed while others keep weekday hours. Stores tend to stay open later in the neighborhoods downtown.

Public Holidays

Major NYC holidays and special events may force the closure of many businesses

or attract crowds, making dining and accommodations reservations difficult.

New Year's Day January 1

Martin Luther King Day Third Monday in January

Presidents' Day Third Monday in February

Easter March/April

Memorial Day Late May

Gay Pride Last Sunday in June

Independence Day July 4

Labor Day Early September

Rosh Hashanah and Yom Kippur Mid-September to mid-October

Halloween October 31

Thanksgiving Fourth Thursday in November

Christmas Day December 25

New Year's Eve December 31

Safe Travel

Crime rates in NYC are still at their lowest in years. There are few neighborhoods where you might feel apprehensive no matter what time of night it is (they're mainly in the outer boroughs). Subway stations are generally safe, too, though again, especially in the outer boroughs, some can be dicey. There's no reason to be paranoid, but it's better to be safe than sorry, so use common sense: don't walk around alone at night in unfamiliar, sparsely populated areas, especially if you're a woman. Carry your daily walking-around money somewhere inside

Practicalities

Newspapers

New York Post (www.nypost.com) The *Post* is known for screaming headlines, conservative political views and its popular Page Six gossip column.

New York Times (www.nytimes.com) 'The gray lady' has become hip in recent years, adding sections on technology, arts and dining out.

Magazines

New York Magazine (www.nymag.com) A biweekly magazine with feature stories and great listings about anything and everything in NYC, plus an indispensable website.

New Yorker (www.newyorker.com) This highbrow weekly covers politics and culture through its famously lengthy works of reportage; it also publishes fiction.

Time Out New York (www.timeout.com/newyork) A free weekly magazine, with listings on restaurants, arts and entertainment.

Radio

WNYC (820AM and 93.9FM; www.wnyc.org) NYC's public radio station is the local NPR affiliate and offers national and local talk and interview shows, with a switch to classical music in the day on the FM station.

Smoking

Smoking is strictly forbidden in any location that's considered a public place; this includes subway stations, restaurants, bars, taxis and parks.

Telephone

Phone numbers within the US consist of a three-digit area code followed by a seven-digit local number. If you're calling long distance, dial ✆1 + three-digit area code + seven-digit number. To make an international call from NYC, call ✆011 + country code + area code + number. When calling Canada, there is no need to use the ✆011.

Area Codes

No matter where you're calling within New York City, even if it's just across the street in the same area code, you must always dial ✆1 + the area code first.

Cell Phones

Most US cell (mobile) phones, besides the iPhone, operate on CDMA, not the European standard GSM – make sure you check compatibility with your phone service provider. North Americans should have no problem, though it's best to check with your service provider about roaming charges.

If you require a cell phone, you'll find many store fronts – most run by Verizon, T-Mobile or AT&T – where you can buy a cheap phone and load it up with prepaid minutes, thus avoiding a long-term contract.

Time

New York City is in the Eastern Standard Time (EST) zone – five hours behind Greenwich Mean Time (London). Almost all of the USA observes daylight-saving time: clocks go forward one hour from the second Sunday in March to the first Sunday in November, when the clocks are turned back one hour (it's easy to remember by the phrase 'spring ahead, fall back').

your clothing or in a front pocket rather than in a handbag or a back pocket, and be aware of pickpockets, particularly in mobbed areas, like Times Square or Penn Station at rush hour.

Toilets

Considering the number of pedestrians, there's a noticeable lack of public restrooms around the city. You'll find spots to relieve yourself in Grand Central Terminal, Penn Station and Port Authority Bus Terminal, and in parks, including Madison Square Park, Battery Park, Tompkins Square Park, Washington Square Park and Columbus Park in Chinatown, plus several places scattered around Central Park. The good bet, though, is to pop into a Starbucks (there's one about every three blocks) or a department store (Macy's, Century 21, Bloomingdale's).

Tourist Information

You'll find infinite online resources to get up-to-the-minute information about New York. In person, try one of the official bureaux of NYC & Company:

City Hall (Map p246; ☎212-484-1222; www.nycgo.com; City Hall Park, at Broadway; 🕐9am-6pm Mon-Fri, 10am-5pm Sat & Sun; [S]4/5/6 to Brooklyn Bridge-City Hall; R to City Hall; J/Z to Chambers St)

Macy's Herald Square (Map p252; ☎212-484-1222; www.nycgo.com; Macy's, 151 W 34th St, at Broadway; 🕐9am-7pm Mon-Fri, from 10am Sat, from 11am Sun; [S]B/D/F/M, N/Q/R to 34th St-Herald Sq)

Times Square (Map p252; ☎212-484-1222; www.nycgo.com; Seventh Ave, at 44th St, Midtown West; 🕐9am-6pm; [S]N/Q/R, S, 1/2/3, 7 to Times Sq-42nd St)

The **Brooklyn Tourism & Visitors Center** (☎718-802-3846; www.nycgo.com; 209 Joralemon St, btwn Court St & Brooklyn Bridge Blvd, Downtown; 🕐10am-6pm Mon-Fri; [S]2/3, 4/5 to Borough Hall) 🍃 has all sorts of info on this much-loved borough.

Neighborhood Tourism Portals

Many of the city's most popular neighborhoods have their own websites (either official or 'unofficial') about exploring the area:

Chinatown (www.explorechinatown.com)

Lower East Side (www.lowereastsideny.com)

Soho (www.sohonyc.com)

Upper East Side (www.uppereast.com)

Williamsburg (www.freewilliamsburg.com)

Travelers with Disabilities

Federal laws guarantee that all government offices and facilities are accessible to people with disabilities. Mayor's **Office for People with Disabilities** (☎212-639-9675; www.nyc.gov/mopd; 🕐9am-5pm Mon-Fri) Contact for information on specific places and a free copy of its *Access New York* guide.

NYC & Company (www.nycgo.com/accessibility) [FREE] A good list of planning tools.

Big Apple Greeter (www.bigapplegreeter.org/what-is-the-access-program) [FREE] This excellent program has over 50 volunteers with physical disabilities on staff who are happy to show off their corner of the city.

Accessibility Line (☎511; http://web.mta.info/accessibility/stations.htm) Call or visit the website for detailed information on subway and bus wheelchair accessibility.

Lonely Planet (http://lptravel.to/AccessibleTravel) Free downloadable Accessible Travel guide.

Visas

The US Visa Waiver Program (VWP) allows nationals from 38 countries to enter the US without a visa, provided they are carrying a machine-readable passport. For an up-to-date list of countries included in the program and requirements, see the **US Department of State website** (www.travel.state.gov).

Citizens of VWP countries need to register with the US Department of Homeland Security (www.cbp.gov/travel/international-visitors/esta) three days before their visit. There is a $14 fee for registration application; when approved, registration is valid for two years or until your passport expires, whichever comes first.

Transportation

Arriving in New York City

With its three bustling airports, two main train stations and a monolithic bus terminal, New York City rolls out the welcome mat for millions of visitors who come to take a bite out of the Big Apple each year.

Direct flights are possible from most major American and international cities. Figure on six hours from Los Angeles, seven hours from London and Amsterdam, and 14 hours from Tokyo. Consider getting here by train instead of car or plane to enjoy a mix of bucolic and urban scenery en route, without unnecessary traffic hassles, security checks and excess carbon emissions.

Flights, cars and tours can be booked online at lonelyplanet.com.

John F Kennedy International Airport

John F Kennedy International Airport (JFK; 🖉718-244-4444; www.kennedyairport.com; 🖂), 15 miles from

Midtown in southeastern Queens, has eight terminals, serves nearly 50 million passengers annually and hosts flights coming and going from all corners of the globe.

Taxi A yellow taxi from Manhattan to the airport will use the meter; prices (often about $60) depend on traffic – it can take 45 to 60 minutes. From the airport, taxis charge a flat rate of $52 to any destination in Manhattan (not including tolls or tip), while to/from a destination in Brooklyn, the metered fare should be about $45 (Coney Island) to $65 (downtown Brooklyn). Note that the Williamsburg, Manhattan, Brooklyn and Queensboro–59th St Bridges have no toll either way, while the Queens–Midtown Tunnel and the Hugh L Carey Tunnel (aka the Brooklyn–Battery Tunnel) cost $8 going into Manhattan.

Vans & Car Service Shared vans, like those offered by Super Shuttle Manhattan (www.supershuttle.com), cost around $20 to $26 per person, depending on the destination. If traveling to the airport from NYC, car services have set fares from $45.

Express Bus The NYC Airporter (www.nycairporter.com) runs to Grand Central Station, Penn Station or the Port Authority Bus Terminal from JFK. The one-way fare is $17.

Subway The subway is the cheapest but slowest way of reaching Manhattan. From the airport, hop on the AirTrain ($5, payable as you exit) to Sutphin Blvd-Archer Ave (Jamaica Station) to reach the E, J or Z line (or the Long Island Rail Road).

To take the A line instead, ride the AirTrain to Howard Beach station. The E train to Midtown has the fewest stops. Expect the journey to take at least 1½ hours to Midtown.

Long Island Rail Road (LIRR) This is by far the most relaxing way to arrive in the city. From the airport, take the AirTrain ($5, as you exit) to Jamaica Station. From there, LIRR trains go frequently to Penn Station in Manhattan or to Atlantic Terminal in Brooklyn (near Fort Greene, Boerum Hill and the Barclay Center). It's about a 20-minute journey from station to station. One-way fares to either Penn Station or Atlantic Terminal cost $7.50 ($10 at peak times).

LaGuardia Airport

Used mainly for domestic flights, **LaGuardia** (LGA; 🖉718-533-3400; www.panynj.gov) is smaller than JFK but only 8 miles from midtown Manhattan; it sees about 26 million passengers per year.

Taxi A taxi to/from Manhattan costs about $42 for the approximately half-hour ride.

Car Service A car service to LaGuardia costs around $35.

Express Bus The NYC Airporter (www.nycairporter.com) costs $14 and goes to/from Grand Central, Penn Station and the Port Authority Bus Terminal.

Subway & Bus It's less convenient to get to LaGuardia by public transportation than the other airports. The best subway link is the 74 St–Broadway station (7 line, or the E, F, M and R lines at the connecting Jackson Heights-Roosevelt Ave station) in Queens, where you can pick up the new Q70 Express Bus (about 10 minutes to the airport).

Newark Liberty International Airport

Don't write off New Jersey when looking for airfares to New York. About the same distance from Midtown as JFK (16 miles), **Newark** (EWR; ☎973-961-6000; www.panynj.gov) brings many New Yorkers out for flights (there's some 36 million passengers annually).

Car Service & Taxi A car service runs about $45 to $60 for the 45-minute ride from Midtown – a taxi is roughly the same. You'll have to pay a whopping $15 to get into NYC through the Lincoln (at 42nd St) and Holland (at Canal St) Tunnels and, further north, the George Washington Bridge, though there's no charge going back through to NJ. There are a couple of cheap tolls on New Jersey highways, too, unless you ask your driver to take Hwy 1 or 9.

Subway/Train NJ Transit (www.njtransit.com) runs a rail service (with an AirTrain connection) between Newark airport (EWR) and New York's Penn Station for $13 each way. The trip takes 25 minutes and runs every 20 or 30 minutes from 4:20am to about 1:40am. Hold onto your ticket, which you must show upon exiting at the airport.

Express Bus The Newark Liberty Airport Express (www.newarkairportexpress.com) has a bus service between the airport and Port Authority Bus Terminal, Bryant Park and Grand Central Terminal in Midtown ($16 one-way). The 45-minute ride goes every 15 minutes from 6:45am to 11:15pm and every half hour from 4:45am to 6:45am and 11:15pm to 1:15am.

Climate Change & Travel

Every form of transport that relies on carbon-based fuel generates CO_2, the main cause of human-induced climate change. Modern travel is dependent on planes, which might use less fuel per mile per person than most cars but travel much greater distances. The altitude at which aircraft emit gases (including CO_2) and particles also contributes to their climate change impact. Many websites offer 'carbon calculators' that allow people to estimate the carbon emissions generated by their journey and, for those who wish to do so, to offset the impact of the greenhouse gases emitted with contributions to portfolios of climate-friendly initiatives throughout the world. Lonely Planet offsets the carbon footprint of all staff and author travel.

Port Authority Bus Terminal

For long-distance bus trips, you'll leave and depart from the world's busiest bus station, the **Port Authority Bus Terminal** (Map p252; ☎212-564-8484; www.panynj.gov; 41st St, at Eighth Ave; [S]A/C/E, N/Q/R, 1/2/3, 7), which sees over 65 million passengers each year. Bus companies leaving from here include the following:

Greyhound (Map p252; ☎800-231-2222; www.greyhound.com) Connects New York with major cities across the country.

Peter Pan Trailways (☎800-343-9999; www.peterpanbus.com) Daily express services to Boston, Washington, DC, and Philadelphia.

Short Line Bus (☎212-736-4700; www.shortlinebus.com) Serves northern New Jersey and upstate New York, focusing on college towns such as Ithaca and New Paltz; part of Coach USA.

Penn Station

Train

Penn Station (33rd St, btwn Seventh & Eighth Aves; [S]1/2/3, A/C/E to 34th St-Penn Station) is the departure point for all Amtrak trains and various other services.

Amtrak (Map p252; ☎800-872-7245; www.amtrak.com) services include the Acela Express to Princeton, NJ, and Washington, DC (note that this express service will cost twice as much as a normal fare). All fares vary, based on the day of the week and the time you want to travel. There's no baggage-storage facility at Penn Station.

Long Island Rail Road (LIRR; ☎511; www.mta.info/lirr; furthest zone one-way off-peak/peak $20.50/28.25) The Long Island Rail Road serves over 300,000 commuters each day, with services from Penn Station to points in Brooklyn

Subway Cheat Sheet

A few tips for understanding the madness of the New York subway:

MetroCard All buses and subways use the yellow-and-blue MetroCard, which you can purchase or add value to at one of several easy-to-use automated machines at any station. You can use cash or an ATM or credit card. Tip: if you're not from the US, when the machine asks for your zip code, enter 99999. The card itself costs $1.

Numbers, letters, colors Color-coded subway lines are named by a letter or number, and most carry a collection of two to four trains on their tracks.

Express and local lines A common mistake is accidentally boarding an 'express train' and passing by a local stop you want. Know that each color-coded line is shared by local trains and express trains; the latter make only select stops in Manhattan (indicated by a white circle on subway maps).

Getting in the right station Some stations have separate entrances for downtown or uptown lines (read the sign carefully). If you swipe in at the wrong one – as even locals do on occasion – you'll either need to ride the subway to a station where you can transfer for free, or just lose the $2.75 and re-enter the station (usually across the street).

Weekends All the rules switch on weekends, when some lines combine with others, some get suspended, some stations get passed, others get reached. Locals and tourists alike stand on platforms confused, sometimes irate. Check www.mta.info for weekend schedules.

and Queens, and on Long Island. Prices are broken down by zones. A peak-hour ride from Penn Station to Jamaica Station (en route to JFK via AirTrain) costs $9.50 if you buy it at the station (or $16 onboard).

NJ Transit (☎973-275-5555; www.njtransit.com) Also operates trains from Penn Station, with services to the suburbs and the Jersey Shore.

New Jersey PATH (☎800-234-7284; www.panynj.gov/path) An option for getting into NJ's northern points, such as

Hoboken and Newark. Trains ($2.50) run from Penn Station along the length of Sixth Ave, with stops at 33rd, 23rd, 14th, 9th and Christopher Sts, as well as at the World Trade Center site.

Budget Buses

A number of budget bus lines operate from locations just outside Penn Station:

BoltBus (☎877-265-8287; www.boltbus.com; 🛜) Services from New York to Philadelphia, Boston, Baltimore and Washington, DC. The earlier you purchase

tickets, the better the deal. Notable for its free wi-fi, which occasionally actually works.

megabus (www.us.megabus.com; 🛜) Travels from New York to Boston, Washington, DC, and Toronto, among other destinations. Free (sometimes functioning) wi-fi.

Vamoose (Map p252; ☎212-695-6766; www.vamoosebus.com; Ⓢ1 to 28th St; A/C/E, 1/2/3 to 34th St-Penn Station) Buses head to Arlington, VA, near Washington, DC.

Grand Central Terminal

The last line departing from Grand Central Terminal, the **Metro-North Railroad** (www.mta.info/mnr) serves Connecticut, Westchester County and the Hudson Valley.

Getting Around

Check the **Metropolitan Transportation Authority** (MTA; ☎511; www.mta.info) website for public transportation information (buses and subway), including a handy travel planner and regular notifications of delays and alternate travel routes during frequent maintenance.

Subway

The New York subway system, run by the Metropolitan Transportation Authority, is cheap, round-the-clock and often the fastest and most reliable way to get around the city. It's also safer and (a bit) cleaner than it used to be. A single ride, regardless of the distance, is $2.75 with a MetroCard. A 7-Day Unlimited Pass costs $31.

It's a good idea to grab a free map from a station attendant. If you have a smartphone, download a useful app (such as the free Citymapper), with subway map and alerts of service outages.

Bicycle

Hundreds of miles of designated bike lanes have been added over the past decade. Add to this the excellent bike-sharing network **Citi Bike** (www.citibikenyc.com; 24hr/7 days $11/27), and you have the makings for a surprisingly bike-friendly city. Hundreds of Citi Bike kiosks in Manhattan and parts of Brooklyn house the iconic bright blue and very sturdy bicycles, which have reasonable rates for short-term users.

To use a Citi Bike, buy a 24-hour or seven-day access pass at any Citi Bike kiosk. You will then be given a five-digit code to unlock a bike. Return the bike to any station within 30 minutes to avoid incurring extra fees. Reinsert your credit card (you won't be charged) and follow the prompts to check out a bike again. You can make an unlimited number of 30-minute check-outs during those 24 hours or seven days.

Ferry

Hop-on, hop-off services are offered by **New York Waterway** (800-533-3779; www.nywaterway.com) and **New York Water Taxi** (212-742-1969; www.nywatertaxi.com; hop-on, hop-off 1-day pass $31), while **East River Ferry** (www.eastriverferry.com; 1-way $4-6) runs a year-round commuter service connecting a variety of locations in Queens and Brooklyn with Manhattan.

Another bigger, brighter ferry is the commuter-oriented **Staten Island Ferry** (Map p246; www.siferry.com; Whitehall Terminal, 4 South St, at Whitehall; 24hr; S1 to South Ferry) FREE, which makes free journeys across New York Harbor.

Bus

Buses are convenient during off hours – especially when transferring between the city's eastern and western sides. The bus network uses the MetroCard; prices as per the subway.

Taxi

Hailing and riding in a cab are rites of passage in New York – especially when you get a driver who's a neurotic speed demon, which is often (don't forget to buckle up). Still, most taxis in NYC are clean and, compared to those in many international cities, pretty cheap. Meters start at $2.50 and increase roughly $5 for every 20 blocks. Tips are expected to

be 10% to 15%, but give less if you feel in any way mistreated; be sure to ask for a receipt and use it to note the driver's license number. See www.nyc.gov/taxi for more information.

Boro Taxi

Green Boro Taxis operate in the outer boroughs and Upper Manhattan. These allow folks to hail a taxi on the street in neighborhoods where yellow taxis rarely roam. They have the same fares and features as yellow cabs, and are a good way to get around the outer boroughs (from, say, Astoria to Williamsburg, or Park Slope to Red Hook). Drivers are reluctant (but legally obligated) to take passengers into Manhattan as they aren't legally allowed to take fares going out of Manhattan south of 96th St.

Car Service

These services are a common taxi alternative in the outer boroughs. Fares differ depending on the neighborhood and length of ride, and must be determined beforehand, as they have no meters. These 'black cars' are quite common in Brooklyn and Queens, however, it's illegal if a driver simply stops to offer you a ride – no matter what borough you're in. A couple of car services in Brooklyn include Northside in Williamsburg and Arecibo in Park Slope.

Behind the Scenes

Acknowledgements

Climate map data adapted from Peel MC, Finlayson BL & McMahon TA (2007) 'Updated World Map of the Koppen-Geiger Climate Classification', *Hydrology and Earth System Sciences*, 11, 163344.

Illustration pp40–1 by Javier Zarracina.

This Book

This book was curated by Regis St Louis and researched and written by Regis St Louis, Cristian Bonetto and Zora O'Neill. This guidebook was commissioned in Lonely Planet's Melbourne office, and produced by the following:

Destination Editor Rebecca Warren
Series Designer Katherine Marsh
Cartographic Series Designer Wayne Murphy
Senior Product Editor Catherine Naghten
Product Editor Alison Ridgway
Book Designer Katherine Marsh
Senior Cartographer Alison Lyall
Assisting Editors Victoria Harrison, Charlotte Orr, Gabrielle Stefanos, Saralinda Turner
Assisting Book Designers Kerrianne Jenkins
Cover Researchers Campbell McKenzie, Naomi Parker
Associate Product Director Liz Heynes
Thanks to Indra Kilfoyle, Anne Mason, Kate Mathews, Jenna Myers, Kathryn Rowan, Dianne Schallmeiner, Luna Soo

Send Us Your Feedback

We love to hear from travelers – your comments keep us on our toes and help make our books better. Our well-traveled team reads every word on what you loved or loathed about this book. Although we cannot reply individually to postal submissions, we always guarantee that your feedback goes straight to the appropriate authors, in time for the next edition. Each person who sends us information is thanked in the next edition, the most useful submissions are rewarded with a selection of digital PDF chapters.

Visit lonelyplanet.com/contact to submit your updates and suggestions or to ask for help. Our award-winning website also features inspirational travel stories, news and discussions.

Note: We may edit, reproduce and incorporate your comments in Lonely Planet products such as guidebooks, websites and digital products, so let us know if you don't want your comments reproduced or your name acknowledged. For a copy of our privacy policy visit lonelyplanet.com/privacy.

A – Z
Index

000 Map pages

High Line (p54)

MATT MUNRO / LONELY PLANET ©

New York City Maps

West & East Villages, Chinatown & Lower Manhattan

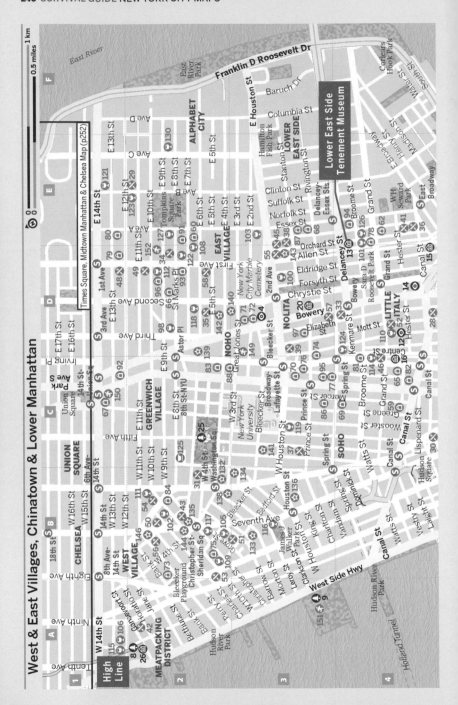

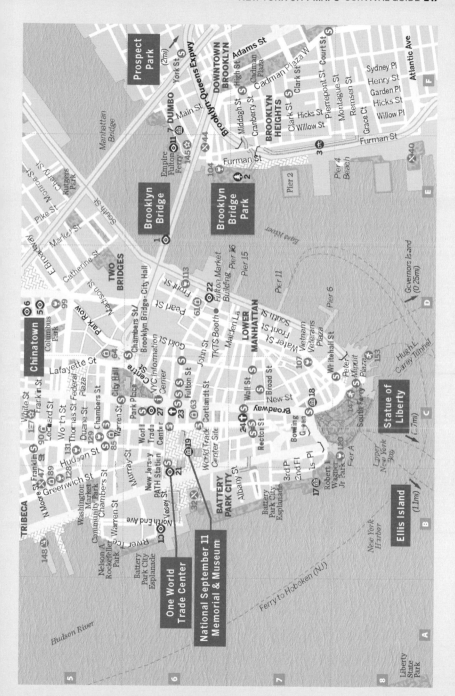

Prospect Park

(2km)

York St S

DOWNTOWN BROOKLYN

Adams St

DUMBO

Main St

7

Cadman Plaza W

Cadman Plaza

Empire Fulton Ferry

11 7

145

X 44

Middagh St

High St S

Cranberry St

Clark St/za W

Clark St S

BROOKLYN HEIGHTS

104

Furman St

2

Brooklyn Bridge

Brooklyn Bridge Park

Willow St

Hicks St

3 S

Pier 2

Furman St

Sydney Pl

Henry St

Garden Pl

Hicks St

Willow Pl

Grace Ct

Montague St

Pierrepont St Court St S

Remsen St

Pier 4 Beach

X 40

F

E

Manhattan Bridge

Cherry St

Rutgers Park

Monroe St

Pike St

South St

E Broadway

Market St

Catherine St

Madison St

TWO BRIDGES

1

East River

Pier 15

Pier 16

Governors Island (0.25mi)

D

Chinatown

6

5

Columbus Park

Park Row

Chambers St

Brooklyn Bridge-City Hall

Front St

113

Fulton Market Building

22

Pier 11

Pier 6

Lafayette Ct

64

Centre St

NYC Information Center

Pearl St

Front St

LOWER MANHATTAN

Maiden La

John St

Water St

Front St

Vietnam Veterans Plaza

White St

Franklin St

17

90

Worth St

Thomas St

Federal Plaza

Duane St

City Hall

Park Place

World Trade Center

27

23

TKTS Booth

63

Fulton St

Cortlandt St

69

Wall St

Broad St

New St

Broadway

18

S

Veterans Plaza

107

Whitehall St

Peter Minuit Plaza

S

153

Statue of Liberty

(2mi)

Hugh L Carey Tunnel

C

TRIBECA

148

127

Leonard St

N Moore St

47

89

131

128

Hudson St

Chambers St

Greenwich St

85

Warren St

Murray St

New Jersey PATH Station

19

21

24

S

Rector St

Bowling Green

S

120

Robert F Wagner Jr Park

South Ferry

Pier A

107

B

One World Trade Center

National September 11 Memorial & Museum

Washington Market Community Park

Nelson A Rockefeller Park

Battery Park City Esplanade

Chambers St

Warren St

River Tce

North End Ave

Vesey St

32

Albany St

BATTERY PARK CITY

Battery Park City Esplanade

3rd Pl

2nd Pl

1s Pl

17

Upper New York Bay

New York Harbor

Ellis Island

(1.1mi)

Liberty State Park

Hudson River

Ferry to Hoboken (NJ)

A

5

6

7

8

West & East Villages, Chinatown & Lower Manhattan

Central Park & Uptown

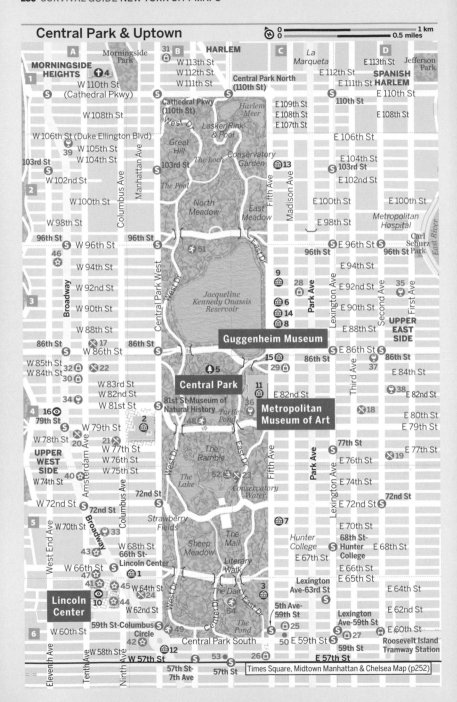

0   1 km
0   0.5 miles

MORNINGSIDE HEIGHTS ⓘ4

HARLEM

SPANISH HARLEM

Jefferson Park

Morningside Park

31 B W 113th St
W 112th St
W 111th St

E 113th St

La Marqueta

E 112th St

E 111th St

W 110th St (Cathedral Pkwy)

Central Park North (110th St)

110th St

E 110th St

W 108th St

Cathedral Pkwy (110th St)

West Dr

Harlem Meer

Lasker Rink & Pool

E 109th St
E 108th St
E 107th St

E 108th St

W 106th St (Duke Ellington Blvd)

39

W 105th St
W 104th St

Great Hill

The Loch

Conservatory Garden

E 106th St

E 104th St

103rd St

W 102nd St

103rd St

The Pool

103rd St

⓭13

E 103rd St
E 102nd St

W 100th St

North Meadow

East Meadow

E 100th St

E 100th St

W 98th St

Madison Ave

East Dr

E 98th St

Metropolitan Hospital

Carl Schurz Park

96th St

46

W 96th St

96th St

51

E 96th St

96th St

96th St

East River

W 94th St

Columbus Ave

Manhattan Ave

Central Park West

E 94th St

Second Ave

First Ave

W 92nd St

9

28

E 92nd St

35

W 90th St

West Dr

Jacqueline Kennedy Onassis Reservoir

⓭6

⓭14

E 90th St

UPPER EAST SIDE

W 88th St

8

E 88th St

Guggenheim Museum

86th St

17

W 86th St

86th St

15

86th St

E 86th St

86th St

86th St

W 85th St

W 84th St

32

22

30

5

29

37

E 84th St

34

Central Park

11

E 82nd St

38

E 82nd St

16

81st St-Museum of Natural History

Turtle Pond

36

Metropolitan Museum of Art

18

E 80th St

79th St

W 79th St

2

48

E 79th St

W 78th St

20

21

The Ramble

77th St

E 77th St

19

UPPER WEST SIDE

Amsterdam Ave

W 77th St
W 76th St
W 75th St

West Dr

East Dr

Fifth Ave

Park Ave

E 76th St

W 74th St

40

The Lake

52

23

Conservatory Water

E 74th St

W 72nd St

72nd St

72nd St

E 72nd St

72nd St

Strawberry Fields

⓭7

E 70th St

Hunter College

68th St-Hunter College

W 70th St

33

West End Ave

Broadway

Columbus Ave

W 68th St

66th St-Lincoln Center

Sheep Meadow

The Mall

E 67th St

E 68th St

43

E 66th St

W 66th St

47

Literary Walk

Lexington Ave-63rd St

E 65th St

41

45

W 64th St

24

3

E 64th St

Lincoln Center

10

44

The Dairy

54

5th Ave-59th St

E 62nd St

W 62nd St

Center Dr

East Dr

Lexington Ave-59th St

59th St-Columbus Circle

49

25

50

E 59th St

27

Roosevelt Island Tramway Station

42

The Pond

59th St

E 60th St

W 60th St

⓭12

Central Park South

53

26

E 57th St

Eleventh Ave

Tenth Ave

Ninth Ave

W 58th St

W 57th St

57th St-7th Ave

57th St

Times Square, Midtown Manhattan & Chelsea Map (p252)

Central Park & Uptown

◎ Sights
1 American Folk Art Museum B5
2 American Museum of Natural History B4
3 Arsenal C6
4 Cathedral Church of St John the
   Divine A1
5 Central Park B4
6 Cooper-Hewitt National Design
   Museum C3
7 Frick Collection C5
8 Guggenheim Museum C3
9 Jewish Museum C3
10 Lincoln Center A6
11 Metropolitan Museum of Art C4
12 Museum of Arts & Design B6
13 Museum of the City of New York C2
14 National Academy Museum C3
15 Neue Galerie C4
16 Zabar's A4

◈ Eating
17 Barney Greengrass A3
18 Beyoglu D4
19 Boqueria D4
20 Burke & Wills A4
   Café Sabarsky .... (see 15)
21 Dovetail A4
22 Jacob's Pickles A4
23 Loeb Boathouse C5
24 The Smith B6
   The Wright .... (see 8)

⊕ Shopping
25 Barneys C6
26 Bergdorf Goodman C6
27 Bloomingdale's D6
28 Blue Tree C3
29 Encore C4

30 Magpie A4
31 Trunk Show Designer
   Consignment B1
32 West Side Kids A4

⊖ Drinking & Nightlife
33 Barcibo Enoteca A5
34 Dead Poet A4
35 Drunken Munkey D3
   Manhattan Cricket Club .... (see 20)
36 Metropolitan Museum Roof Garden
   Café & Martini Bar C4
   Robert .... (see 12)
37 The Daisy D4
38 The Penrose D4
39 West End Hall A2

⊕ Entertainment
40 Beacon Theatre A5
41 Elinor Bunin Munroe Film Center A6
   Film Society of Lincoln Center .... (see 10)
   Frick Collection .... (see 7)
42 Jazz at Lincoln Center B6
43 Merkin Concert Hall A5
   Metropolitan Opera House .... (see 10)
44 New York City Ballet A6
45 New York Philharmonic A6
46 Symphony Space A3
47 Walter Reade Theater A5

⊕ Activities, Courses & Tours
48 Belvedere Castle B4
49 Bike and Roll B6
50 Central Park Conservancy C6
51 Central Park Tennis Center B3
52 Loeb Boathouse B5
53 Municipal Art Society B6
54 Wollman Skating Rink B6

Times Square, Midtown Manhattan & Chelsea

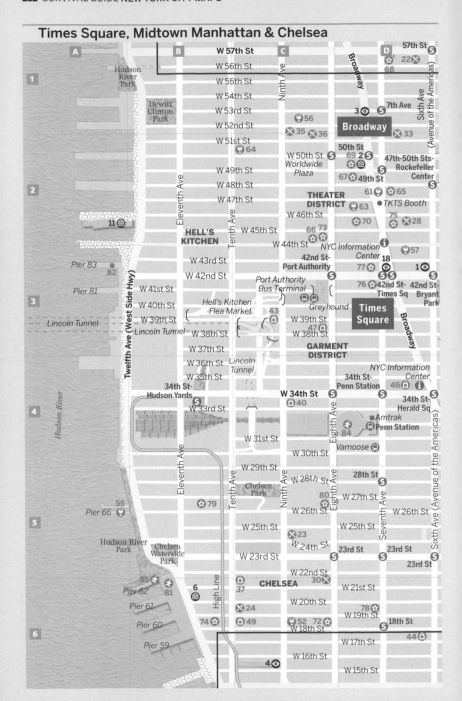

1 km
0.5 miles

E 57th St
50
9
E 56th St

Central Park & Uptown Map (p250)

E 55th St

E 54th St

MoMA
Fifth Ave-
53rd St
13
E 53rd St
51

Lexington Ave-
53rd St

Rockefeller
Center
E 51st St
15
17
16
48
E 49th St

E 52nd St

First Ave

Sutton Pl

West Rd

East Rd

Roosevelt
Island

Southpoint
Park

East Channel
East River

Franklin D
Roosevelt Four
Freedoms Park

E 50th St

Park Ave

Third Ave

Second Ave

E 48th St

7 THE
DIAMOND
DISTRICT
E 45th St
58

E 47th St

E 46th St

Vanderbilt Ave

Grand
Central
Terminal
10

E 43rd St

5

E 44th St

E 42nd St
Bryant
Park 14
21 5th Ave

42nd St-
Grand Central

E 41st St

United
Nations

East River

Queens-Midtown Tunnel

E 40th St

E 39th St

E 38th St
Fifth Ave

Second Ave

E 37th St

E 36th St

E 35th St

Empire State
Building
8
KOREATOWN

E 34th St
33rd St

Tunnel Entrance St

St Vartan
Park

Franklin D Roosevelt Dr

East River

Madison Ave
20
32
28th St
39
28th St

E 33rd St

E 32nd St
MURRAY
HILL

E 31st St

E 30th St

LITTLE
INDIA
71
E 26th St

E 29th St

E 28th St

E 27th St

Bellevue
Hospital
Center

Second Ave

First Ave

Broadway
54

FLATIRON
DISTRICT
34 26
83
27
Park Ave S
12
29

Madison
Square Park
23rd St
23rd St

E 25th St

E 24th St

E 23rd St

E 22nd St

GRAMERCY

24th St
Park

53
45
62
42
Fifth Ave
31 25
38 41 60

E 21st St

GRAMERCY
PARK

E 20th St

E 19th St

E 18th St

STUYVESANT
TOWN

West & East Villages, Chinatown & Lower Manhattan Map (p246)

UNION
SQUARE
14th St-
Union Sq
19

Irving Pl
E 17th St

E 16th St
Stuyvesant
Square
E 15th St

Times Square, Midtown Manhattan & Chelsea

Symbols & Map Key

Look for these symbols to quickly identify listings:

- ◉ Sights
- ⊕ Activities
- ⊖ Courses
- ⊙ Tours
- ✪ Festivals & Events
- ⊗ Eating
- ⊖ Drinking
- ✪ Entertainment
- ⊙ Shopping
- ❶ Information & Transport

These symbols and abbreviations give vital information for each listing:

🍃 Sustainable or green recommendation

FREE No payment required

- ☎ Telephone number
- ☺ Opening hours
- P Parking
- ⊝ Nonsmoking
- ✳ Air-conditioning
- @ Internet access
- 📶 Wi-fi access
- 🏊 Swimming pool

- 🚌 Bus
- ⛴ Ferry
- 🚋 Tram
- 🚆 Train
- 🗒 English-language menu
- 🥗 Vegetarian selection
- 👪 Family-friendly

Find your best experiences with these Great For... icons.

 Budget

🍽 Food & Drink

 Drinking

 Cycling

 Shopping

 Sport

🖼 Art & Culture

✨ Events

📷 Photo Op

🔭 Scenery

👨‍👩‍👧 Family Travel

 Short Trip

🔀 Detour

🥾 Walking

💬 Local Life

📖 History

🎫 Entertainment

🏖 Beaches

❄ Winter Travel

☕ Cafe/Coffee

 Nature & Wildlife

Sights
- 🏖 Beach
- 🐦 Bird Sanctuary
- ☸ Buddhist
- 🏰 Castle/Palace
- ✝ Christian
- ☯ Confucian
- 🕉 Hindu
- ☪ Islamic
- 卐 Jain
- ✡ Jewish
- 🗽 Monument
- 🏛 Museum/Gallery/ Historic Building
- 🏚 Ruin
- ⛩ Shinto
- 🔱 Sikh
- ☯ Taoist
- 🍇 Winery/Vineyard
- 🐾 Zoo/Wildlife Sanctuary
- ◉ Other Sight

Points of Interest
- 🏄 Bodysurfing
- 🏕 Camping
- ☕ Cafe
- 🛶 Canoeing/Kayaking
- • Course/Tour
- 🤿 Diving
- 🍸 Drinking & Nightlife
- ⊗ Eating
- 🎭 Entertainment
- ♨ Sento Hot Baths/ Onsen
- 🛍 Shopping
- ⛷ Skiing
- 😴 Sleeping
- 🤿 Snorkelling
- 🏄 Surfing
- 🏊 Swimming/Pool
- 🥾 Walking
- 🏄 Windsurfing
- ⊕ Other Activity

Information
- $ Bank
- 🏛 Embassy/Consulate
- ✚ Hospital/Medical
- @ Internet
- 👮 Police
- ✉ Post Office
- ☎ Telephone
- 🚻 Toilet
- ❶ Tourist Information
- ● Other Information

Geographic
- 🏖 Beach
- ⊢◀ Gate
- 🏠 Hut/Shelter
- 🗼 Lighthouse
- 🔭 Lookout
- ▲ Mountain/Volcano
- 🌴 Oasis
- 🌳 Park
-)(Pass
- 🧺 Picnic Area
- 💧 Waterfall

Transport
- ✈ Airport
- 🚇 DART station
- ⊗ Border crossing
- 🚊 Boston T station
- 🚌 Bus
- 🚠 Cable car/Funicular
- 🚲 Cycling
- ⛴ Ferry
- Ⓜ Metro/MRT station
- 🚝 Monorail
- P Parking
- ⛽ Petrol station
- 🅢 Subway/S-Bahn/ Skytrain station
- 🚕 Taxi
- 🚉 Train station/Railway
- 🚋 Tram
- ⊖ Tube Station
- Ⓤ Underground/ U-Bahn station
- ● Other Transport

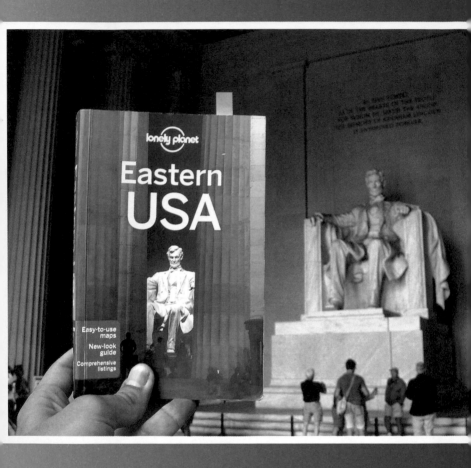

LONELY PLANET IN THE WILD

Cristian Bonetto

Cristian has played both visitor and local in New York City, a place that won his heart way back in his *Sesame* Street diaper days. Indeed, his passion for the city saw *New York Magazine* name him one of the 'Reasons to Love New York' in 2014. Gotham's constant reinvention continues to feed an insatiable curiosity, one that has seen the one-time scriptwriter shed light on everything from lesser-known art collections to cognoscenti dumpling dens. Cristian tweets at twitter.com/cristianbonetto.

Zora O'Neill

Zora moved to New York City in 1998, and moved immediately to Astoria, Queens. She still loves it every day, because she can eat great food and buy fresh produce 24 hours a day. Zora has written guidebooks since 2002; for Lonely Planet, she has covered Amsterdam, southern Spain and Egypt. She is the author of *All Strangers Are Kin*, a travel memoir about studying Arabic and traveling in the Arab world. She is online at www.zoraoneill.com.

Our Story

A beat-up old car, a few dollars in the pocket and a sense of adventure. In 1972 that's all Tony and Maureen Wheeler needed for the trip of a lifetime – across Europe and Asia overland to Australia. It took several months, and at the end – broke but inspired – they sat at their kitchen table writing and stapling together their first travel guide, *Across Asia on the Cheap*. Within a week they'd sold 1500 copies. Lonely Planet was born.

Today, Lonely Planet has offices in Dublin. Melbourne, London, Oakland, Franklin, Delhi and Beijing, with more than 600 staff and writers. We share Tony's belief that 'a great guidebook should do three things: inform, educate and amuse'.

Our Writers

Regis St Louis

A Hoosier by birth, Regis grew up in a sleepy riverside town where he dreamed of big-city intrigue and small, expensive apartments. In 2001, he settled in New York, which had all that and more. Since then he has explored vast swaths of the city, from the Bronx to Brighton Beach, ever in search of both classic and bizarre NYC experiences. Regis' work has appeared in more than 50 Lonely Planet guidebooks, and he has also written for many other organizations, including the BBC, the *Telegraph* and the *Chicago Tribune*. When not on the road, Regis splits his time between Brooklyn and New Orleans.

← ———————— More Writers ←

STAY IN TOUCH LONELYPLANET.COM/CONTACT

EUROPE Unit E, Digital Court, The Digital Hub, Rainsford St, Dublin 8, Ireland

AUSTRALIA Levels 2 & 3 551 Swanston St, Carlton, Victoria 3053
☎ 03 8379 8000, fax 03 8379 8111

USA 150 Linden Street, Oakland, CA 94607
☎ 510 250 6400, toll free 800 275 8555, fax 510 893 8572

UK 240 Blackfriars Road, London SE1 8NW
☎ 020 3771 5100, fax 020 3771 5101

 twitter.com/ lonelyplanet

 facebook.com/ lonelyplanet

 instagram.com/ lonelyplanet

 youtube.com/ lonelyplanet

 lonelyplanet.com/ newsletter